ZULU
WAR

IAN KNIGHT & IAN CASTLE

ZULU
WAR

IAN KNIGHT & IAN CASTLE

First published in Great Britain in 2004 by Osprey Publishing,
Elms Court, Chapel Way, Botley, Oxford OX2 9LP, UK
Email: info@ospreypublishing.com

www.ospreypublishing.com

Previously published as Elite 32: *British Forces in Zululand 1879*; Elite 21:
The Zulus and Campaign 14: *Zulu War 1879*

© 2004 Osprey Publishing Limited

ISBN 1 84176 858 8

Editor: Gerard Barker
Index by Alan Thatcher

Origination by The Electronic Page Company, Cwmbran, UK
Printed in China through World Print Ltd.

04 05 06 07 08   10 9 8 7 6 5 4 3 2 1

Contents

Zulu War 1879, Twilight of a Warrior Nation

British Forces in Zululand 1879

The Zulu War

On 4 March, 1878 at King William's Town, British Kaffraria, Gen. Sir Arthur Cunynghame handed over supreme command of the British forces in southern Africa to his successor, Lt. Gen. Sir Frederic Thesiger. It was hardly a plum job. It was a fact of Imperial life that commanders in the Colonies were expected to achieve the maximum result with a minimal expense of resources, and southern Africa was going through a troublesome period of its history.

A war against the Xhosa people—the Ninth, and last, Cape Frontier War—was about to enter its final phase of dismal skirmishing, but across the region the African population was restless. The Basotho, upset by the attempts of Cape authorities to disarm them, were stirring, and one chief, Moorosi, was already moving towards confrontation. In 1877, as part of its Confederation policy— an attempt to rationalise its political and economic interests in the area—Britain had annexed and occupied the bankrupt Transvaal, the most inward-looking and Anglophobe of the Boer Republics. The Boers had reacted with sullen resentment, and a steady stream of troops were despatched across the monotonous 'high-veld' to garrison the more significant settlements. With the Transvaal had come a festering border dispute with the Pedi Chief Sekhukhune, which threatened to drag Britain into yet another small African war.

Yet none of these problems can have been uppermost in Thesiger's mind as 1878 wore on, since his political master, the High Commissioner, Sir Henry Bartle Frere, had another more pressing task for him to consider. Frere was convinced that one solution to the complex problems which beset the region was to overthrow the last powerful independent black kingdom bordering British possessions—the Zulu kingdom of King Cetshwayo kaMpande.

A prospective war with the Zulus posed Thesiger a number of clear strategic questions. The aggressive intent was all Britain's: Cetshwayo had remained on the political defensive, and was keen to avoid a confrontation. Thesiger would therefore have to take the war across the border of Colonial Natal and wage it in Zululand. Yet Zululand was a vast and difficult country; it covered some 15,000 square miles, most of it rolling downland dropping in a series of terraces from inland heights to a sub-tropical belt bordering the Indian Ocean. It was well-watered, but its majestic river systems had cut many deep gorges on their passages through the

Lieutenant-General Sir Frederic Augustus Thesiger, 2nd Baron Chelmsford, the British commander in the Anglo-Zulu War. He is wearing his campaign uniform of blue patrol jacket and riding breeches. The helmet puggaree was not authorised for use in South Africa, but does seem to have been worn by senior officers. (S. Bourquin)

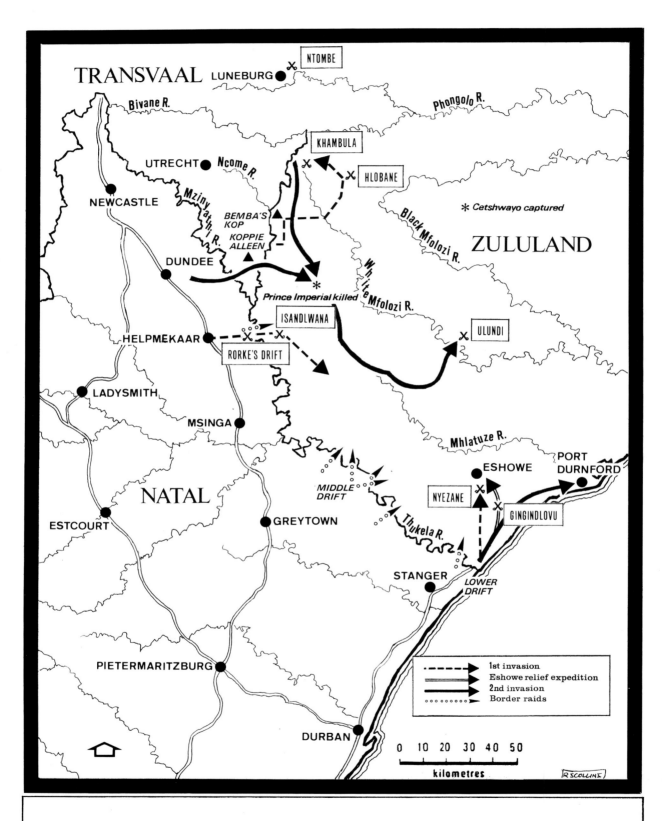

The British Invasion of Zululand · 1879

hills. Much of it was covered in bush or forest, large tracts of it were unmapped, and there were only a few traders' wagon tracks to serve as roads. The border with Natal was over 200 miles long, marked by the Mzinyathi (Buffalo) and Thukela Rivers, which might be crossed at dozens of points by the Zulu army, but which remained very real obstacles to more encumbered European troops.

Thesiger's initial strategy called for five separate columns to be massed at points stretching from the mouth of the Thukela in the south-east up to the Transvaal in the north. Yet he had remarkably few troops available for such an enterprise. Six infantry battalions were already in South Africa, mopping up the Cape Frontier or garrisoning the Transvaal—the 2/3rd, 1/13th, 1st and 2nd/24th, 80th and 90th—and another, the 88th, was arriving in a steady trickle from Mauritius. There were two artillery batteries available, N/5 and 11/7; a solitary company of Royal Engineers; and an absurdly small Transport staff, to whom the enormous burden of ensuring that supplies were ferried in the wake of the advance would fall. There were no regular cavalry, only two squadrons of Mounted Infantry and a handful of small Volunteer units drawn from the settler community. Natal's large black population, for the most part hostile to the Zulus, was a potential source of levies, but clearly manpower remained in short supply. Thesiger appealed to the home government for reinforcements; but the Colonial Office did not support Frere's war-mongering, and the general was sent only two more infantry battalions (the 2/4th and 99th) and two Engineer companies (2nd and 5th).

By late 1878 Frere had manipulated a diplomatic crisis with the Zulus. Thesiger—who succeeded to the title Lord Chelmsford on the death of his father in October—completed his plans. He retained the concept of five columns, but reduced two of them to defensive border garrisons, leaving three to act as an invasion force to converge on the Zulu capital at Ulundi. Three advancing columns were much easier to supply than two; they risked diluting Chelmsford's greatest asset—the massed firepower of his infantry battalions—but allowed the Zulus little room for manoeuvre in the counterstrike against Natal.

The Right Flank Column (No. 1) was comman-

Col. Henry Evelyn Wood, commander of the Right Flank Column, in his service dress. He is wearing the officers' undress frock of the 90 LI (buff collar and regimental badge). His rank is indicated by the braid on his sleeve and by the star and crown badges on his collar. His helmet bears the splendid 1878 pattern plate and fittings, although sketches of him in the field show him to be wearing a less conspicuous dyed helmet with no fixtures. (Royal Collection)

ded by Col. Charles Pearson of the 3rd Foot, and collected at the Lower Drift, just inland from the mouth of the Thukela. Number 2 Column, consisting largely of African troops under Lt. Col. Anthony Durnford RE, would be based on the Natal side of the Middle Drift of the Thukela. The Centre Column (No. 3) would cross over from its supply depot at the Rorke's Drift mission station on the Mzinyathi. It was commanded by Lt. Col. Richard Glynn of the 24th, but accompanied by the general himself, and was intended as the main striking arm. The Left Flank Column (No. 4) was commanded by Col. H. Evelyn Wood, 90th LI, and would cross the Ncome (Blood) River into Zululand from the Transvaal. The final column, No. 5, under Col. Hugh Rowlands, 34th Foot, would remain further north on the Transvaal border, where it could keep an eye not only on the Zulus but on the Boers and Pedi as well.

The timing of the campaign would also be significant. Most of the rain in Natal and Zululand falls in the summer months—December, January and February. During that time the rivers are swollen and tracks can easily be churned to greasy quagmires; but the grass is tall and fresh, and there would be a minimal chance of the Zulus lighting grass fires. In 1878 the whole region was suffering from a drought, so Chelmsford might have had the best of both worlds; in addition, the late rains were delaying the harvests, and there was the possibility that the Zulus might be distracted in a summer campaign by the need to gather their crops. Accordingly, Frere timed his showdown with Cetshwayo to give Chelmsford all the benefits of a summer campaign.

General Sir Garnet Wolseley, who superseded both Chelmsford and Frere at the end of the war, in the uniform he wore as Special Commissioner for Southern Africa, with both civil and military powers. (Author's Collection)

Officers of the Buffs photographed in Natal shortly before the start of the campaign. They are wearing either the blue patrol jacket or the scarlet frock, and forage caps or foreign service helmets. The brass spikes and chin-chains visible here were not worn on campaign (Canterbury City Museum)

Zulu representatives were summoned to a meeting at the Lower Drift and presented with an ultimatum with which, Frere knew, they could not possibly comply. The time allotted for compliance with the ultimatum expired on 11 January 1879. During the last few weeks the troops were marched into position and the stores amassed. A small Naval contingent from HMS Active was landed to join Pearson's column. No news came from Cetshwayo. The war began.

* * *

From the start, it did not go well. The drought finally broke, and Chelmsford's columns began their advance amongst torrential downpours. The general had voiced a fear that he might have trouble forcing the Zulus to fight, but he had underestimated his enemy. Once King Cetshwayo realised that he could not avoid a confrontation he had taken steps to deal with the British strategy. Local elements from his army were ordered to harass the flanking columns, while the main Zulu strike force was despatched to confront Chelmsford. By 20 January the two armies were drawing close to one another. Chelmsford misread the situation, and on the 21st split his force, leaving one portion in the camp at Isandlwana while marching out himself with the other. As an afterthought he scribbled a note to Durnford asking him to bring his column up to support the camp. Durnford's men had scarcely entered the camp on the 22nd when they stumbled upon the main Zulu impi, and precipitated a battle which ended in the massacre of the camp's defenders. The defence of the depot at Rorke's Drift by a single company of the 2/24th against attacks by the Zulu reserve could not obscure the magnitude of the disaster. Chelmsford's initial plan was smashed; in the aftermath he could do little but fall back on Natal, try to shore up his defences, and hope the Zulus did not launch a further foray into Natal.

The flank columns were left high and dry. Pearson had also been engaged on the 22nd—he had broken a Zulu attempt to block his advance on the hills above the Nyezane River—and had pushed forward to the deserted mission station at Eshowe. Here he dug in to await developments, while the Zulus gathered in increasing numbers in the hills around him, laying him under siege. Only Evelyn Wood was free in the north, and he relentlessly harried the Zulu clans in his vicinity.

Yet the main Zulu army did not cross into Natal. Isandlwana had exhausted them, and the king still hoped to win political advantage by waging a defensive war. Chelmsford was allowed the respite he needed to regroup. The home government, embarrassed by Isandlwana, sought to restore British honour by despatching more reinforcements than even Chelmsford had asked for. He received six further infantry battalions (2/21st, 57th, 58th, 3/60th, 91st and 94th); two full artillery batteries (M/6 and N/6); a company of Engineers (30th); three companies of the Army Service Corps (3, 4 and 5); and a company of the Army Hospital Corps. Where before he had no cavalry except what he could scrape together locally, now he was sent the 17th (Duke of

The blue patrol jacket and forage cap: 2nd Lt. Macarthy of the 4th Regiment. The badge on the forage cap is the number '4' surmounted by the 'Lion of England'. (King's Own Regimental Museum)

Officers of the 88th Regiment (Connaught Rangers) at Fort Pearson, Lower Drift, prior to the second invasion. This picture shows something of the variety of officers' service dress; Lt. Col. Hopton, centre, is wearing an OR's frock, as are the officers on either end of the front row. The two on either side of Hopton are wearing officers' frocks, and one has buttoned canvas or leather leggings. Patrol jackets are also in evidence, and headgear is the glengarry or forage cap. (National Army Museum)

Cambridge's Own) Lancers and the 1st (King's) Dragoon Guards. In addition there were drafts to make good his losses, miscellaneous support services, more Naval contingents, and no less than four major-generals.

As the troops arrived, so Chelmsford began to reassert control of the military stalemate. In March he moved to relieve Eshowe. Ordering his commanders along the border to make what diversionary attacks they could, he crossed the Thukela once more at the Lower Drift, and on 2 April defeated a Zulu force sent to confront him at Gingindlovu. Eshowe was relieved the next day, and within a week Chelmsford had brought his men back into Natal. In the meantime another decisive battle had already taken place at the other end of the country. Cetshwayo, too, had regrouped his forces, and this time sent them against Wood's column. Wood's intelligence reports had included

rumours of their advance, but nevertheless Wood had decided to press ahead with an attack, timed to support Chelmsford, on the Zulu mountain stronghold of Hlobane. The attack, on 28 March, was badly co-ordinated, and turned into a rout on the appearance of the main Zulu army. Wood's men were only able to extricate themselves with heavy losses. The next day, however, the Zulu force attacked Wood's fortified camp at Khambula, and was driven off after hours of heavy fighting.

The battle of Khambula was the turning point of the war. The Zulus had attacked confident that, after Isandlwana, the British were no match for them, and they had been severely defeated. It was clear to the king and his generals that the war could not be won. Chelmsford was now in a position to begin his invasion afresh, making the most of his new resources. His new plan involved a much stronger column, designated the First Division, advancing from the Lower Drift and up the coastal lowlands. A second column, the Second Division, would cross into Zululand several miles north of Rorke's Drift and, skirting Isandlwana, cut across to join the old Centre Column's planned line of advance. Along the way it would affect a juncture with Wood's Column, now redesignated the Flying Column. The First Division was intended largely as support for a combined push by the Second Division and Flying Column.

The advance began in May, slowly groping forward, establishing small stone or earthwork forts every few miles to guard the supplies and the convoys that laboriously trundled back and forward to fetch them. There was constant skirmishing, but the Zulu army did not commit itself until Chelmsford finally reached Ulundi. Here, on 4 July, he formed his troops up in a huge hollow rectangle, and watched with satisfaction as the Zulu charges dashed themselves hopelessly against a hail of artillery and volley fire.

Chelmsford's conduct of the war was not without its critics, and the home government had at last lost patience, sending out Gen. Sir Garnet Wolseley to replace him. But Chelmsford had snatched his victory before Wolseley could reach the front, and by the time Sir Garnet arrived there was little to do beyond supervising the capture of Cetshwayo and suppressing the last patches of Zulu resistance. The Dragoons ran the king to earth in a remote hideaway in northern Zululand in August and led him away to exile; and at the beginning of September Wolseley imposed a settlement on Zululand and began to withdraw. By the end of the month the evacuation was complete.

According to the official record, during the campaign 76 officers and 1,007 men had died in action, together with 604 black auxiliaries, though this figure is a substantial underestimate. Thirty-seven officers, 206 men and 57 auxiliaries were

Rank distinction, infantry officers' undress frock. The braid is that of a major; note the looped 'bullet-hole' braid. (Author's Collection)

Infantry officers' forage cap, showing the oak-leaf braid and button design on top. A regimental badge and numeral would have been worn on the front. (Author's Collection)

wounded, and 17 officers and 330 men died of disease. A further 99 officers and 1,286 men were invalided 'from the command for causes incidental to the campaign'. The total cost of the war was estimated at the time as £5,230,323.

Perhaps 7,000 Zulus had been killed in war, and countless hundreds more wounded.

Infantry

The Cardwell Reforms

The standard battlefield tactical unit of the 1870s was not the regiment, but the infantry battalion. Since Edward Cardwell had become Secretary of State for War in Gladstone's first cabinet in 1870 he had pushed through a process of reform and modernisation, often in the face of bitter opposition from the military establishment, and the result was a gradual change in the composition and outlook of the Army. Flogging in peacetime was abolished immediately (it was retained as a punishment in the field, and was used during the Zulu War), easing one of the more brutalising factors in the Other Ranks' lot. Two years later, active service was shortened from twelve years with the Colours to six with the Colours and six on reserve. This was intended both to attract a better quality of recruit—and standards of literacy in the

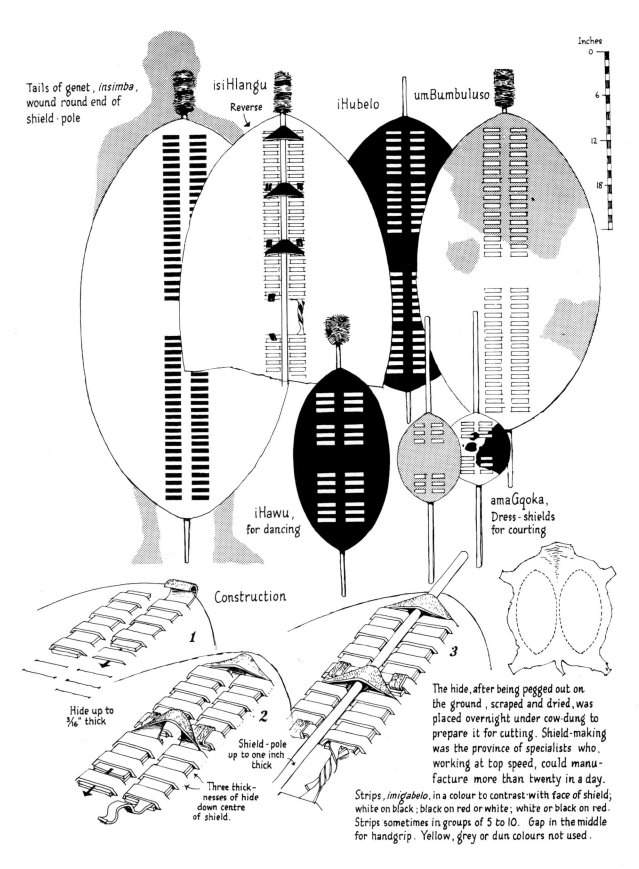

Tails of genet, *insimba*, wound round end of shield-pole

isiHlangu

Reverse

iHubelo

umBumbuluso

Inches
0
6
12
18

iHawu, for dancing

amaGqoka, Dress-shields for courting

Construction

1

Hide up to ³⁄₁₆" thick

2

Shield-pole up to one inch thick

Three thicknesses of hide down centre of shield.

3

The hide, after being pegged out on the ground, scraped and dried, was placed overnight under cow-dung to prepare it for cutting. Shield-making was the province of specialists who, working at top speed, could manufacture more than twenty in a day.

Strips, *imigabelo*, in a colour to contrast with face of shield; white on black; black on red or white; white or black on red. Strips sometimes in groups of 5 to 10. Gap in the middle for handgrip. Yellow, grey or dun colours not used.

14

lower ranks did increase markedly over the decade—and to provide a large pool of well-trained reservists who were still young.

The move attracted considerable criticism on the grounds that it replaced toughened veterans in the ranks with inexperienced youngsters, and it is interesting to note that experience in the Zulu War tends to bear this out. Many observers were struck by the youth of the short-service men, particularly those sent out after Isandlwana, who seemed to have been rather too impressed by the Zulus' fearsome reputation, and who remained prone to false alarms, particularly at night. Such alarms were not only wearing on the nerves; they could be dangerous, and on more than one occasion night piquets were mistaken for the enemy, and shot.

There was a change, too, amongst the officer class. The system by which officers had purchased their commissions, leading to a hierarchy based on personal fortune rather than competence or experience, was abolished in 1871. Many senior officers still held commands acquired under the old system, and the necessity of a private income meant that they remained a social élite, but there was an increasing emphasis on proficiency and training among junior officers. New, more fluid tactical theories were beginning to replace the rigid columns and lines of the Napoleonic era, which in turn encouraged greater self-reliance and flexibility. Such theories were largely intended for the European theatre, but in fact the British Army found itself employed in the role of Imperial policeman, where no two opponents or circumstances were exactly alike. Although over-confidence and inexperience often resulted in defeats early in such campaigns, the Army learned the hard way how to adapt to particular conditions.

Another of Cardwell's reforms, in 1873, was to link infantry battalions in pairs and tie them to a specific district within the United Kingdom where their recruitment and training was to be based. The 109 Line Infantry Regiments were identified by numbers, but many also had a subsidiary title reflecting their regional links. The 3rd Regiment, historically known as 'the Buffs' because of the colour of their facings, were the East Kents; the 24th Regiment were the 2nd Warwickshires, and so on. The first 25 regiments were each composed of two battalions, the remainder of one. In 1881 this process would be taken to its logical conclusion and several of the single-battalion regiments were amalgamated to form a single regiment; e.g. the 88th Regiment, the Connaught Rangers, were joined with the 94th to form the 1st and 2nd Battalions of the Connaught Rangers. In theory, one battalion was always supposed to be stationed at the depot whilst the other served overseas, but in fact the demands of Empire meant that significantly more were overseas at any given time.

It was most unusual for battalions of the same regiment to be serving together, though the 24th achieved this distinction, and it is interesting to note the effects of Cardwell's reforms upon them. The 1/24th had been sent overseas in 1867, and had arrived at the Cape from Gibraltar in 1875. Most of its men had enlisted under the old long-service system and, although nearly half of them were replaced by drafts from home before the start of the Zulu War, as many as 80% of its NCOs

OR's glengarry badge, 24th Regt. (above), and officers' belt clasp. (Collection of Keith Reeves)

course, but its composition was markedly different. It arrived in South Africa in March 1878, and was employed 'mopping up' on the Frontier. The soldiers were mostly short-service men whose youth struck observers in marked contrast to their sister battalion, and they included a much higher proportion of men with Welsh accents, bearing witness to the success of recruiting drives around the depot in Brecon. They, too, however, soon learned their craft amongst the kloofs and bush of the Frontier, which gave them a considerable advantage over their counterparts later in the war who had no experience to offset against their opponents' reputation.

Organisationally, each battalion consisted ideally—according to *Regulations for Field Forces, South Africa 1878*—of 30 officers and 866 men, though few were ever up to strength because of casualties, sickness and so on; on the eve of campaign the 1/24th, for example, had less than 700 men available for duty. Each battalion included a band—who were employed as stretcher-bearers in action—and was divided up into eight lettered companies, each ideally consisting of 107

Two splendid portraits of colour-sergeants wearing the dress tunic. Above is Col. Sgt. Anthony Booth, 80th Regt., who won the VC for his part in the action at Ntombe Drift in March 1879; right is Col. Sgt. Smith, 90th LI, who won the DCM during the Ninth Cape Frontier War. Note that Light Infantry wear the chevrons on both sleeves. Smith is also wearing the home service Light Infantry shako, and has a 'marksman' badge above his left cuff. Although the 90th wore their facing colours on the tunic collar and cuffs, there was no facing panel on the cuff of the frock. As well as being excellent uniform references, these portraits suggest something of the character of such men. (Royal Collection)

remained, and company photographs show a large number of men with Long Service and Good Conduct stripes. The men were perfectly acclimatised, and well used to serving under their officers and NCOs. They had fought throughout the Ninth Cape Frontier War, including the battle of Centane in February 1878, where their concentrated volley fire had broken a massed Xhosa attack. Gen. Cunynghame had been most impressed: 'there was no duty whatever to which the 24th Regiment could not be found equal to'.

The 2/24th would earn its own eulogies in due

Other Ranks and three officers—a captain, a lieutenant and a second lieutenant. The remaining officer establishment consisted of a lieutenant-colonel (in command), two majors, an adjutant, a paymaster and a quartermaster.

Infantry Uniforms

Although there had been experiments with dull and neutral-coloured clothing in the 1850s, khaki remained in service in India only, and the troops in Zululand went into action in a variety of traditional scarlets, blues and greens. There were concessions to practicality, however, in that both officers and ORs had a choice of jackets, for smarter occasions or for when duties required a practical working dress.

Officers

The officers' tunic, with its regimental facing colours on the collar and cuffs and its ornate gold braid, appears only in formal photographs and was not worn in the field. Instead, officers wore either a blue patrol jacket or a scarlet frock, the latter being sometimes known as the Scarlet

The OR's 1877-81 pattern tunic, showing the collar patches, cuff panels, trefoil braid, piping, collar badge and shoulder numeral. This particular tunic was worn by the 7th Royal Fusiliers who did not serve in Zululand, though the pattern is the same as for those who did. The practice of wearing Long Service and Good Conduct chevrons on the right sleeve was switched to the left shortly after the Zulu War. (National Army Museum)

Patrol, or the India-Pattern Frock, reflecting its origins.

The patrol jacket was of dark blue cloth, edged all round by flat, black 1in. mohair braid. It was decorated across the front with four rows of black $\frac{1}{4}$in. flat mohair plait; each double row had an eye loop in the centre (above and below) and ended in a double drop-loop. The jacket fastened down the front with hooks and eyes, but there were four netted olivets on the right side which fastened through the braid loops on the left. The cuffs were ornamented with Austrian knots in the same braid, and the back seams each had a double row of braid ending at each end in a crow's foot design, and with double eyes in the centre. Prior to 1881 the patrol jacket had no shoulder straps.

The undress frock was made of light cloth or serge, and was fastened by five regimental buttons down the front. The cuffs and shoulder straps were also scarlet, but the collar was completely in the regimental facing colour. The facing colours for

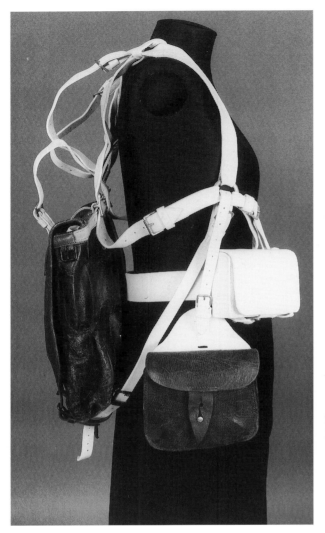

the regiments who fought in Zululand were as follows: 2/3rd buff, 2/4th blue, 1/13th blue, 2/21st blue, 1st and 2nd/24th green, 57th yellow, 58th black, 80th yellow, 88th green, 90th buff, 94th Lincoln green, and 99th yellow (the 3/60th Rifles and 91st Highlanders wore distinctive uniforms described below). The frock was piped down the front, up the back skirt vents, and round the shoulder straps in white. The shoulder straps also bore the regimental number, embroidered in gold. Rank was indicated by gold braid on the cuff and by collar badges. A single line of braid around the cuff, with an Austrian knot above and below the cuff, was worn by lieutenants and second lieutenants. Captains wore a double row of braid, with the same knots above and below. Majors also had a double row, but with a second line of looped 'bullet

hole' braid above the upper row. Lieutenant-colonels and above had a similar looped row below the second row.

The universal rank system signified rank by a series of badges on either side of the collar opening. A gold embroidered crown indicated lieutenant-colonel, a star major, and a crown and star captain. In theory a crown on its own indicated a lieutenant, and a star on its own a second lieutenant, but in practice neither of these ranks wore badges on the frock. In some regiments—certainly the 4th and 24th—junior officers wore regimental badges in place of rank ones. On the blue patrol jackets, only lieutenant-colonels and above seem to have worn collar rank badges. On the full dress tunic the badges were silver.

In practice, there was considerable variation in

The Valise pattern equipment. The exact design of these buff waist pouches post-dates the Zulu War, but in all other respects it is correct for 1879. The two looped straps at the back retained the rolled greatcoat, with the mess tin strap below. The valise itself was not usually worn on the march in Zululand, but carried on the regimental transport. The black expense pouch was often worn at the back in its place. (National Army Museum)

the design of frocks, often within the same regiment. A photograph of officers of the 90th during the campaign shows both piped and unpiped frocks, and several have breast pockets. Certain styles obviously followed a regimental fashion. Officers of the 80th Regiment appear to have worn unpiped frocks, with the shoulder straps replaced by leather pads. It was quite common for officers to wear the OR's frock; and there is a tantalising suggestion (supported by a surviving example and by analysis of photographs of Lt. G. Bromhead in

the field) that the 2/24th preferred OR's frocks stripped of all decoration except the collar facing-tab.

Officers' headgear varied between the dark blue glengarry side-cap with black ribbons and red tourie, worn with a regimental badge on the left; a dark blue peaked forage cap; and the foreign service helmet. The forage cap had a square black leather peak, and a wide band of black oak-leaf pattern lace all round, with a black cord button and design on the top. It was worn with the regimental badge over the numeral on the front.

The foreign service helmet was white with a brass spike and chin-chain, though on campaign these were replaced with a white 'cap' and leather strap repectively. The regimental badge was authorised for wear on the front. In 1878 a new star plate, with the regimental number in front and surmounted by a crown, had been approved, but, with the possible exception of a few senior officers, it does not seem to have been issued to the troops before the start of the Zulu campaign. Instead the old 1869-78 shako plate was retained; this consisted of a laurel wreath surmounted by a crown, with the numeral cut out in the centre. In practice, the combination of white helmet and brass plate proved the most conspicuous part of the soldiers' uniform, an obvious and tempting target, and all ranks used to remove the plate and dull down the helmet with improvised dyes ranging from tea, coffee, and boiled mimosa bark to cow-dung. Again, there was considerable variation between regiments regarding the wearing of helmet plates. In some it was the fashion for officers alone to retain them. A number of plates have been recovered from the battlefield of Isandlwana, but very few, bearing no relationship with the number of casualties, and making any conclusion about their distribution impossible.

Officers' trousers were dark blue with a thin red stripe down the outer seam. For mounted duties it was common to wear buff Bedford cord riding breeches. Boots were of black leather, although, again, there was considerable variation, brown leather riding boots and leggings or leather or canvas being common.

Officers' weapons consisted of the 1822 pattern Infantry Officers' Sword, with a steel scabbard, carried suspended by two slings from a white leather sword-belt, fastened with a gilt Regimental clasp. A number of privately purchased revolvers were carried, of which the 1872 pattern Adams was the most popular. The Sam Browne belt, which was becoming increasingly popular within the British Army, does not seem to have been worn in Zululand. Instead, officers carried their revolvers in a brown leather holster either on a strap over the shoulder, or attached to a waist belt. Waist belts usually had a snake-hook fastener, and small ammunition pouches were commonly worn on them. Field glasses were also carried in leather cases.

Other ranks

The Other Ranks' tunic was scarlet, and fastened down the front by seven brass general service buttons (bearing the royal arms). The facing colours were displayed on a pointed tab on either side of the collar, and on a pointed cuff panel. The cuffs were edged in white tape forming a trefoil knot above the point. The tunic was piped round the bottom edge of the collar, down the front, and up the back vents of the skirt. The shoulder straps were also piped, and bore the regimental numeral in either brass or white metal. A Regimental badge was worn on the collar tabs. The badges for those Regiments which fought in Zululand were: 2/3rd, the Dragon of Cadwalladar; 2/4th, the Lion of England; 1/13th, a bugle and strings surmounted

OR's buff leather waist belt and ammunition pouch, 24th Regiment, of the type worn in Zululand. (National Army Museum)

by a crown; 2/21st, a grenade with a thistle on the ball; 1st and 2/24th, a sphinx; 57th, a laurel wreath and scroll bearing the honour 'Albuhera'; 58th, the Castle and Key of Gibraltar; 80th, the Staffordshire knot; 88th, a crowned harp; 90th, a stringed bugle; 94th, an elephant; 99th, the Duke of Edinburgh's cypher, two 'A's on either side of a coronet.

In Line Infantry regiments rank chevrons were worn on the right sleeve only, but Fusiliers, Rifles, Highlanders and Light Infantry wore them on both sleeves. The distinctions were as follows: one white worsted chevron, lance corporal; two white chevrons, corporal; three white chevrons, lance sergeant; three gold lace chevrons, sergeant; three gold chevrons surmounted by a crown, staff sergeant; three gold chevrons surmounted by a cross Union Flag device, colour sergeant; four gold chevrons surmounted by a crown, worn above the cuff, sergeant major. Long Service and Good Conduct stripes were awarded to qualifying privates and lance corporals, to a maximum of seven badges, for 2, 5, 12, 16, 18, 21 and 26 years' service. The badge itself was a white chevron point uppermost, worn above the right cuff. Various trade and proficiency badges were also worn.

The OR's frock was of similar design, but had only five buttons, and was not piped down the front. In theory both the collar tabs and cuff facings should have been retained, but this varied from regiment to regiment, some preferring to leave off the cuff facing. The 3rd, 21st and 90th had plain red cuffs (but retaining the white tape

trefoil), though the 24th seem to have retained the facing colour.

Both the tunic and frock appear in photographs of the Zulu War. Whilst it is possible that the tunic was only worn for the photographer, it seems likely both were worn in the field even within the same regiment, though the frock was undoubtedly the more common as it was more practical.

OR's headgear consisted of the glengarry cap, with regimental badge; and the foreign service helmet, usually denuded of its fittings, and dyed, as described for the officers. OR's trousers were dark blue with a red stripe down the outer seam. Boots were black, and worn in marching order with black leather leggings, which were fastened down the outside by a series of loops passing through one another, and fixed at the top by a strap.

Infantry equipment was the 1871 Valise Pattern. This consisted of a buff leather waist belt, fastened by a regimental clasp. On either side of it were two buff ammunition pouches carrying 20 rounds apiece. Carried on a leather sling over the left shoulder was the Oliver pattern water-bottle, a small coopered D-section barrel with a screw stopper. A white haversack was worn over the left shoulder. In full marching order a waterproofed black canvas valise was designed to be carried at the small of the back, supported by braces attached to the waist belt. A rolled grey greatcoat was carried across the shoulders, with a mess-tin below, usually in a black container; the glengarry was usually tucked under the straps on the outside of the greatcoat. A black leather 'expense' pouch containing a further 30 rounds of ammunition was carried below the right-hand buff pouch. In practice, the troops in Zululand do not seem to have worn their valises, which were usually carried on the regimental transport instead. The expense pouch was often therefore carried in place of the valise, at the back of the belt. It also seems fairly common for the greatcoat to have been carried *en banderole*.

Two of the battalions which fought in Zululand were Light Infantry—the 1/13th and 90th—but their uniforms were the same as Line regiments' except in the areas discussed. They also had green glengarries rather than the Line's blue. The 90th were also nominally a Scottish Regiment (Perthshire Volunteers), but this was not reflected in

Unidentified private. 4th Regiment, 1879. He is wearing the undress frock, with a LS & GC stripe on the right cuff and a marksman badge on the other. The collar badge is the Lion of England. The helmet spike and chin-chain were not worn on active service. (Keith Reeves Collection)

their uniform in any way, except the title 'Perthshire' on their badge.

Scottish uniforms

Three of the other battalions—the 2/21st, 91st and 99th—also had Scottish associations. The 2/21st (Royal Scots Fusiliers) wore the same as Line Infantry with a number of minor differences. Both glengarries and officers' forage caps had a distinctive diced band of red, white and green (the last where the two lines of red crossed). Officers' frocks were similar to their Line equivalents, but instead of shoulder straps had twisted crimson cords, and the regiment's grenade badge was also worn on the collar in place of rank badges. Officers, but apparently not Other Ranks, also seem to have retained the grenade helmet plate.

The battalion also maintained pipers, who feature in at least one contemporary engraving showing troops on the march in Zululand. They wore the usual helmet, but with a Scottish jacket with rounded skirt front and gauntlet cuffs, and the kilt. The jacket was dark blue, and fastened by white metal diamond-shaped buttons. There were three buttons on each cuff, and three on each shaped pocket flap on the front skirts. The jacket was piped red around the bottom of the collar, around the cuffs, and in line with each of the buttons on the cuffs and skirts. A white metal

The Oliver pattern water-bottle. (Author's Collection)

grenade badge was worn either side of the collar opening. The kilt was of Royal Stewart Tartan, with a red rosette on the right side of the kilt. The hose were red with a blue diamond pattern, and the sporran was white with black tassels. A black leather waist belt with a white metal plate bearing the regimental device was worn, as were the ordinary haversack and water-bottle. The pipe-bag and ribbons were also of Royal Stewart Tartan. Alas, though the 21st played a significant part at Ulundi, there is no evidence to suggest that the pipes were played during the battle.

The 91st (Princess Louise's Argyllshire) Highlanders did wear a characteristic Highland uniform, although this regiment wore trews rather than the kilt. Contemporary photographs show officers wearing both the dress doublet and the frock in the field. The doublet had gauntlet cuffs and shaped Inverness skirt-flaps. It was scarlet with yellow cuffs and collar, and fastened by eight regimental buttons down the front. There was a band of gold lace around the top of the collar and around the cuffs, with three loops of gold braid and three buttons on each cuff and skirt-flap. The shoulder cords were also of twisted gold braid. There was white piping around the bottom of the collar, down the front, and in a double row round the Inverness skirt-flaps. Rank distinctions were worn on the collar by all ranks; and there were further distinctions indicated by the cuff braid, colonels having four extra narrow bands of braid, majors three, captains two, and lieutenants one. The frock was also scarlet, but with only five buttons down the front, and the facing colour on the collar only. The Inverness skirts were omitted, and instead the skirts were rounded at the front with a pocket flap on either side. Cuffs were again of the gauntlet style, with three buttons, and there were also three buttons on the skirt pockets. The bottom edge of the collar, down the front and around the skirts, pocket flaps, shoulder straps and lines to cuff and pocket buttons were piped with narrow gold braid. The cuffs were edged with a slightly wider gold braid.

Even within the same photograph, there is considerable variation in the style of frocks evident. One officer has six buttons rather than five, while another has diamond-shaped buttons rather than round. Of two officers wearing the doublet, one has a breast pocket, the other does not. Headgear is the ubiquitous helmet, mostly without decoration, though one officer appears to be wearing a puggaree of animal skin, and another has an object attached on one side which appears to be a small plume or animal tail. The helmets generally appear to have been stained, and the bands around them appear very dark. Most of the officers are wearing the usual paraphernalia of straps and haversacks, as well as the undress sword belt, which was white with a regimental clasp. Swords are the 1865 pattern Scottish broadsword with a crossguard rather than the basket hilt, carried in a steel scabbard. Trousers were of the Campbell of Cawdor tartan, and tucked into knee-boots, which may well have been 'veld boots' of local manufacture—these were of brown leather, and laced part of the way up the front, with a strap at the top on the outside.

ORs of the 91st wore the undress frock, which was scarlet with a yellow collar, rounded skirts with pocket flaps, and gauntlet cuffs. The piping around the base of the collar, cuffs and in line with the cuff and skirt buttons was white. The regimental badge—a boar's head—was worn on the collar, and the numerals '91' in brass on the shoulder straps. Trews were as for officers, and leggings, boots and all other equipment were as for Line Infantry. A photograph of the battalion lined up in Zululand, however, shows that, with the exception of one man who has buff ammunition pouches, all the others have black pouches of a slightly older design.

Like the 21st, the 99th (Duke of Edinburgh's) Regiment had little about their uniform to suggest their Scottish connections, apart from a diced band (red, white and yellow) on the glengarry and officers' forage cap. However, despite the fact that the regiment sailed straight from Chatham in November 1878 in response to Chelmsford's request for reinforcements on the eve of the campaign, a photograph of them at the Lower Drift early in the war indicates that they were still wearing outdated items no longer common to the other regiments. In particular, they are wearing an 1872 pattern undress frock; this lacked the collar patches and cuff trefoil of the later pattern. Instead, the whole collar was the facing colour (yellow for the 99th), and the cuffs were plain, with

White foreign service helmet (the top vent on this example has sunk slightly with age), bearing the shako plate of the 57th (West Middlesex) Regiment. (Keith Reeves Collection)

a single loop of white braid. The bottom edge of the collar and the shoulder straps were edged white, and the regimental numerals and collar badges were worn as normal. The equipment is Valise pattern, but with the black ammunition pouches described earlier. In the photograph the helmets appear clean and the shako plate is clearly visible, although at this point the battalion had not been in the Colony long, and may well have followed the usual practice of removing the plate and dying the helmet and equipment straps later. Unfortunately no evidence has come to light of the uniform worn by officers in the field, but there is no reason to suppose it would have been different from that of Line Infantry.

The Rifles

The 3/60th were the only Rifle battalion to take part in the campaign, arriving in March 1879 and taking part in the Eshowe relief expedition and the advance of the 1st Division. Their uniform was extremely distinctive. Officially it consisted of very

A company of the 99th Regiment crossing the Thukela at the Lower Drift. The single loop of cuff braid identifying the pattern of frock worn by this regiment can clearly be seen, right. Note that the men retain their helmet plates. (Local History Museum, Durban)

dark 'rifle green' jacket and trousers; however, due to problems with finding a suitable dye which did not fade, the true colour was very close to black. Officers wore an undress frock, fastened with four black buttons. There were no shoulder straps, and the collar was red, but this was largely obscured by two wide bands of black braid around the top and bottom. Trousers were of the same colour, with black boots and leggings. Field officers wore black riding breeches reinforced on the inside with black dyed buckskin, and black boots with steel spurs. The helmet was the standard foreign service type, dyed brown, but unlike most other regiments the 60th did not remove their helmet plates. These were an inconspicuous black metal Maltese cross, with a bugle centre device, on a red field. Officers' equipment consisted of black leather waist belts, fastened with a snake hook or square buckle—both painted black—and with a black leather revolver holster, and a sword with a steel hilt and black leather knot in a black scabbard. Any other

equipment—field glasses, water-bottle etc—would have been predominantly black.

The uniform of the ORs was similarly sombre. They wore the same helmet, and a dark frock fastened by five black bakelite buttons. The bottom edge of the collar was piped red, and there was a loop of braid on the cuffs. The battalion number was embroidered in scarlet on the shoulder strap. Rank chevrons, worn on both sleeves for Rifle regiments, were black on a red background. Trousers were black with no stripe. Leggings and boots were black, and the equipment was the Valise pattern but with all straps black and all buckles of brass. The waist belt was fastened by a snake-hook rather than the usual locket. The haversack, worn over the right shoulder, was black, as were the water-bottle straps. The greatcoat, however, was the more usual grey. All Other Ranks were armed with the sword-bayonet, and the slings on the rifle were black leather.

Infantry Colours

Each infantry battalion carried two Colours, the Queen's Colour and the Regimental Colour. The Colours were six feet flying by five feet six inches deep, and had fringes, cords and tassels of mixed gold and crimson. The pike was topped either by a brass or gilt device of a lion surmounting a crown, or a less complex spearhead. The Queen's Colour was basically the national standard, the Great Union Flag, and bore a gold embroidered Imperial crown in the centre above the regimental numeral. Thus the famous Queen's Colour of the 1/24th, which Lts. Melvill and Coghill tried to save at Isandlwana, was the Union flag with a crown above the numeral XXIV. The 2/24th's Queen's Colour was similar but with a scroll beneath the numeral bearing the title II Battalion. The Regimental Colour was unique to each battalion. It was of the regimental facing colour, with a small Union flag in the dexter canton (the top corner abutting the pike), and a regimental device and battle honours. For example, the Queen's Colour of the 58th (Rutlandshire) Regiment was the Union with a crown above the numeral LVIII; but the Regimental Colour was black with the Cross of St George, the Union in the dexter canton, a red and gold LVIII in the centre, surrounded by RUTLANDSHIRE with the Union wreath around, a crown above, and the motto MONTIS INSIGNIA CALPE below. In 1879 it had ten battle honours on scrolls

on either side of the central device. The Buffs carried their Colours into action at Nyezane, and several battalions carried them at Ulundi, including the 58th, who achieved the distinction, at Laing's Nek two years later in the Transvaal War, of being the last infantry regiment to carry their Colours into action. When not in action, the Colours were furled and protected by a heavy leather case with a brass top.

Appearance in the field

It is interesting to note that there seems to have been no provision for replacing worn out or damaged clothing during the campaign. Zululand's climate can be one of extremes, and this was certainly the case in 1879, when baking days alternated with sudden chilling downpours during the summer months, and a biting frost was common on winter nights. Much of the country is covered in thornbush, and the rigours of life in the open took a heavy toll on soldiers' uniforms.

Infantry Colours. The Regimental Colour of the 94th, left, and Queen's Colour of the 21st Royal Scots Fusiliers. Although this photograph was taken in 1881 during the Transvaal War, where these Colours had an interesting history, the same Colours were also carried in Zululand. (National Army Museum)

Of the 1/13th one observer wrote: 'their uniforms were in rags, and patched with different colours, some had no boots . . . their helmets . . . were covered in old shirts . . . and their belts and rifles dirtied to order'. The regimental history of the 2/21st states: 'Each man endeavoured as best he could to repair the rents and holes in his apparel; but the material obtainable was most unsuitable, being neither the colour nor texture of the material itself. Patches of biscuit bags, blankets, waterproof sheets, may cover deficiencies, but they do not add to the splendours of a soldier's uniform!'

There is no reason to suppose that the experience of these two regiments was in any way unique. Sketches by Lt. W. W. Lloyd of the 24th show men of his regiment in patched uniforms, with battered helmets or civilian hats; and Pte. Gissop of the 17th Lancers wondered 'what people would have thought could they only have seen us with our clothes torn and patched, belts and saddles dirty, bits rusty, boots without blacking or grease, and so lamentable in appearance from the Regiment which left England so clean and smart such a short time ago'. Photographs on campaign show both officers and men wearing civilian hats instead of helmets—clearly this was as much a matter of necessity as of choice.

A night piquet of the 94th Regiment, Upoko River, Zululand. The men are wearing their equipment buckled over the greatcoats. (Author's Collection)

Weapons

The standard infantry weapon was the 1875 Mark II pattern Martini-Henry rifle, the earlier version of which had begun to replace the Snider from 1871. It was a single shot breech-loader with a simple mechanism, activated by lowering a lever behind the trigger guard. This caused the breech-block to drop, allowing the cartridge to be inserted into the chamber at the top of the breech. The cartridge was a .45in. Boxer type, with a hardened but unjacketed lead bullet of 480 grains. The barrel had seven grooves and the bullet emerged with a muzzle velocity of 1,350 feet per second. It was sighted up to 1,000 yards, but its effective battlefield range was half that, and it was particularly deadly at 350 yards. By the time of the Zulu War it was in service around the world, and had proved itself on the Eastern Cape at Nyumaxa in January 1878. Sir Arthur Cunynghame had been impressed: 'At no time had the power of the Martini-Henry rifle been more conspicuously shown; indeed, it was perhaps the first occasion when it had been fairly used by the British army.' It was considered to possess the necessary stopping-power to lay out a charging warrior in his tracks, and the heavy bullet certainly inflicted the ghastly wounds associated with its type—small entry holes with horrific exit wounds.

It was not without its faults, however. With frequent use the barrel became hot and fouled, exaggerating the already pronounced recoil. The

The 91st Highlanders on the march in Zululand. Note the pipers, centre left, and the fact that blankets are worn 'en banderole'. (National Army Museum)

extractor grip might tear through the soft brass of the cartridge, causing it to jam; and since the forestock did not encircle the barrel over-heating could mean burnt fingers on the left hand. To counter this veterans of the Cape Frontier War sewed bullock hide around the forestock.

The Martini-Henry weighed 9lb., was 4ft 1½ins. long, and had a buff leather sling. ORs below the rank of sergeant carried a triangular socket bayonet 21½ins. long, which gave a combined reach of over six feet; the bayonet was nicknamed 'the lunger' as a result. It was carried in a black leather scabbard with brass fittings on the left rear of the waist belt. Sergeants and above carried the 1871 pattern sword bayonet, which had a steel hilt with a chequered leather grip, and a blade with a double curve; it was carried in a black scabbard with steel fittings.

In view of the controversy surrounding the question of the supply of ammunition at Isandlwana, it is worth considering the design of the boxes used to contain the battalion supplies. As early as 1874 the *Treatise on Ammunition* provided plans of the Small Arms Ammunition Box, Mark IV, which was capable of carrying 560 Snider rounds or 600 Martini-Henry rounds. This was modified slightly by the Mark V and VI models of 1875. In each case, the boxes were made of teak or mahogany, and lined with tin to protect the contents on overseas service. Each pattern was encircled by two copper retaining bands, screwed into place; but it was *not* necessary to remove the bands in order to gain access to the ammunition. Access was via a grooved sliding panel in the lid; this was held in place by one screw, but it was generally recognised that in times of emergency a sharp blow, or even a kick, to the outer edge would snap the screw and dislodge the panel. The tin liner could be pulled back by means of a handle situated at the panel opening. It is not clear which pattern of boxes were in use at Isandlwana—Mark IV, V or VI—but in each case the quartermasters would have known better than to waste time unscrewing the retaining bands.

Logistics

Before leaving the infantry, it is worth considering the logistical back-up necessary to maintain a battalion in the field. Each battalion had to carry its own ammunition, tents (the eight-man Bell tent—after the man who invented it, rather than its shape), entrenching tools and medical equipment, not to mention rations. In Zululand these usually consisted of 'mealies' (local corn carried in 200lb. bags), tough army biscuit in heavy wooden boxes, and tinned 'bully beef'. Fresh meat was usually 'on the hoof' and vegetables were procured where available. Wood's column included a field bakery. These requirements alone could take up 17 wagons, without the luxury of the officers' personal baggage, and the men's bottled beer. If there was no fuel around, that too would have to be transported. For cavalry regiments, whose British-bred horses would not eat coarse local grasses, fodder, too, would have to be carried.

There were a limited number of Army General Service wagons available, but they were not ideal, since their narrow carriage, intended for European roads, made them unstable in southern Africa. The solution was to purchase local transport, which Chelmsford's harassed and inexperienced transport staff did, often at inflated prices. The wagons themselves were large and heavy, sometimes tented, often with a half-tent covering the rear portion only. They required between 16 and 18 oxen apiece to pull them; and if the oxen were to remain healthy they needed 16 hours each day for rest and grazing, which reduced their travelling potential to about ten miles per day. On trackless country, roads seamed by dongas or turned into a quagmire by sudden rain, it was much less.

Shortage of transport remained a major head-ache throughout the war, and it is impossible to ignore the extent to which it dominated Chelmsford's strategy. The camp at Isandlwana was unlaagered because the wagons were about to return to Rorke's Drift to fetch supplies; Rorke's Drift proved so defensible simply because those same supplies were available to build barricades. The Second Invasion moved at such a methodical pace so that forts could be erected to guard the staging posts as the convoys slogged back and forth along the lines of communication. Even in battle the wagons formed the surest means of defence, the *laager*. This was based on the Boer practice of circling wagons for protection in hostile country at the end of a day's trek. In 1879, especially after Isandlwana, transport wagons were drawn into one or more linked square laager, which was often entrenched. The usual method was to dig a trench several paces beyond the wagon line, piling the earth up inside to form a parapet. The troops would then sleep between the parapet and the wagons at night, and man the parapet at times of alarm. The wagon-drivers themselves were usually civilian contractors, with African *Voorloopers*, who walked at the head of the train, controlling the oxen with long whips.

Another Transvaal War photo, this time of the 3/60th Rifles at Mount Prospect Camp. The uniform is the same as worn in Zululand; the single loop of braid on the cuffs is clearly visible, as are NCOs' chevrons. Most of the helmets here have both the Maltese Cross badge and the spike. The 1879 medal ribbon is just visible on most of the jackets. (Royal Greenjackets Museum, Winchester)

Cavalry

At the beginning of the campaign Chelmsford had no regular cavalry regiments at his disposal— something of a drawback given the cavalry's traditional roles of scouting and pursuit. He did, however, have two understrength squadrons of Mounted Infantry, who were distributed throughout the invading columns. The MI consisted of selected soldiers from infantry regiments mounted on locally acquired horses. They wore the foreign service helmet, with no fittings, and the undress frock of their battalions, with buff Bedford cord riding breeches, leggings and boots. Instead of infantry equipment they carried loop-style ammunition bandoliers over the left shoulder. Waist belts, water-bottles and haversacks may have been worn on occasions. Officers wore cord riding breeches, boots, and patrol jackets or frocks from their own battalions. Despite the mixed origins of this force it performed extremely well, and paved the way for greater reliance on Mounted Infantry units in later campaigns.

When news of the Isandlwana débâcle reached London, two full regiments were embarked for South Africa: the 1st (King's) Dragoon Guards,

and the 17th (Duke of Cambridge's Own) Lancers. Both created a mixed reaction when they arrived in Natal. The settlers were impressed that such dashing regiments had been sent to their aid, but sceptical about the value of British-bred horses. The heavy cavalry mounts had indeed suffered badly on the long voyage out, and once ashore refused to eat the local grasses. The regiments were therefore allowed to make their way up country slowly to allow the horses time to recover; they did not reach the front until May. Here they were brigaded together to form the Cavalry Brigade under Maj.-Gen. Marshall, and attached to the 2nd Division. Both emerged from the campaign with distinction; the 17th, with one squadron of Dragoons, charged from the square at Ulundi to turn the Zulu retreat into a rout, and it was a patrol of the Dragoons who finally captured King Cetshwayo.

Each cavalry regiment consisted of four squadrons, each of 120 privates, 22 NCOs (including four artificers and two trumpeters), and six officers; and a headquarters staff, to a nominal total of 653 men. The Dragoon Guards were almost up to strength with 649, the 17th slightly under with 622.

Lancer officers' uniform

In neither regiment did the Dress Regulations make many concessions to the practicalities of service in the field beyond replacing home service headgear with the inevitable helmet. The officers of the 17th Lancers wore their full dress 1876 pattern tunic. This was dark blue with a white plastron front, white collar and cuffs, and white piping along the leading edge of the skirt, around the bottom, and along the back and arm seams. It was double-breasted, with two rows of gilt buttons bearing the regimental death's head device, the rows being eight inches apart at the top and four inches at the waist; the last two buttons were flattened to fit under the waist girdle. There were two more buttons at the back above the slashed skirt panels, which bore three more buttons, and were edged all round with gold cord. A small button on each shoulder secured a loop of gold braid. There was a one-inch band of gold lace around the top of the collar and around the pointed cuffs. Field officers had a double row of

The .45 Martini-Henry Rifle, Mark 2; the standard infantry arm during the Zulu War. (National Army Museum)

gold around the cuffs and a narrow band around the bottom of the collar. Rank badges (in silver) were worn on the collar by all officers. Trousers were dark blue with a double white stripe with a blue line between.

Dress Regulations called for officers to wear a gold waist girdle with two crimson stripes, but this was not worn in Zululand. There were other unofficial practical modifications, too. It is hard to imagine anything more conspicuous in the bright African sun than a glaring white helmet and plastron. When photographed in Natal the Lancers' helmets were still pristine, but by the time they were in Zululand they had achieved the same

The Mark V Small Arms Ammunition box, showing the copper retaining straps. Access to the ammunition was via a sliding centre panel, missing on this example. For overseas garrisons the box was lined with tinfoil. (Royal Regiment of Wales, Brecon)

muddied look as those of the infantry, and no doubt by the same means. The plastron was obscured simply by buttoning it over to reveal the less conspicuous blue reverse side.

The officers' dress pouch belt does seem to have been retained in action, however. This was gold, with a white centre line; the plate, chain, pickers, buckle tip and slide were all of silver. The pouch itself was blue leather with a silver top engraved round the edge and with an entwined 'VR' cypher in gilt. Individual portraits suggest that it was fashionable within the regiment to wear the belt with the plate high in the centre of the chest and the top mount under the shoulder cords. The dress sword belt, carrying the 1822 Light Cavalry sabre in a steel scabbard, was gold with a white centre line and a snake clasp, the slings being the same but with gilt buckles. It was officially supposed to be worn under the tunic, though photographs in Zululand show several officers wearing it outside. Indeed, many seem to have preferred unofficial

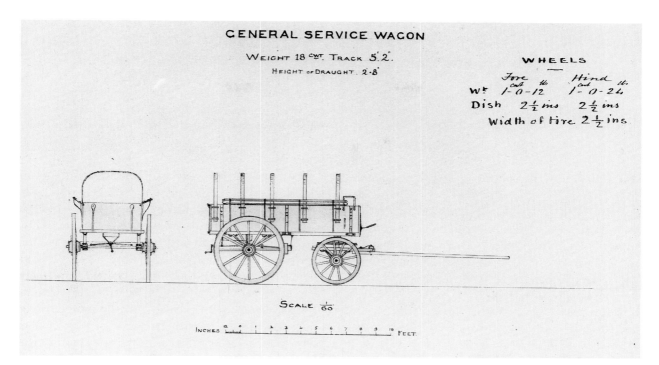

GENERAL SERVICE WAGON

WEIGHT 18 CWT. TRACK 5'.2".
HEIGHT OF DRAUGHT. 2'.8'

WHEELS
Wt. Fore 1-0-12 cwt. lb.   Hind 1-0-24 cwt. lb.
Dish 2½ ins   2½ ins
Width of tire 2½ ins

SCALE 1/60

INCHES 9 0 1 2 3 4 5 6 7 8 9 10 FEET

brown leather belts with revolver holsters. Some also discarded their trousers in favour of the popular cord riding breeches.

The General Service wagon, the standard transport wagon of the British Army. From a series of sketches depicting transport vehicles during the Zulu War. (National Army Museum)

Lancer OR's uniform

The OR's tunic was of similar pattern to the officers': blue, with a white plastron front, white collar, pointed cuffs, and white piping down the leading edge of the skirt, round the bottom, along the back seams and around the back skirt flaps. The buttons were of brass and regimental pattern. The shoulder cords were single loops of yellow braid. NCOs' chevrons were gold, worn on the right sleeve only, and Long Service and Good Conduct stripes were yellow, and worn above the right cuff. Trousers were dark blue with a double white stripe. The official waist girdle was yellow worsted with two red stripes, but it was not worn on campaign, and nor were the yellow body lines. Like the officers, the ORs reversed their plastrons to show the blue side.

A white canvas haversack was worn over the right shoulder, and a white pouch belt, with brass fittings and black leather pouch, was worn over the left shoulder, as was the Oliver pattern water-bottle. The sword belt was of white leather with a brass snake-hook fastener. The 1864 Cavalry Trooper's Sword was carried in a steel scabbard.

Photographs of the regiment on campaign show buff ammunition pouches worn on either side of the waist belt buckle, since in addition to the lance the men carried Martini-Henry carbines. The main weapon, the lance, was the 1868 pattern— nine feet long, and made of 'male' bamboo, which has less pith and is therefore stronger than the more common 'female' bamboo. The blade was of cast steel, as was the shoe. A red-over-white pennon was fixed to the wood just below the blade, and there was a white rawhide grip at the point of balance.

There is very little evidence concerning horse furniture, but both Lancers and Dragoons were issued some of the new 1878 pattern 'Angle Iron Arch' saddles, though they were not favourably received. The bulk of the remaining saddles were presumably the 1856 'Universal Wood Arch', with the 1860 pattern bridle. Blue cavalry cloaks, with a white lining for officers, were carried strapped over the wallets in front of the saddle. The blue valise, piped white around the ends, bearing '17' above the letter 'L', was strapped behind the saddle, with a mess tin on top.

Dragoon uniforms

Like the Lancers, the Dragoons wore a modified dress uniform, including tunics, but with the foreign service helmet. The officers' tunic was scarlet with blue velvet collar and cuffs, fastened down the front by eight regimental pattern buttons. Lieutenants and captains had a ¾in. band of gold lace around the top of the collar, and field officers had lace all round. Rank badges were worn on either side of the collar opening. The cuffs were edged in gold cord ending in an Austrian knot design—three rows of cord for field officers (extending to 11ins. from the cuff), a double row for captains (extending to 9ins.), and a single row for lieutenants (extending to 7ins.). A gold twisted cord was worn on each shoulder, fastened by two small regimental buttons. There were two further buttons above the centre of the skirts at the rear and three on each shaped panel, which were edged in gold braid. The tunic was piped blue down the front, and the skirts lined white. Breeches were dark blue with a wide gold stripe down the outside, and were reinforced on the inside. Boots were

Chelmsford's existing transport was completely inadequate for his needs; civilian wagons, of which this is a typical pattern, were purchased or hired to make up the shortfall. (National Army Museum)

black, with steel spurs. Unlike the Lancers, Dragoon officers seem to have worn an undress pouch belt very similar to the ORs', with a white belt and black pouch. The sword belt was white with a gilt rectangular buckle bearing the regimental badge. The sword itself was the 1856 pattern Heavy Cavalry Officers' Sword, carried in a steel scabbard. Various unofficial brown belts may also have been worn.

The ORs' tunic was also scarlet, with velvet collar, cuffs and shoulder straps. The collar was edged all round with yellow worsted, as were the cuffs, which ended in an Austrian knot device. The shoulder straps were edged in yellow worsted all round except on the seam, and bore '1' and 'DG' in yellow embroidery. The back skirt flaps were edged in yellow and decorated with three buttons. OR's breeches were blue with a wide yellow stripe. The sword belt was white with a snake-clasp, carrying the 1864 pattern sword. Like the Lancers, the Dragoons carried ammunition pouches for their Martini-Henry carbines. No doubt this would have been most uncomfortable after prolonged riding and a photograph of a 1st KDG private visiting Isandlwana in June 1879 suggests a solution—he has his belt casually slung around his shoulder rather than at the waist.

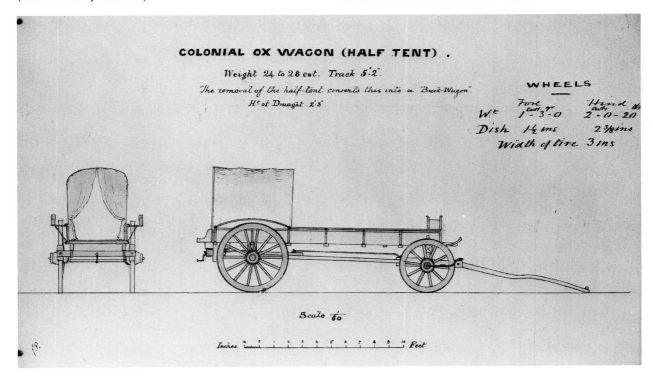

COLONIAL OX WAGON (HALF TENT).

Weight 24 to 28 cwt. Track 5'2"

The removal of the half-tent converts this into a 'Buck-Wagon'.

Ht of Draught 2'5"

WHEELS

	Fore	Hind
Wt	1-3-0	2-0-20
Dish	1½ ins	2⅜ ins
Width of tire	3 ins	

Scale 1/60

Inches. Feet

1: Infantry private
2: Infantry officer
3: Officer, Royal Artillery
4: Bombardier, Royal Artillery

A

The 1/24th firing line, Isandlwana, 22 January 1879:
1: Sergeant, 24th Regiment
2: Lieutenant, 24th Regiment
3: Private, 24th Regiment
4: Bandsman, 24th Regiment

B

Isandlwana, 22 January 1879:
1: Battalion Quartermaster, 24th Regiment
2: Mounted Infantry private
3: Lt.Col. Anthony Durnford, RE
4: Trooper; Buffalo Border Guard
5: Trooper; Natal Carbineers
6: Trooper; Natal Mounted Police

C

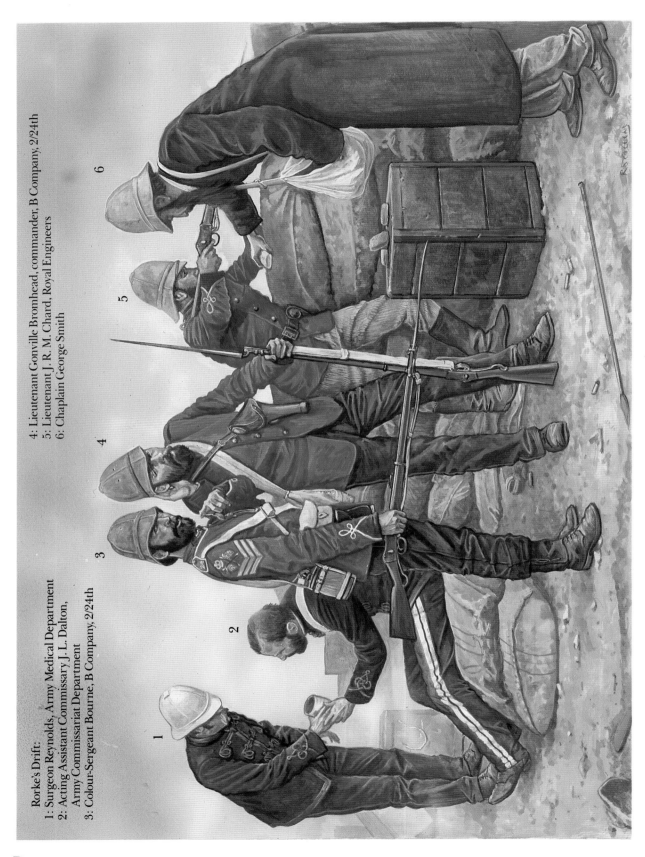

Rorke's Drift:
1: Surgeon Reynolds, Army Medical Department
2: Acting Assistant Commissary J. L. Dalton,
   Army Commissariat Department
3: Colour-Sergeant Bourne, B Company, 2/24th

4: Lieutenant Gonville Bromhead, commander, B Company, 2/24th
5: Lieutenant J. R. M. Chard, Royal Engineers
6: Chaplain George Smith

D

The Battle of Nyezane, 22 January 1879:
1: Private, 99th Regiment
2: Sapper, Royal Engineers
3: Trooper, Durban Mounted Rifles
4: Trooper, Stanger Mounted Rifles

E

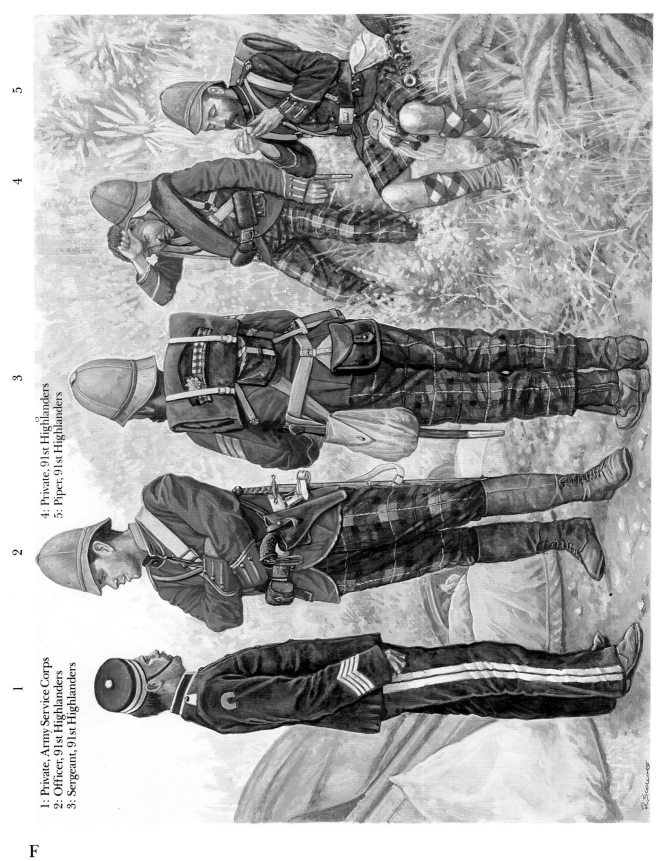

F

1: Private, Army Service Corps
2: Officer, 91st Highlanders
3: Sergeant, 91st Highlanders

4: Private, 91st Highlanders
5: Piper, 91st Highlanders

1 2 3 4 5

The Naval Brigade at Gingindlovu, 2 April 1879:
1: Sailors, HMS *Boadicea*
2: Private, Royal Marine Light Infantry
3: Officer, Royal Naval landing party
4: Sailor, HMS *Shah*

G

The descent of the 'Devil's Pass',
Battle of Hlobane, 28 March 1879:
1: Trooper, Frontier Light Horse
2: Lt.Col. Redvers Buller
3: Officer, Frontier Light Horse
4: Trooper, Frontier Light Horse
5: Sergeant, Transvaal Volunteers

H

The death of Lieutenant and Adjutant F. J. Cockaye Frith,
17th Lancers, Upoko River, 5 June 1879:
1: Private, 17th Lancers
2: Corporal, 17th Lancers
3: Lt. and Adj. Frith
4: Officer, 17th Lancers

I

The Battle of Ulundi, 4 July 1879; inside Lord Chelmsford's square:
1: Privates, Army Hospital Corps
2: Officer, 2/21st Royal Scots Fusiliers
3: Col. Henry Evelyn Wood
4: Lieutenant-General Lord Chelmsford

J

Natal Native Troops searching the field after Ulundi
1: Trooper, Natal Native Horse
2: Warrior, Natal Native Contingent
3: Swazi Warrior

K

King Cetshwayo kaMpande in captivity, August 1879:
1: Sergeant, 3/60th Rifles
2: Officer, 3/60th Rifles

3: King Cetshwayo kaMpande
4: Trooper, 1st (King's) Dragoon Guards
5: Major, King's Dragoon Guards

1 2 3 4 5

Artillery

Despite experiments with breech-loading models in the 1860s, the British Army of the 1870s was still primarily armed with muzzle-loading guns. In Zululand, RA batteries were armed with either 7-pdr. or 9-pdr. 8cwt. Rifled Muzzle-Loading guns.

The Mark IV 7-pdr. was intended for use as a mountain gun. It had a steel barrel with three rifling grooves, and a maximum range of 3,100 yards. Designed to be mounted on the small, narrow 'Abyssinian' carriage, it could either be dragged by three mules in tandem, or dismantled and carried on pack mules. Its narrow carriage had advantages in bush country, but it was unstable on more open tracks and easily overturned. As a result, so-called Colonial or Kaffrarian carriages were introduced for use in southern Africa. These were modified versions of the carriage used for the 9-pdr. 8cwt. model. It is sometimes surprisingly difficult to tell from contemporary evidence which guns were used where, but Lt. Lloyd's guns of 11/7 (11 Battery, 7th Brigade), which accompanied Pearson's column and fought at Nyezane, are listed in the official history as 'two 7-pdrs., mule'; whilst N/5, who lost two guns at Isandlwana, had them mounted on Kaffrarian carriages. When mounted on the latter they were drawn by the 16-pdr. Armstrong Limber, which also drew the 9-pounders. Generally, the 7-pdr. did not prove very successful in Zululand. By mounting it on a heavy carriage, much of

its chief asset, its manoeuvrability, was lost. It had a low muzzle velocity, which rendered shrapnel largely ineffective, and the small bursting charge meant that the destructive power of the common shell was negligible. On the whole, it was felt that if the 7-pdr. had to be mounted on a 9-pdr. carriage to be practical, they might as well have had the 9-pdr. in the first place.

The 9-pdr. 8cwt. RML was the standard RA field gun of the 1870s, and distinguished itself in the Zulu War, where its contributions to the decisive battles of Khambula and Ulundi were of major importance. The barrel was of wrought-iron, and could throw a shell a maximum of 3,500 yards.

With the many reinforcements who began to arrive at Durban from March onwards came the two Gatlings of 10/7 RA, the first battery in the British Army to have Gatlings. The Gatling was a cumbersome, hand-cranked machine-gun invented by an American, Dr. Richard Gatling, during the Civil War. The British War Office tested the weapon at the beginning of the decade, and was favourably impressed, ordering a number of .45in. Gatlings for Army use and heavy .65in. Gatlings for the Navy.

The artillery version was mounted on a carriage similar to the field guns, and received its rounds from a hopper which fitted above the breech. The British Gatling was designed to take standard

Small Arms ammunition, the Boxer cartridge. This was not entirely suitable, since the soft metal often tore under pressure from the extractor grip, fouling the breech and causing jamming. At Ulundi the bolts slipped out and were hard to find in the long grass, rendering the guns ineffective at a crucial stage of the battle. Nevertheless, when it was working, the Gatling more than made up for its faults. It was ideally suited for use on the open terrain of Zululand against the Zulu massed charge, and those who saw it in action were fascinated by the way it chopped lines clean through the attacking force.

Also used in Zululand were a number of 9-pdr. Hales Rocket Troughs. Rockets had first been used by the British Army during the Napoleonic Wars, where they differed little in principle from an ordinary firework, propelled by a slowly burning charge of black powder. Since a tube is inherently unstable in flight, and will cartwheel over and over, some form of stabilising system is necessary. During the Napoleonic Wars, this was nothing more than a stick, and the range and accuracy of the projectile was barely worth the effort of its invention. During the 1860s, however, William Hale, a mechanic at the Royal Arsenal, invented a stick-less rocket, whose charge ignited through three vents at the base end, where three curved baffles were used to deflect the force and twist the rocket on its central axis. After extensive trials both 9-pdr. and 24-pdr. rockets were approved. The latter were originally intended for siege purposes, but were largely taken up by the Navy, where a tube was developed for on-ship use.

On land the 9-pdr. rockets were launched from a three-legged trough which included an adjustable arm for elevation. The rocket was ignited by means of a friction tube attached to a lanyard and inserted into one of the vents. The gunner firing the rocket had to 'bring . . . the lanyard up under the hollow of his left foot, which should be placed close to the hind rest of the trough, and pull . . . upwards with his right hand with a steady pull'. What happened next was unpredictable. The elevation system of the trough was intended for use on level ground, and in the field it was difficult to set the range with anything approaching accuracy—a calculation further hindered by the erratic burning rate of the black powder. Rockets were known

to sail clear over the heads of their targets or, striking some obstacle, to be deflected wildly off course, even bouncing back at their crew. When they did strike home, they had no warhead as such, and their charge might fail to explode altogether. None the less they were considered useful in Colonial warfare, where the terrifying howl they made in flight, and the sparks and smoke they trailed across the sky, were thought to be of tremendous psychological advantage.

There is no evidence that the Zulus were impressed by them; they never stalled an attack

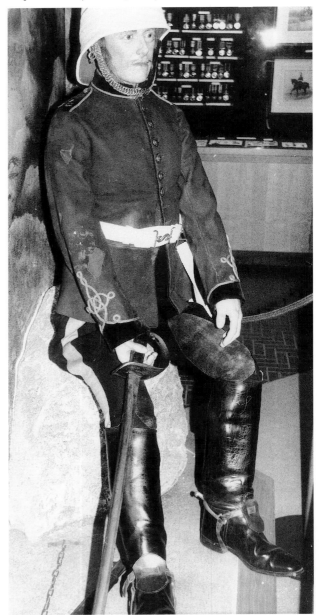

before one, and simply called them 'paraffin', a white man's combustible material with which they were familiar through the activities of traders. The *Manual of Field Artillery Exercises* specified that 'the (crew) detachment consists of one non-commissioned officer and four gunners'. In fact Maj. Russell's rocket battery, attached to Durnford's No. 2 Column, consisted of one RA bombardier and eight members of the 24th to man three troughs, which were carried on mules. During the battle of Isandlwana they were overrun by the Zulus.

Artillery uniforms

During the Zulu War RA officers seem to have worn the blue patrol jacket almost without exception. This fastened down the front with hooks and

The uniform of an OR of the 1st (King's) Dragoon Guards; an impressive collection displayed at Cardiff Castle. On campaign the brass chin-chain would have been replaced by a leather strap. (Cardiff Castle)

A close-up of the same display, showing the blue cuffs and yellow worsted braid, and details of the sword belt—here without the scabbard. (Cardiff Castle)

eyes and olivets, and was bordered all round with 1in. black mohair braid. There were five rows of flat plait mohair braid across the chest, ending in crow's foot knots and olivets. The cuff was edged in the same braid, ending in crow's foot knots, as were the back seams, which had a knot at each end and two eyes at equal distances. The stand-and-fall collar was edged in wide, flat braid, and no rank badges were worn. Trousers were blue with a 2in. scarlet stripe. Headgear was the inevitable dyed helmet. The sword belt was white with a gilt regimental plate, and photographs indicate that many officers wore leather holster belts, after the manner of the infantry.

Like the infantry, RA rankers seem to have favoured the undress frock; this was dark blue, and fastened by five buttons. The collar was red with yellow worsted piping around the bottom edge; the shoulder straps were piped yellow all round, and the cuff bore a yellow trefoil. The shoulder straps bore the brigade number and a grenade badge embroidered in yellow. NCOs' chevrons were in gold, and sergeants and above had gold

10/7 Battery RA, the first Gatling battery in the British Army, with its guns. The two men centre, with chevrons above their cuffs, are staff sergeants. Note the officer in blue patrol. The men appear to be wearing the undress frock. (S Bourquin)

worsted. The OR's frock, which does feature in a few isolated campaign photos, was of a similar pattern, but with nine buttons down the front. It was piped scarlet, and the scarlet collar was edged all round in yellow worsted. The cuffs bore a more ornate Austrian knot design. Shoulder straps were piped scarlet with grenade badge and number in yellow. All rank chevrons were gold lace, and sergeants and above had gold lace instead of worsted. Photographs show NCOs wearing brown leather revolver holsters and sword belts. Regulations specified a white leather belt for ORs with the brass universal locket. Trousers were dark blue with a wide scarlet stripe, and leggings and boots were black.

Departmental Corps

At the start of the war Chelmsford had just one Company of **Royal Engineers**—a theoretical strength of six officers and 194 NCOs and sappers.

He received two more in the build-up prior to hostilities, and one final reinforcement after Isandlwana.

Photographs of Engineer officers in the war show them wearing either the blue patrol jacket or the undress frock. The blue patrol had Garter-blue velvet collar and cuffs, and was edged all round with 1in. black mohair braid. It was fastened down the front by hooks and eyes, and there were five double rows of black flat plait mohair across the chest, looping over olivets in the centre, and ending with olivets and crow's foot knots. The cuffs were also edged in the same braid, ending in a crow's foot knot, as were the back seams. The basic design of the RE patrol jacket was very similar to the RA one, the chief distinction being the velvet collar and cuffs.

The officers' undress frock was scarlet with blue velvet collar and cuffs, and fastened by five regimental buttons. The collar was edged all round with narrow gold braid, as was the cuff, ending in a trefoil or crow's foot. There was a thin twist of gold cord on the shoulder, fastened by a small regimental button.

Trousers were dark blue with a wide red stripe, though officers on mounted duties often preferred cord breeches. Headgear was the usual helmet.

Swords were the 1856 Engineer Officers' pattern, though it seems unlikely, in such a practical profession, that they would have been much carried. No doubt RE officers carried revolvers, field glasses, water-bottles and so on in the same way as infantry officers.

The OR's undress serge was scarlet with blue collar and cuffs. The collar was edged all round with yellow worsted braid, and the cuffs had a single yellow loop. Shoulder cords were of yellow braid held in place by a small button. OR's trousers were dark blue with a red stripe down the outside leg. When on the march infantry-pattern equipment was worn. The men were armed with the Martini-Henry rifle. At the battle of Nyezane sappers of Capt. Wynne's No. 2 Company were improving a river drift while Pearson's column was crossing, when the Zulus attacked. The Zulu left horn advanced rapidly to threaten the drift, and the Engineers were called away to assist in driving them off. At Ulundi Chelmsford used RE men as a reserve within his square, moving them up to support sections of the firing line as they were threatened.

Small detachments from the **Army Hospital Corps** served throughout the war. It was a corps without officers—these being formed separately into the Army Medical Department, though in 1884 the two were brought together and in 1898 amalgamated under the new title of the Royal Army Medical Corps. Typically, the men seem to have worn the undress frock in Zululand. This was dark blue, fastened with five buttons; the collar was piped all round with scarlet braid, as were the shoulder straps. There was a braid trefoil on each cuff, terminating in a curl at each side by the sleeve–back seam, above which were two buttons. The collar badges were brass crowns, and the letters 'AHC', also in brass, were mounted on the shoulder straps. All ranks wore a white arm badge on the right arm, bearing the red cross of Geneva, and edged in gold for senior sergeants and yellow for ORs. Rank chevrons were gold for senior sergeants, and red for lance sergeants and below; they were worn on the right sleeve below the red cross badge. Trousers were dark blue with a narrow red stripe. Gaiters were of the infantry lace-up pattern, and boots were black. Equipment consisted of a brown leather waist belt with snake

clasp, with a white haversack and Oliver pattern water-bottle suspended from a brown leather strap. Headgear in the field seems to have been the ubiquitous helmet; or the forage cap, which was peaked, with a gold band, for sergeants only. However, a photograph of a private of the AHC in South Africa in 1879 shows him to be wearing a peaked forage cap, apparently with a white cover.

Information on the **Army Service Corps** at the time of the war is scarce, but there do exist two good photographs of troops in the field. These show at least two different types of jacket, a tunic and an undress frock. The former was dark blue with a blue velvet collar; it was fastened by eight buttons, but was completely plain apart from a white edging to the collar and twisted white shoulder cords (although a number of men in the group have conspicuous white LS & GC chevrons above the right cuff, as well as trade badges). The frock was similar but with a plain blue collar, five buttons, and edging around the collar and shoulder cords. A third pattern of jacket seems to be in evidence, which was plain blue with four buttons—this may have been some sort of working jacket. Forage caps were dark blue with gold button and double gold band for sergeants, and white for lower ranks. Helmets were also worn. Equipment was a brown leather belt with snake-hook fastener; staff sergeants wore swords, and ORs carried sword bayonets.

A 9-pdr. Hales rocket trough, used in Zululand. One arm of the trough is missing, and this rocket seems to be a larger 24-pdr. type. (Natal Museum)

Naval Brigades

Naval Brigade landing parties were a feature of Victorian campaigns and the Zulu War was no exception. The first party was landed by HMS *Active* in November 1878; it was 230 strong, including 34 Royal Marine Light Infantry and eight Royal Marine Artillery. This detachment was present at the reading of the ultimatum to the Zulu envoys at the Lower Drift on 11 December, and subsequently fought with Pearson's Column. A small detachment from HMS *Tenedos* was landed on 1 January 1879; this was only 61 strong, with 15 Marines, including three RMA. In the aftermath of Isandlwana HMS *Shah* was diverted from a homeward journey and landed most of its ship's complement at Durban, a total of 378 men. On 20 March HMS *Boadicea* also landed a brigade of ten officers and 218 men. About 100 Marines were included in the last two detachments. Because, of necessity, Naval Brigades were landed on the coast, they fought throughout the war with the coastal operations.

The uniforms of the sailors seem to have varied slightly between each detachment. The *Active* men appear to have worn blue Navy jumpers with black silk neckerchiefs, white trousers and white caps. The *Tenedos* men wore blue jumpers (their collars are clearly plain and unstriped), neckerchiefs, blue trousers and blue covers to their caps. The *Boadiceas*, however, wore white jumpers with plain white collars and black neckerchiefs, and white trousers, with blue covers over their caps. Only HMS *Shah*'s men seem to have worn straw sennet hats with the name of their ship on a band; they also wore blue jumpers and trousers.

Equipment does seem to have been uniform, however. Canvas leggings with a leather trim were worn by both officers and men. Waist and shoulder belts were brown leather, as were the ammunition pouches. Weapons were the Martini-Henry rifle with a cutlass bayonet, a fearsome looking weapon

Plan of the 9-pdr. RML gun and its carriage, the standard field piece of the Zulu War. The 7-pdr. RML was sometimes mounted on 9-pdr. carriages with very little modification. (Royal Artillery Institute, Woolwich)

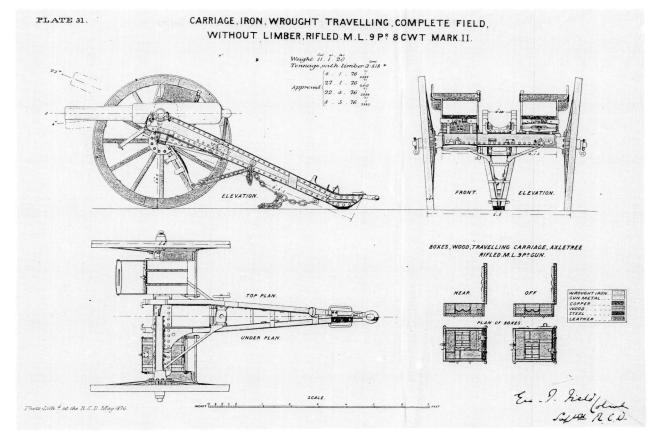

PLATE 31.

CARRIAGE, IRON, WROUGHT TRAVELLING, COMPLETE FIELD,
WITHOUT LIMBER, RIFLED. M.L. 9 PR 8 CWT MARK II.

ELEVATION.

FRONT. ELEVATION.

TOP PLAN.

UNDER PLAN.

BOXES, WOOD, TRAVELLING CARRIAGE, AXLETREE RIFLED. M.L. 9 PR GUN.

NEAR. OFF.

PLAN OF BOXES.

SCALE.

which differed scarcely from the ordinary cutlass except in the provision of fittings to enable it to be attached to the rifle.

Officers wore blue single-breasted jackets with rank indicated by rings around the cuff. Trousers were either blue or white, and headgear was either the peaked cap (blue without a cover, white with), or the ordinary foreign service helmet, dyed brown. Swords were Naval Officers' pattern, carried in black leather scabbards with gilt mounts from a black sword belt. Revolvers worn on shoulder straps also appear common.

The Royal Marine Infantry wore a dark blue working jacket on active service in Zululand. There were four brass buttons down the front, with two small ones retaining twisted scarlet shoulder cords. Collar badges were an embroidered red bugle device. Rank chevrons were worn on both arms, and were gold for senior sergeants and red worsted for below. The uniform of the Royal Marine Artillery differed only in having a grenade badge instead of the bugle and different pattern buttons. Trousers were dark blue with a narrow

red stripe for the RMLI and a wide stripe for the RMA. Photographs of Marines in Zululand show the RMLI to be wearing glengarries, and the RMA forage caps. The glengarry was blue with the regimental badge, whilst the forage cap was blue with a yellow band for men and gold for sergeants, and a small grenade badge at front. No doubt in action both would have worn the usual helmet.

Equipment was the 1871 Valise pattern but with black ammunition pouches. The rifle was the Martini-Henry, and all ORs carried the infantry sergeants' pattern sword bayonet. Leggings were black as for infantry. A photograph of Lt. Dowding, RMLI, of the *Active* detachment shows him wearing an infantry-style patrol jacket and blue trousers with a narrow red stripe. He is armed with a regimental pattern sword, and a revolver strap with a conspicuous ammunition pouch.

The Naval detachments brought with them

The 16-pdr. RML limber, used in Zululand to pull the 9-pdr. RML. (Royal Artillery Institute, Woolwich)

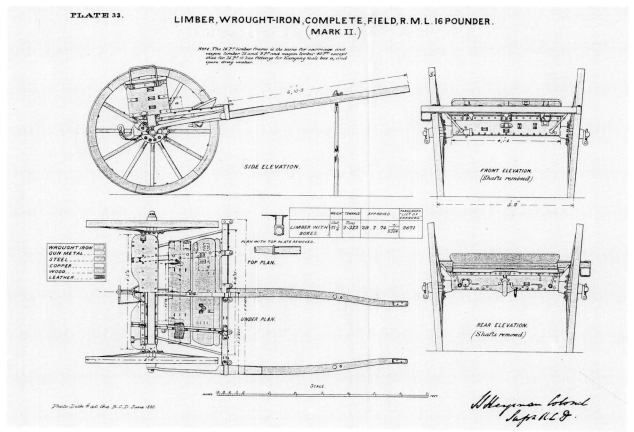

PLATE 33.

LIMBER, WROUGHT-IRON, COMPLETE, FIELD, R.M.L. 16 POUNDER.
(MARK II.)

their own artillery, including Gatlings which were used to good effect at Nyezane and Gingindlovu. Unfortunately it is not possible to be certain about the calibre of these guns. Regulations specified .65in. Gatlings for Naval use, but due to a delay in the supply of these the Navy had also acquired a number of Army .45in. calibre weapons. What is certain is that Naval Brigade Gatlings were mounted on different carriages from their Army counterparts, these being narrower and minus the axle-tree boxes. The Navy also landed some of its field guns, including 12-pdr. Armstrongs, but these were replaced by 7-pdrs.—presumably the standard RML model—for the actual advance into Zululand.

They also had a number of Hale's rockets. These were heavy 24-pdrs., fired from tubes rather than the Army's troughs. In 1869 Lt. John Fisher RN had invented a 'sea service rocket tube Mark II'. This was designed to be bracketed onto the side of

a ship; but by 1879 a modified version replaced the bracket with a tripod for land service, and the Fisher tube was the type used in Zululand. The 24-pdr. rocket certainly had more power than the 9-pdr. version; and, though it seems to have been just as unpredictable in flight, it scored some notable successes. At Nyezane a well-aimed rocket went right through a homestead occupied by the enemy, setting it on fire, and causing Cdr. Campbell to comment in his report: 'All were remarkably steady under fire . . . Boatswain John Cotter was most successful with the rockets I placed in his care.'

Volunteers and Irregulars

On the eve of the Zulu War the Colony of Natal maintained the quasi-military Natal Mounted Police and eight Volunteer units. These had begun to spring up among the settler community in the 1850s when it became clear that the home govern-

Details of the harness equipment used to pull the 16-pdr. RML limber. (Royal Artillery Institute, Woolwich)

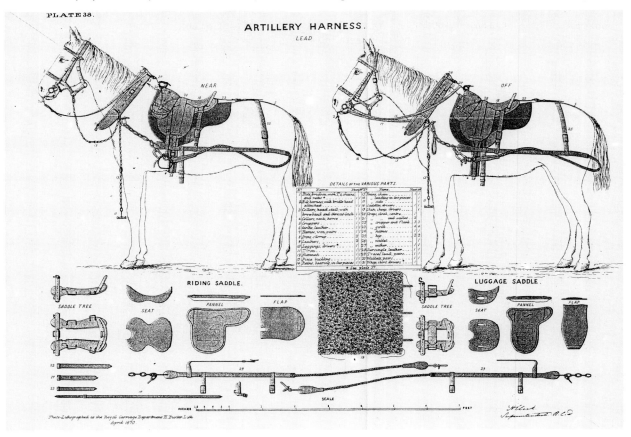

ment would not be prepared to maintain a large permanent garrison in the Colony. The Volunteer movement was stimulated by reports of the Rifle Volunteer Movement at home, although the nature of the country meant that the majority of the units were cavalry rather than infantry. Each unit elected its own officers and provided its own uniforms, whilst the government provided weapons and ammunition.

The Natal Mounted Police, a permanent police force used to regulate the behaviour of both black and white inhabitants of Natal, and the closest thing the Colony had to regular troops, was only 80 strong in 1879, and most of the Volunteer units were smaller: 20 for the Alexandra Mounted Rifles, 38 for the Buffalo Border Guard, 40 for the Stanger Mounted Rifles. In the main these volunteers were enthusiastic; they met to train regularly, they were often good shots and good horsemen, and they were certainly used to the country, so their military value outweighed their paucity of numbers, especially in a force chronically short of cavalry. Uniforms varied from unit to unit, but dark blue or black braided uniforms were popular, with forage caps or helmets, whose fittings seem to have been retained on active service.

From the moment plans were announced by the War Office to introduce Swinburne-Henry carbines amongst regular troops the authorities in Natal campaigned vigorously to be allowed to issue them to their Volunteers. They were told that regular troops had priority and that they would have to wait. Instead they received a Snider carbine, of a pattern with a particularly short stock (presumably to reduce the weight and facilitate use from the saddle). By the time the war with the Zulus loomed, however, the home government relented, and the Sniders were replaced by Swinburne-Henrys—again with shorter stocks than on the standard model—just before the start of the campaign. NCOs and officers also carried swords, and ORs a Bowie knife which could be attached to the end of the carbine to form a

Plans of the .45in. Royal Artillery Gatling, its carriage and limber (Royal Artillery Institute, Woolwich)

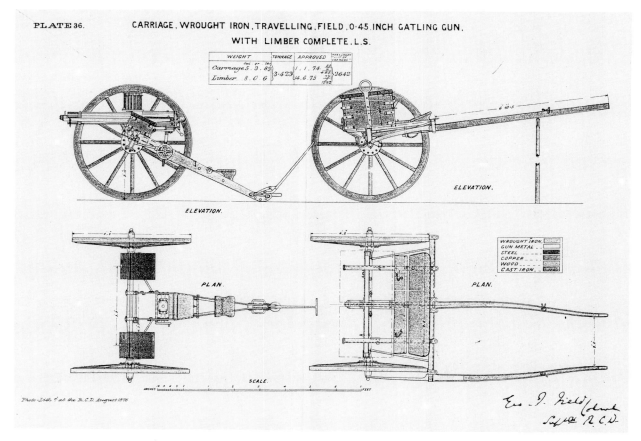

bayonet. Equipment also seems to have been issued centrally, and consisted of brown leather ammunition belt and pouch and a white haversack.

It is worth noting that the Natal Volunteers had been enlisted for the defence of Natal, and could not technically be employed outside the borders of the Colony. The Lieutenant-Governor of Natal, Sir Henry Bulwer, the senior administrator of the province, was deeply opposed to the Zulu War, and constantly tried to thwart Chelmsford's plans whenever they interacted with Natal's administrative system. He insisted that Chelmsford allow the Volunteers to vote on whether they would serve in Zululand. They did.

In addition to the Natal Volunteer units, Chelmsford had at his disposal a number of Irregular cavalry units. Unlike the Volunteers these were not men who were part of an existing system, but who simply joined up for a short period of service instead. Perhaps the most famous of these were the Frontier Light Horse, a unit some 200 strong originally raised on the Eastern Cape Frontier. They seem to have started out in smart uniforms, though details are scarce and contradic-

tory. They seem to have worn buff cord jackets with several rows of narrow braid across the chest, ending in a trefoil knot. Trousers were black with a red stripe. A second uniform existed which was of black cord with flat black mohair edging, and black braid around the cuffs. This may have been worn by officers, although photographs exist of Sgt. O'Toole, VC, and Trooper Brown, DCM, both wearing it. (However, this may reflect a desire to look smart for the camera rather than general practice.) Equipment consisted of a bandolier and carbine. By the time the Zulu War broke out most men were wearing civilian clothes with a red puggaree around the hat.

Of the other Irregular units it is very difficult to be sure. Those raised in the Transvaal were issued riding breeches, boots, a jacket, a hat with a puggaree, and a carbine and bandolier. The puggaree was probably red, or possibly white, a colour favoured in the Transvaal, and the jacket almost certainly a dark brown civilian type. Uniform details were minimal—ranks were probably indicated by white tape chevrons. There was certainly no provision for replacement clothing once it became worn out, so no doubt civilian items would have been substituted.

Finally, Evelyn Wood's Column had the service of the Boer leader Piet Uys. Most Boers along the Zululand border were hard-line republicans, bitterly anti-British, and content to see them slog it

Royal Naval detachment from HMS *Tenedos* on top of Fort Pearson, overlooking the Lower Drift of the Thukela, with Gatling (left) and limber (right). The Navy Gatling was mounted on a narrower carriage than the RA version, without the axle-tree boxes. The sailor centre is carrying an ammunition hopper. (Local History Museum, Durban)

out with their old enemies the Zulus; Boer support for the British invasion was therefore minimal. However, Piet Uys, a respected farmer in the 'disputed territory' on the Transvaal/Zululand border, whose family had a history of struggle against the Zulus, did come forward with 32 of his family and followers. They fought at Hlobane, where unfortunately Uys was killed. His men were disheartened and returned to their farms the next day, taking no further part in the campaign.

Natal's African Troops

When the first whites arrived in Natal in the 1820s the area was largely depopulated by the persistent raiding of the Zulu king Shaka. Once the whites had secured an official title to the land the survivors of these raids began to return, and the land began to fill up. This process was accelerated over the years by vast numbers of refugees fleeing successive political crises within Zululand itself. By the eve of the Zulu War Natal's black population was over 300,000. Many of these had a traditional hostility towards the Zulus which made them potentially good recruits for Chelmsford's army. The Lieutenant-Governor, Sir Henry Bulwer, was opposed to the idea of raising levy units, realising that it might sour relations between Natal blacks and the neighbouring Zulus for generations; and a sector of Colonial society was always worried about arming the African population because of the danger of revolt. Chelmsford overcame Bulwer's objections and was able to raise three

Officers and men from HMS *Tenedos'* Naval Brigade, wearing blue uniform with blue covers on their caps, and brown leather equipment. Note the Marines, right, in frocks and glengarries. (Africana Museum, Johannesburg)

regiments of the Natal Native Contingent, but the issue of black troops remained a contentious one throughout the war.

The 1st Regiment, NNC, had three battalions, and the other two regiments two each. Each battalion consisted of ten companies of nine European NCOs and 100 levies. Any promise the regiments may have had, however, was largely vitiated through lack of money. It had been hoped to issue each man with a red coat, but this proved impractical, so the universal badge of African troops became a red rag around the head. The men were also issued with blankets and woollen comforter caps, and many turned out in items of cast-off European clothing. Only one in ten was issued with a firearm, often of obsolete pattern, and ammunition was limited to a few rounds to prevent wastage. For the most part the men carried their own shields and spears, though there is a tantalising (if unconfirmed) reference to pikes being issued. Companies also seem to have improvised their own flags.

Officers were drawn largely from Imperial regiments, or from settlers with some experience of command, and wherever possible staff officers, at least, spoke Zulu. The NCOs were generally of poor calibre, since many of the better volunteers had already joined the more prestigious mounted units. Those who remained were often European immigrants who spoke little English and less Zulu, and who treated their men with contempt. Most

Members of the Natal Carbineers (left) and Natal Native Horse, in camp c.1879. The general appearance of the NNH men is well conveyed. The man in white (right) may be a member of the magistrate's black police (Natal Archives)

NNC officers wore infantry-style patrol jackets, riding breeches, and a wide-brimmed hat with a red puggaree—a uniform popular with officers throughout the Irregular units. It is difficult to be certain what the NCOs wore; they appear in photographs with dark, probably brown, jackets, cord trousers, and hats.

The reputation of the NNC has suffered unfairly at the hands of historians, largely because it received an undue amount of blame for the Isandlwana débâcle. Well led and intelligently employed, much could have been made of it. Its primary duties were scouting and mopping up after a battle, and at these it excelled; it was never intended as front-line material. After Isandlwana the 3rd Regiment was so badly shaken that it was disbanded, and the remaining regiments were reorganised into independent battalions. Belatedly, they were given a higher proportion of firearms.

Rather more successful from the first were five troops of mounted blacks, each of about 50 men, known collectively as the Natal Native Horse. Three of these troops were drawn from the amaNgwane clan, who lived in the Drakensburg foothills in Natal and who were old enemies of the Zulus. They were known to the British as the Sikhali Horse after their Chief Zikhali. One of the other troops was composed of Tlokwa Basothos, led by Hlubi Molife, an old friend of Col. Durnford. The last one was drawn from the black Christian community at Edendale. All the NNH wore European clothing with a red rag round their hats. Most preferred to ride barefoot, with their toes grasping the stirrup, but the Edendale men were booted and spurred. All were armed with carbines, and some carried hide quivers of assegais behind their saddles.

One unit which was uniformed was the Natal Native Pioneers. This was 273 strong, divided into five companies, the companies being distributed amongst the columns during the first invasion. The Pioneers carried carbines as well as picks and shovels, and seem to have been given the old 1872 pattern frock with the single loop of braid on the cuffs, and the collar torn out. The trousers were white canvas and extended to the knee only. Forage caps appear to have been blue with a white band.

In addition to the NNC Chelmsford also organised less permanent black units for border defence. A small number of black policemen kept an eye on the major river crossings on behalf of district magistrates. There are tantalising references to them being uniformed, and they may have worn a white canvas shirt and trousers; they were armed with old percussion rifles. Border Guards, raised from clans living along the frontier and placed under white levy-leaders, were stationed in companies of 100, with 200 more in reserve, near the more important drifts. Finally, there was a Border Levy, again drawn from local clans, who were expected to turn out to defend their district should the Zulus attack. All of these men carried their own weapons, and at the most wore no more uniform than a red headband. White levy-leaders, often border magistrates or men well used to the area, improvised their own uniforms to achieve a military look, patrol jackets of various patterns being popular.

In the northern theatre Wood was able to recruit both friendly Zulus and Swazi warriors. The Zulus were mostly followers of the Zulu prince Hamu kaNzibe, who defected to the British with his followers. They were drafted into a unit known as Wood's Irregulars, along with a number of Swazis. The Swazis, who lived north of Zululand, were traditional enemies of the Zulus and were content to join the war in the hope of plunder. Both photographs and engravings indicate that they wore their full ceremonial regalia into action.

British Columns in Zululand, 1879

First Invasion

Number One Column (Colonel Pearson)
Royal Artillery, 2 7-pdrs.
Royal Engineers, No. 2 Company
2nd Battalion, 3rd Foot
99th Foot (6 companies)
Naval Brigade
No. 2 Squadron, Mounted Infantry
Natal Hussars
Durban Mounted Rifles
Alexandra Mounted Rifles
Stanger Mounted Rifles
Victoria Mounted Rifles
2nd Regiment, Natal Native Contingent
(2 battalions)
Natal Native Pioneers, No. 2 Company

Number Two Column (Lt. Col. Durnford)
Rocket Battery
1st Regiment, Natal Native Contingent
(3 battalions)

NCOs of the Durban Mounted Rifles. They are carrying Snider carbines, which were replaced just before the Zulu War with Swinburne-Henrys. (Natal Archives)

A family reunion in the Natal Volunteer Corps on the eve of the Zulu War: Lt. W. E. Shepstone (seated left) and fellow officers of the Durban Mounted Rifles are visited by his brother, 'Offy' Shepstone of the Natal Carbineers (seated right). The man in the foreground is also a Carbineer officer, and both are wearing the NC's braided blue patrol jacket with white facings. (Natal Archives)

Sikali Horse
Natal Native Pioneers, No. 3 Company

Number Three Column (Colonel Glyn)

N/5 Battery, Royal Artillery (7-pdrs.)
Royal Engineers, No. 5 Company
1st Battalion, 24th Foot
2nd Battalion, 24th Foot
No. 1 Squadron, Mounted Infantry
Natal Mounted Police
Natal Carbineers
Newcastle Mounted Rifles
Buffalo Border Guard
3rd Regiment, Natal Native Contingent
(2 battalions)
Natal Native Pioneers, No. 2 Company

Number Four Column (Colonel Wood)

11/7 Battery, Royal Artillery (7-pdrs.)
1st Battalion, 13th Foot
90th Foot
Frontier Light Horse
Wood's Irregulars

Note: following the disaster at Isandlwana a number of Irregular units were transferred to this Column from No. 5 Column. Several other units (Boer Volunteers, Baker's Horse, Kaffrarian Rifles) joined this Column during the course of the First Invasion.

Number Five Column (Colonel Rowlands)

80th Foot
Schutte's Corps
Eckersley's Contingent
Raaf's Corps
Ferreira's Horse
Border Horse
One Krupp gun, two 6-pdr. Armstrongs

Second Invasion

First Division (Major-General H. H. Crealock)

1st Brigade
2nd Battalion, 3rd Foot (8 companies)
88th Foot (6 companies)
99th Foot (8 companies)
2nd Brigade
57th Foot (8 companies)
3 Battalion, 60th Rifles (7 companies)
91st Highlanders (8 companies)
Divisional troops
Naval Brigade, with 3 guns
4th Battalion, Natal Native Contingent
5th Battalion, Natal Native Contingent
John Dunn's Scouts
Natal Volunteers (as per original No. 1 Column)
M/6 Battery, RA (7-pdrs.)
8/7 Battery, RA (2 7-pdrs.)
11/7 Battery, RA (2 7-pdrs.)
0/6 Battery, RA (Ammunition Column)
Royal Engineers, 30th Company

Second Division (Major-General Newdigate)

1st Brigade
2nd Battalion, 21st Foot (6 companies)

58th Foot (6 companies)
2nd Brigade
1st Battalion, 24th Foot (7 companies)
94th Foot (6 companies)
Divisional Troops
N/5 Battery, RA (7-pdrs.)
N/6 Battery (9-pdrs.)
0/6 Battery, RA (Ammunition Column)
Royal Engineers, No. 2 Company
Bettington's Natal Horse
Shepstone's Basothos
2nd Battalion, Natal Native Contingent
Army Service Corps
Army Medical Department
Cavalry Brigade
(Attached to 2nd Division)
1st Dragoon Guards
17th Lancers

Flying Column (Brigadier-General Wood)
1st Battalion, 13th Foot
80th Foot
90th Foot

Men of the Stanger Mounted Rifles (with large badges on their forage caps) and Victoria Mounted Rifles. The VMR's uniform was dark blue with red facings, including a red band around their forage caps. The influence of the British Rifle Volunteer Movement on these men's uniforms is very clear (Natal Archives)

11/7 Battery, RA (4 7-pdrs.)
10/7 Battery, RA (Gatlings)
Royal Engineers, No. 5 Company
Mounted Infantry
Frontier Light Horse
Transvaal Rangers
Baker's Horse
Natal Native Horse
Natal Native Pioneers
Natal Light Horse
Wood's Irregulars

Note: this list gives the nominal strength of each column at the start of the First and Second Invasions, and does not reflect the order of battle in individual engagements. A complete list of all British troop dispositions, including details of specific engagements, troops deployed on lines of

communications, reinforcements and reorganisations, can be found in the official history, the *Narrative of Field Operations Connected with the Zulu War of 1879* (HMSO, 1881, reprinted 1907, 1989).

The Plates

A1: Infantry private
Wearing a greatcoat and based on sketches by Lt. W. W. Lloyd, 24th Regt. Lloyd shows men in greatcoats on wet days or on night picket duty. Blankets were worn *en banderole* with light equipment; a waist belt with one ammunition pouch, and haversack.

A2: Infantry officer
He is also in a greatcoat, again after Lloyd. The officers' greatcoats were double-breasted, and the sword and revolver belt were apparently worn over the top.

A3: Officer, Royal Artillery
This figure is based on a portrait of Maj. F. B. Russell, who was killed in action commanding the rocket battery at Isandlwana. He is wearing a typical RA officer's uniform; the blue patrol jacket with revolver carried by a shoulder strap, and sword.

A4: Bombardier, Royal Artillery
The rocket battery was manned at Isandlwana by one bombardier and eight privates from the 24th. This man is wearing the OR's undress frock, and is explaining the system of the 9-pdr. rocket trough. The rockets themselves were painted red and the launchers black.

B: The 1/24th firing line, Isandlwana, 22 January 1879:
B1: Sergeant, 24th Regiment
This figure is wearing the undress frock and typical 'fighting kit'—the waist belt with buff ammunition pouches and black expense pouch at rear, and haversack and water-bottle. The chevrons for Line regiments are worn on the right sleeve only. Note the bullock-hide guard sewn over the stock to protect the left hand from an over-heated barrel. Although Queen's Regulations stated that only

A self-portrait by Lt. W. Fairlie showing his uniform as an officer in the Natal Native Horse. He is wearing a blue infantry patrol jacket, buff riding breeches, and a slouch hat with a red puggaree—a uniform favoured by many Irregular officers. (National Army Museum)

moustaches were to be worn, this was relaxed on campaign where full beards were the norm.

Commandant Piet Uys (centre) and his sons. Uys was the only Boer leader to support the British invasion of Zululand; he was killed at the battle of Hlobane. (S. Bourquin)

B2: Lieutenant, 24th Regiment

Wearing the officers' undress serge, demonstrates it was common practice for only field officers and above to wear rank badges on the collar, and in the 24th junior officers wore a regimental badge instead.

B3: Private, 24th Regiment

Again, he is wearing the undress frock, with Long Service and Good Conduct chevrons on the right sleeve, and a 'marksman' badge on the other, reflecting the experience of many of the 1st Battalion men.

B4: Bandsman, 24th

Bandsmen were used as stretcher bearers in battle. Band uniforms were apparently unique to each battalion, some having quite ornate uniforms,

others ordinary tunics or frocks. This winged tunic with bandsman's badge is based on photographs of the 1/24th's band in King William's Town in 1878. The cap is the standard glengarry with regimental badge.

C: Isandlwana, 22 January 1879:

C1: Battalion Quartermaster, 24th Regiment

Each infantry battalion had a Quartermaster, a commissioned officer who had risen through the ranks. He was usually given an honorary rank, often lieutenant; as such he would have worn the same uniform as his fellow officers, with the exception of the black leather belt. In this case he is wearing a forage cap and the blue, infantry pattern patrol jacket. No doubt, like other officers, he might also have carried a revolver.

C2: Mounted Infantry private

The MI were made up of infantrymen drawn from a number of battalions, who wore their regimental serge (this man is from the 80th) with cord riding breeches. The carbine is the Swinburne-Henry.

C3: Lt. Col. Anthony Durnford, RE

Durnford was one of the British commanders at Isandlwana and was killed with one of the 'last stands'. This is based on his own description of his service uniform. He is wearing an Engineer officer's patrol jacket with rank badges. His left arm, disabled by a wound years before, is tucked into his jacket. He wears a wide-brimmed hat with red puggaree, reflecting his command of black troops, and riding breeches.

C4: Trooper, Buffalo Border Guard

One of the Natal Volunteer units, the BBG, who fought at Isandlwana, wore a black cord uniform which, unlike its counterpart in the Natal Mounted Police, retained its colour. For undress troopers wore a black forage cap with a distinctive buffalo-head badge, but it seems likely that in action they wore the helmet with full fittings.

C5: Trooper, Natal Carbineers

The premier Natal Volunteer unit, the Carbineers wore a blue uniform with white facings. The officers' tunics had five rows of black lace across the front, ending in trefoil knots, and no buttons.

C6: Trooper, Natal Mounted Police

The NMP's uniform was also black, though the dye seems to have been unable to withstand the rigours of field use, and there are several references to the uniform fading to brown. Note the carbine bayonet. Officers and NCOs carried swords.

D: Rorke's Drift:

D1: Surgeon Reynolds, Army Medical Department

Reynolds was in charge of the hospital at Rorke's Drift, and during the battle greatly distinguished himself tending the wounded. We have shown him wearing the AMD's patrol jacket, which was of infantry pattern, and have assumed that he would have worn the foreign service helmet.

D2: Acting Assistant Commissary J. L. Dalton, Army Commissariat Department

Dalton was one of the Commissary staff in charge of the supply depot before the fight. He played an active role in planning the defences, and was wounded whilst manning the barricades. He later returned to the fight to hand out ammunition. He is wearing the infantry pattern patrol jacket and undress trousers, which had a double white stripe down the outside seam.

D3: Colour-Sergeant Bourne, B Company, 2/24th

Colour-Sergeant Bourne received the DCM for his part in the defence. Based on contemporary company photographs, our reconstruction shows him

wearing the undress frock with colour sergeant's chevrons.

D4: Lieutenant Gonville Bromhead, commander, B Company, 2/24th
Based on contemporary photographs; we show him wearing an OR's serge stripped of all insignia except the collar patches. He is known to have used both a rifle and a revolver during the fight.

D5: Lieutenant J. R. M. Chard, Royal Engineers
Chard was the senior officer at Rorke's Drift. Based on a careful sifting of the evidence, we have reconstructed him in an undress frock with riding breeches. Like Bromhead, he is known to have used both a revolver and a rifle during the fight, the former presumably his own, the latter probably a 24th spare.

D6: Chaplain George Smith
Smith was the vicar of Escourt in Natal, who had accompanied the Centre Column to Rorke's Drift. During the battle he went the rounds handing out ammunition, and exhorting the men not to swear. He wore a long black civilian coat, faded to green, and distributed cartridges from a haversack.

E: The Battle of Nyezane, 22 January 1879:
E1: Private, 99th Regiment
Photographs show that the 99th wore the old-style 1872 pattern frock with single-loop cuff design.

Capt. Cecil D'Arcy, VC (left), and Sgt. Edmund O'Toole, VC, of the Frontier Light Horse. D'Arcy is wearing a typical Irregular officers' uniform, while O'Toole is wearing the FLH's black uniform. (Kille Campbell Africana Library)

Since Pearson's column was attacked on the march, we have shown him in full marching order. Note that this battalion also had black ammunition pouches instead of the more common buff type.

E2: Sapper, Royal Engineers
The Engineers were working to improve the riving crossing when the battle began, and were rushed up to assist in driving back the Zulu left horn. This

Unfortunately in poor condition, this fascinating photograph shows men of the Natal Native Horse at Sir Garnet Wolseley's camp at Ulundi in September 1879 at the end of the Zulu War. Most are wearing slouch hats with puggarees, though one (centre) has a forage cap, and another (right) has a Zulu-style leopard-skin headband around his hat. The officers at centre are from the Mounted Infantry and Natal Mounted Police. (John Young Collection)

man is wearing the undress frock with infantry-pattern pouches.

E3: Trooper, *Durban Mounted Rifles*
The DMR wore one of the most colourful Volunteer uniforms with red trim and black braid. Officers wore a similar uniform but with crow's foot knots on the tunic braid and olivets down the front. They carried swords and revolvers.

E4: Trooper, *Stanger Mounted Rifles*
One of the units which most reflected the influence of the Rifle Volunteer movement, the SMR was 40 strong and served with Pearson's column. When the siege of Eshowe began all the Volunteer units present were sent back to Natal; they later accompanied the relief column, and fought at Gingindlovu.

F1: Private, *Army Service Corps*
This private is in undress frock and forage cap. Photographs indicate that the helmet was also widely worn.

F2: Officer, *91st Highlanders*
He is wearing the undress frock which had the facing colour on the collar only, and 'veld boots'. His equipment is the regimental pattern sword belt, and usual holster and other belts.

F3: Sergeant, *91st Highlanders*
The sergeant appears in full marching order. This shows the usual method of wearing the Valise equipment: rolled greatcoat at the top, mess-tin, and expense pouch at the bottom. The valise itself is not carried. Note that Highland NCOs wore chevrons on both sleeves.

F4: Private, *91st Highlanders*
He is wearing the serge frock, and a blanket *en banderole*, as seems to have been popular with this battalion. Note that the ammunition pouches on the waist belt are black rather than buff.

Although this sketch represents the campaign against Sekhukhune in late 1879, it gives an excellent impression of the appearance of the Irregulars from the Transvaal, and of the Swazis, who seem to have fought in their full ceremonial regalia in both campaigns. (Author's Collection)

Maj. Bengough's 2/1st NNC outside Fort Bengough in Natal during the Zulu War. Most of the men have no uniform except a red rag around their heads, though many are wearing items of European clothing. (Natal Archives)

F5: Piper, 91st Highlanders

Based on a photograph of the battalion on the march, he is wearing the undress regimental piper's uniform, with the valise equipment behind.

G: The Naval Brigade at Gingindlovu, 2 April 1879:
G1: Sailor, HMS Boadicea.

The men from the *Boadicea*'s detachment wore white jumpers, trousers and caps. All belts are brown. The rocket equipment is the Fisher launching tube Mark II, for the 24-pdr. Hales rocket. Originally intended for use aboard ship, the Fisher tube was adapted for land service by the addition of a tripod.

G2: Private, Royal Marine Light Infantry

He is wearing the blue working jacket adopted on this campaign, with valise equipment with black ammunition pouches.

G3: Officer, Royal Naval landing party

Most Royal Navy officers, whatever their detachment, seem to have favoured the blue jacket, with either white or blue trousers, and the cap. Revolvers were carried as per infantry officers.

G4: Sailor, HMS Shah

Sketches and engravings of the *Shah*'s men during the battle show them to have worn blue trousers and jumpers, canvas leggings, and straw 'sennet' hats. Note the cutlass bayonet on the Martini-Henry.

H: The descent of the 'Devil's Pass', Battle of Hlobane, 28 March 1879:
H1: Trooper, Frontier Light Horse

Pieced together from confusing contemporary evidence, this shows the FLH's original uniform; a buff braided jacket with black trousers. Some men would still have been wearing this in Zululand, whilst others simply wore civilian clothes with a red rag around the hat. All, however, would have carried a carbine and bandolier.

H2: Lt. Col. Redvers Buller

Wood's dynamic cavalry commander, Buller won the VC for rescuing men in the débâcle at Hlobane. Sketches show that he fought in a practical civilian costume of Norfolk jacket and riding breeches.

H3: Officer, Frontier Light Horse

Many Irregular officers, of whatever unit, preferred to wear the infantry-style patrol jacket, with cord riding breeches, and a wide-brimmed hat with puggaree. Certainly Cecil D'Arcy, who won the VC with the FLH at Ulundi, was pictured in this uniform. Most Irregular officers would also have been armed with both a carbine and revolver.

H4: Trooper, Frontier Light Horse

Based on contemporary photographs, this shows the FLH's black cord uniform—though the exact significance of this uniform remains a mystery.

H5: Sergeant, Transvaal Volunteers

Many of the Irregular units who fought with Wood—Raaf's Transvaal Rangers, the Kaffrarian Rifles, the Border Horse—probably wore little

A 7-pdr. RML gun used in the Zulu War, mounted on a 'Kaffrarian' carriage, a modified version of the 9-pdr. carriage. (S A Museum of Military History, Johannesburg).

more than civilian dress with a coloured puggaree around the hat. If NCO ranks were indicated at all, they were probably marked with white worsted tape.

I: The death of Lieutenant and Adjutant F. J. Cockaye Frith, 17th Lancers, Upoko River, 5 June 1879:

I1: Private, 17th Lancers
This shows the full extent of campaign modifications: the dyed helmet, reversed plastron tunic front, and ammunition pouches worn with the sword belt.

I2: Corporal, 17th Lancers
This corporal clearly shows the detail of the rear of the tunic and equipment. Note that the sword is hooked up to a small hook on the sword belt.

I3: Lt. and Adj. Frith.
Frith was killed in a skirmish on the Upoko in early June and is shown wearing the dress tunic, with plastron reversed, and lieutenant's rank insignia. Note the leather revolver belt worn with the full dress pouch belt. Most illustrations show officers' tunics at this period to have round collars; Frith is unusual in that contemporary portraits clearly show him with a square collar.

I4: Officer, 17th Lancers
As well as the dress tunic, some officers wore patrol jackets. Unlike the infantry, cavalry patrol jackets varied from regiment to regiment. This is the type favoured by the 17th.

J: The Battle of Ulundi, 4 July 1879; inside Lord Chelmsford's square:

J1: Privates, Army Hospital Corps
The AHC seem to have worn both helmets and forage caps on campaign in Zululand; the cap with the white cover is based on a contemporary photo. The jackets are the undress frock; note the distinctive red cross badge (right arm only).

J2: Officer, 2/21st Royal Scots Fusiliers
Although a Scottish regiment the 21st's uniform was largely the same as for Line Infantry; compare this with Fig.B2. One feature of the 21st officers' frock was that it had shoulder cords rather than straps, and the grenade badge was always worn on the collar. The cuff rank distinction is for major. The officers of this battalion also retained the grenade helmet badge, but not the ORs.

J3: Col. Henry Evelyn Wood
Wood commanded the Flying Column troops during the battle. He is wearing the frock of his regiment, the 90th LI, with colonel's rank distinctions; and a dyed helmet rather than the one with elaborate fittings with which he posed for photographs.

J4: Lieutenant-General Lord Chelmsford
He is in his field service kit, a blue patrol jacket with riding breeches, and a helmet with a plain puggaree.

Several regiments which took part in the battle did so with Colours flying. Those in the background are of the 1/13th Light Infantry, with the Queen's Colour to the fore.

K: Natal Native troops searching the field after Ulundi:

K1: Trooper, Natal Native Horse
The NNH wore European clothing with a red rag around their hats. Most preferred to ride barefoot.

They were armed with carbines, and sometimes with spears carried in a holster at the back of the saddle.

K2: Warrior, Natal Native Contingent
He is wearing his issued blanket and red distinguishing rag around the head, with a mixture of European and African clothing. The weapons are his own shield and spear.

K3: Swazi Warrior
Sketches show that the Swazis wore their full regalia into action. This magnificent costume consists of a 'busby' of trimmed ostrich feathers, with *sakabuli* feathers on either side, and streamers of feathers hanging below the otter-skin headband. His body is covered with cow-tail ornaments, and around his waist he wears a skirt of animal skin.

L: King Cetshwayo kaMpande in captivity, August 1879:
L1: Sergeant, 3/60th Rifles
The 60th's uniform was extremely sombre, the rifle green of the jacket and trousers in fact being black. All equipment was of black leather, including the sling on the rifle. Rifle regiments wore chevrons on both sleeves, and all ORs carried the sword bayonet.

L2: Officer, 3/60th Rifles
He is wearing the undress frock. Being less conspicuous than their Line counterparts, the 60th retained their helmet plates but dyed the helmets brown.

L3: King Cetshwayo kaMpande
When the king was captured by a patrol of the

A 9-pdr. RML gun used in the Zulu War. (SA Museum of Military History, Johannesburg).

KDG he was wearing a table-cloth as a cloak. He looked haggard after his ordeal, but accepted his fate with dignity. He was carrying a staff which had once belonged to his great uncle, King Shaka, the founder of the Zulu nation.

L4: Trooper, 1st (King's) Dragoon Guards
Like the Lancers, the Dragoons on campaign carried ammunition pouches with their waist belts, as well as a pouch belt and haversack.

L5: Major, King's Dragoon Guards
This officer is wearing the dress tunic with major's rank distinctions, but with the undress pouch belt and sword belt.

Overleaf: As the Zulu chest advances over the crest of the iNyoni heights, the warriors bunch together in this contemporary engraving. In fact, most of the Zulu attack was executed in open order, with the warriors concentrating only in the final rush. Note the many firearms carried by these men. Although the artist has accurately conveyed the various elements of Zulu dress, it is unlikely that quite so much was retained in action.

The Zulus

The People

'A very remarkable people, the Zulu', the British Prime Minister, Benjamin Disraeli, said on hearing of a fresh disaster in the war of 1879. 'They defeat our generals; they convert our bishops; they have settled the fate of a great European dynasty'. Remarkable, indeed, to have taken on the full might of the British Empire at its height, and won, if not the war, at least some of the battles. Who were the Zulus, and how did they achieve the fame as warriors which they enjoy to this day?

The area now known as Zululand lies on the south-eastern coast of Africa, between the Drakensberg Mountains and the Indian Ocean. It is steep rolling grassland, dropping from cool inland heights to a sub-tropical coastal strip, and intersected by many river systems which have, in places, cut deep, wide gorges. In the valleys thornbush grew luxuriantly, and many of the heights were thickly forested. Until decimated by 19th century hunters, both black and white, the countryside teemed with game—antelope, wildebeest, elephant and lion. Above all, the area was covered with a wide mix of grasses which, with the comparative absence of tsetse fly, made it some of the best cattle country in southern Africa.

Cattle played a crucial rôle in the Zulu scheme of things, not just as a practical asset—a source of food and hides—but also as a means of assessing status and worth. Although African Iron Age deposits have been found across Zululand dating back to the 6th century, the Nguni people, the cultural and racial group to which the Zulu belong, wandered into the area in search of new pastures some time in the 17th century. They spread out over the countryside, slowly peopling it with clan groups who traced their origins to a common ancestor. Oral tradition has it that a man named Zulu established his homestead on the southern bank of the White Mfolozi River in about 1670. The name

Zulu man in everyday dress, carrying both a throwing and a stabbing spear, and—in his right hand—a round-headed knobkerry club of polished wood. His loin-covering is of strips of twisted fur. (Brian Maggs)

Glossary

This is a glossary of Zulu *military* terms; some words have alternative non-military uses, but for clarity we have used only the translation relevant to this book. Proper names are not included here, nor are they italicised in the body of the text. (Source: James Stuart Archive, ed. J. B. Wright and C. de B. Webb.)

amasi ....thick curdled milk

ibandla ....tribal council

ibheshu ....cowskin buttock flap

ibutho,
   pl. amabutho ....age-group guild, thus regiment

ikhanda,
   pl. amakhanda ....military garrison base

iklwa ....large stabbing spear

impi ....(1) body of armed men (2) war

i'mpondo zankhomo ....'beast's horns' formation (see *uphondo*)

induna,
   pl. izinduna ....senior military or civil leader

ingxotha ....brass forearm band

inyanga,
   pl. izinyanga ....doctor

iphovela,
   pl. amaphovela ....headdress of stiff cowhide

isangoma ....diviner, 'witch-smeller'

ishoba,
   pl. amashoba ....tufted ends of cow tails

isicoco ....ornamental headring

isifuba ....centre ('chest') of Zulu army formation

isigaba ....group of associated *amaviyo* companies within regiment

isigodlo ....royal or command residence within a garrison

isihlangu ....large war shield

isijula ....long-bladed throwing spear

isiphapha ....broad-bladed throwing spear

iviyo,
   pl. amaviyo ....company within a regiment

iwisa ....knobkerrie, war club

izikhulu,
   sing. isikhulu ....elders, councillors

ka ....son of

palane ....outsize regiment

udibi ....teenage boys who acted as warriors' servants

umbhumbuluzo ....reduced-size war shield

umkhonto ....spear

umkhumbi ....circle of warriors gathered for orders

umncedo ....genital sheath

umqhele ....fur headband

umthakathi,
   pl. abathakathi ....wizard, witch

umutsha ....fur groin flap

umuzi,
   pl. imizi ....homestead, village

uphondo,
   pl. izimpondo............of Zulu army crescent formation

utshwala ....Zulu beer

Zulu means 'the heavens', and his followers took the name *amaZulu*, 'the people of the heavens'.

At this time the Zulus were no different from their neighbours. They lived in a series of village homesteads (*umuzi*; plural *imizi*) which were basically family units. Each village consisted of a number of huts built in a circle around a central cattle enclosure, and surrounded by a stockade. They were usually built on a slope facing east. The huts themselves were dome-shaped, like old-fashioned beehives. They were made by thatching grass to a wooden framework; the floor inside was made of polished clay, and a raised lip marked out the central fireplace. There was no chimney—the smoke escaped as best it could through the thatch. The layout of an *umuzi* reflected social relationships. The Nguni were polygamous, and a man might have as many wives as his wealth and status would allow. He himself lived at the top of the homestead facing the entrance with the wives and children of his senior house to the right, and those of the subordinate house to the left. Any dependants lived at the bottom, near the gate.

Daily life for the men consisted of tending the cattle and performing the heavier tasks around the homestead. Cultivation of cereal crops, and all household duties, fell to the women. Since beasts were too precious to slaughter merely for food, meat was only eaten on special occasions; the staple diet was curdled milk—*amasi*—and maize, augmented sometimes with pumpkins and sweet potatoes.

These vegetables were grown in small plots near each homestead. The grain was stored for use all year round in large wicker baskets raised on stilts to keep them away from the damp and rats, or in an underground pit sealed with a large stone. For diversion the Zulus had *utshwala*, a thick, rather sour beer; and tobacco, which was dried, crushed and taken as snuff. In general the people lived a healthy, outdoor life—they were neither as markedly tall or short as other African peoples, and in complexion they were, on average, rather light skinned.

Their utensils, the Zulus made of wood, bone, clay, basket-weave and iron. Iron ore was scattered in easily accessible surface deposits across the country, and particular clans gained high reputations as smiths—notably the Mbonambi near the coast, and the Chube in the dark Nkhandla forest overlooking the spectacular Tugela River. It is no coincidence that both these areas are rich in ore and fuel. The smith smelted the ore in a shallow pit, over which a fire was lit. Bellows made of cowhide sacks pumped by hand were used to feed in air via clay nozzles. Once the ore was melted, it was extracted and hammered into shape. Like many African peoples, the Nguni regarded this process with superstitious awe, the more so because the best

Characteristic 19th-century domed 'beehive' huts, typical of both *amakhanda*—garrisons—and ordinary homesteads. These examples have been built by archaeologists over the surviving clay floors of King Cetshwayo's *isigodlo* at Ulundi.

Zulu blacksmiths at work: a famous sketch from the 1840s by George French Angas. The smith works the bellows while his assistants retrieve the ore from the furnace and hammer it into shape. (British Museum)

smiths were said to temper their products with human fat. The smiths made hoes and, of course, spears.

Weapons and Costume

Early spears had a small, leaf-shaped blade with a long shank or tang. Having forged his blade, the smith turned it over to another specialist, the spear-maker. He selected appropriate wood for the shaft, and drilled out the end with an awl. Strong vegetable glues were used to fix the blade in place, and this was bound with a wet fibre. When this was dry, the join was sealed with either split cane, or with a tube of hide cut from a calf's tail. The Zulu word for a spear is *umkhonto*, although there are several different spears, each with its own particular function. The *isiphapha*, for example, was a broad-bladed spear and was used for hunting game; the *isijula* was used in warfare.

For his everyday protection in a wild country, a man would carry a spear and *iwisa*, a knobkerrie made of hardwood with a large polished head. He would also carry a small oval shield made of cowhide, reinforced with a stick held in place by a double row of hide lacing. The top of the stick was usually decorated with a strip of civet or genet fur, wound round.

A man would remain at his father's homestead until he married, when he would establish an *umuzi* of his own. The change in status was considerable and indicated by means of the headring, or *isicoco*, donned by men immediately prior to their first marriage. The *isicoco* was a fibre sewn into the hair, plastered with gum and polished with beeswax. In the 19th century it was fashionable to shave the crown and back of the head, leaving just the hair around the ring. Occasionally the ring was raised up on a pad of hair. Young unmarried men would sometimes tease out their hair and build it up into bizarre shapes with clay and tallow.

Ordinary costume was minimal. A man was required to wear an *umncedo*, a sheath of plaited grass and leaves; with this, he would be considered adequately dressed in all company. However it was usual to wear a loin covering over this: a thin strip of hide around the hips, with an oblong of soft dressed cowskin low on the buttocks (*ibheshu*), and strips of fur (*umutsha*) at the front. Fur from the civet, genet and samango (green) monkey were the most popular types, but sheepskin and antelope were sometimes used. Often two or more skins would be twisted together to resemble tails. Samango monkey tails were sometimes worn either side of the *ibheshu*. Only chiefs were allowed to wear a cloak of leopard skin, with leopard claws as a necklace. Chiefs often carried sticks with carved wooden heads as staffs of office.

Clothing for married women consisted of a large pleated leather skirt. The hair was also worn in a distinctive fashion: a small circular patch was teased out, coloured with red ochre and the head shaved round it. This is the origin of some of the extravagant headdresses which can be seen among married women in Zululand today. Unmarried girls wore a fringe of brown strings low on their hips, or a small leather skirt. Minimal as this was, it always seemed to protect their modesty, as several British officers commented to their chagrin.

Most Zulus loved to ornament themselves. Before the 1840s beads were the prerogative of an important few, but with the arrival of European traders they became very common. Both men and women wore them, particularly unmarried girls, who wore them in strings around the arms and legs and slung around the body. Ingots of brass, perhaps traded from the Portuguese in the north, were worked to produce highly-prized heavy rings, worn around the neck and arms. Both sexes pierced their ears and wore large plugs in the lobes. These were made of ivory, bone, clay and later of sugar-cane. Men often carried snuff-spoons in their ears, or tucked into their headrings. Such spoons were dished at one end and tapered to a point at the other—sometimes two or three such points—which were used to scratch the head. The snuff itself was carried in gourds, horns, or wooden containers from a thong around the neck.

Witchcraft and Warfare

The Nguni lived in great dread of the evil effect of witchcraft, and often wore magical charms—necklaces with special blocks of wood and pouches with magical medicine—to ward off evil. If someone had an accident, or was injured by a wild animal or in war, they would turn to the *inyanga*, a medical doctor who carried a wide range of herbal

remedies and poultices which were often effective. If, however, the problem was beyond the skill of the *inyanga*, it was thought to be the work of *abathakathi*—wizards—who could only be identified by the *isangoma*, or diviner.

The Nguni believed that ancestral spirits watched over their everyday lives, and that misfortunes were either the result of spirits being offended, or of witchcraft. The *isangoma* was able to

A Zulu man carrying a knobkerry; note the twisted-fur loin flap, and the headring marking his status as a married man. (Radio Times Hulton Picture Library)

decide these matters. Ancestral spirits could usually be propitiated by sacrificing a beast, but wizards would have to be 'smelt out' in a grim ceremony. Both men and women could be *isangomas*, but women were thought to have particularly acute powers. They wore their hair in braids, and were dressed in bizarre costumes, slung around with magical charms; they carried gnus' tails as the badge of their profession. At a smelling-out ceremony the suspects would sit chanting in a circle whilst the *isangoma* danced and capered around them. At last, she would strike one with the gnu's tail. This was an accusation which brooked no defence, since even an innocent man might be possessed by *abathakathi* without his knowledge; and the penalty was a gruesome death. A sharpened stick about 18 in. long was driven into the victim's anus. This was the Nguni judicial sanction extreme; ordinary criminal cases were tried before a chief, and a fine in cattle was the usual penalty, although serious offenders might be clubbed to death.

Until the 19th century warfare in Zululand was infrequent and largely bloodless. When disputes did

A Zulu man dressing a friend's hair. Both wear the *isicoco* headring of married men; the one on the left has shaved his head all round the ring, the one on the right has grown the hair below the ring but shaved the crown—both common 19th-century styles. This picture may date from *c.*1865. (Killie Campbell Africana Library)

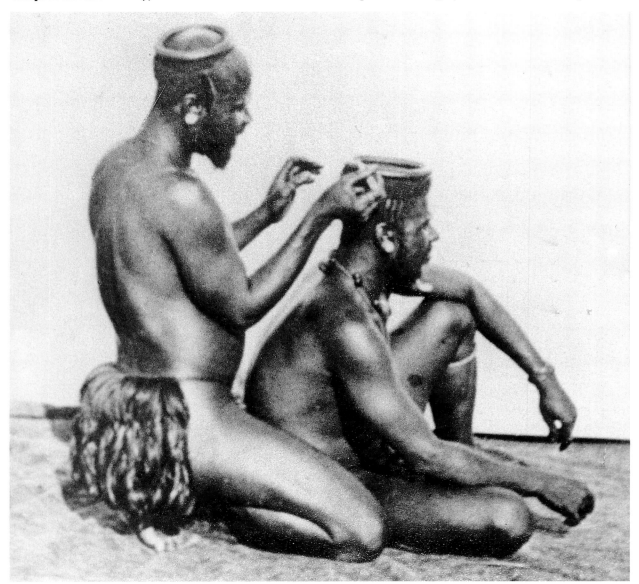

arise, often over grazing rights, the combatants would meet at an appointed time and place, with the women and children turning out to watch. Individual warriors would step out and challenge rivals from the opposing forces to individual combat. Amidst much jeering and cheering, spears would be thrown, and a few casualties sustained. One side would eventually withdraw. It seems likely that, with plenty of unclaimed pasture, a defeated clan could simply move on to find new lands. However, by the late 18th century the

Two married women, probably of King Mpande's court, sketched by Angas; they wear the traditional married woman's long skirt, but not the top-knot of hair also associated with this status. The baskets and gourds are typical Zulu utensils. (British Museum)

population was such that Zululand was becoming congested, and it was no longer possible for clans to have access to good grazing all the year round. Historians still argue the point today, but it seems likely that this competition for natural resources was the cause of the shattering violence which was to follow.

Shaka and 'The Crushing'

The Zulus played little part in this early conflict; they were a minor clan living between two more powerful neighbours, the Mthethwa of King Dingiswayo to the south-east, and the Ndwandwe of King Zwide to the north. Oral tradition has it that Dingiswayo was a wise and just ruler and Zwide a treacherous despot; this may be a case of history being interpreted by the victors, but Zwide does seem to have been the more ruthless, attacking and subduing his northern neighbours.

Then history introduced a new factor, with all the elements of a dark fairy-story. Sometime in 1786 Chief Senzangakhona of the Zulu met a maiden of the eLangeni clan named Nandi, when she was fetching water by a pool. They became lovers; but, when Nandi became pregnant, the Zulu chief's advisors sent her away, saying she was harbouring an *i-shaka*, an intestinal parasite. When she was subsequently delivered of a son Nandi called him Shaka. Senzangakhona was resentful of the responsibility forced upon him, and soon found a reason to drive Nandi and her son away. They ended up among the Mthethwa, where Shaka grew to manhood, and duly enlisted in the Mthethwa army.

It was customary for youths of about 17 to be banded together into guilds, called *amabutho* (sing. *ibutho*), for the ceremonies attendant upon the onset of manhood. The *amabutho* were required to perform duties for the chief, and Dingiswayo used these age group guilds as a basis for military units. Shaka joined the Mthethwa iziCwe *ibutho*, and seems to have found an outlet for his personal frustrations in battlefield aggression. He was not, however, impressed by the style of warfare then practised—he preferred to charge down upon his enemy and engage him in hand-to-hand combat. He found the light throwing spears too flimsy for this purpose, and designed his own broad-bladed spear for close combat. It had a blade about 18 in. long by 1½ in. wide, set into a stout haft 30 in. long. With typical gallows humour, he called it *iklwa*—the sound it was said to make on being withdrawn from a deep body thrust.

Shaka's reputation as a ferocious warrior drew him to Dingiswayo's attention, so much so that when Senzangakhona died in 1816 the Mthethwa chief put Shaka forward as his candidate for the Zulu throne. The legitimate heir was discreetly disposed of.

Shaka called up all the available fighting men—a total of perhaps 400—whom he organised into four regiments grouped according to age, thus completing the militarisation of the *amabutho* system. They were armed with copies of the *iklwa*, and given new, large war shields, called *isihlangu*, which covered

A young Zulu man with his hair shaped into a fantastic crest with clay and tallow—an extreme example of a common practice. He also wears a snuff-spoon through his pierced earlobe, and snuff containers round his neck. (S. Bourquin)

them from shoulder to ankle. It had been customary for men to wear hide sandals: Shaka considered these awkward and ordered his men to discard them; to harden their feet they were required to stamp flat heaps of thorn-bush.

The warriors were trained in a new tactical formation, the *i'mpondo zankhomo*, or 'beast's horns'. One body, the *isifuba* or 'chest', rushed down on the enemy in a frontal assault, whilst flanking parties, the *izimpondo* or 'horns', rushed out on either side to surround them. A further body, the 'loins', was kept in reserve. When they reached the enemy the warriors were supposed to hook the left edge of their shield over the edge of their opponent's, and wrench to the left. This dragged the opponent's shield across his own body, throwing him off balance, and preventing him from using his own spear arm; it also exposed the left side of his body to the Zulu *iklwa*.

Shaka tried out his new army on his neighbouring clans. It was brutally effective. The Zulus had begun their rapid and ruthless rise, a period still known as *mfecane*—'the crushing'.

Gqokli Hill

The sudden emergence of a new power allied to the Mthethwa on his very border was a problem for Zwide of the Ndwandwe. In 1818 he collected an army and moved against Shaka. In less than two years Shaka's army had grown to perhaps 4,000; it was heavily outnumbered by a Ndwandwe host of 8,000 to 10,000, but the Zulu had superior training and weapons.

Shaka took up a position on a rocky knoll known as kwaGqokli, which crested a spur running down to the White Mfolozi River. A jumble of boulders and coarse grass, Gqokli is a tough climb; and a slight shoulder on the summit provides a depression, out of sight from the lower slopes, in which Shaka could hide his reserves. The battle took place some time in April 1818, and began with Shaka attempting to reduce the odds. Small parties of Zulus defended the river crossing, disrupting the Ndwandwe approach, and a large herd of cattle was used to lure further enemy troops away from Gqokli. The Ndwandwe commander then tried repeated frontal attacks on Shaka's warriors, who were drawn up in lines around the summit of Gqokli. These were unsuccessful; the Ndwandwe,

still wearing sandals, still throwing their spears, were taken aback by the fierce close-quarter combat of the Zulus. Finally, the Ndwandwe formed up into a column and attempted to punch a hole through the Zulu lines. With perfect timing, Shaka unleashed his hidden reserves, who streamed out to surround the Ndwandwe column, smashing it in a few minutes' brutal mêlée. The Ndwandwe army began to disintegrate and, although a running fight developed which lasted most of the day, the Ndwandwe finally withdrew.

An *inyanga*, or practitioner of traditional medicine. He carries his remedies in an assortment of horns, gourds and other containers slung around his neck and in the bag in his hand. *Izinyanga* used natural medicines with a degree of success, aided by the faith of their patients. (Brian Maggs)

An *isangoma* or diviner of supernatural phenomena. Although there are suggestions of European influence in her dress, this picture does convey something of the *isangoma's* intimidating appearance. The braided hair, inflated bladders in the headdress, and above all the gnu's tail in her right hand are all traditional badges of her calling. (Royal Engineers Museum)

Gqokli hill was the supreme vindication of the new Zulu tactics; and in the immediate aftermath Shaka consolidated his position by snapping up further clans. A prize plum fell into his lap when Dingiswayo mounted his own campaign against the Ndwandwe, only to fall into Zwide's hands and be put to death. In an ironic reversal of the tactic which had brought him to power, Shaka quickly put forward his own candidate for the Mthethwa throne, and absorbed Dingiswayo's former empire. This was too much for Zwide, who reorganised his troops along Zulu lines, and made an all-out bid to crush the Zulu upstart.

The Second Zulu/Ndwandwe War of 1819 was a turning point in the history of Zululand and, indeed, of black South Africa. The Zulu were once more heavily outnumbered, and Shaka chose to retire before the Ndwandwe advance, taking his cattle with him and emptying grain stores. Since all Nguni armies lived off the land, this caused serious problems for the Ndwandwe. After a week of fruitlessly chasing the Zulus through some of the most rugged parts of the country, the Ndwandwe began to retire. As they crossed the fords of the Umhlatuze River, Shaka launched his attack. The fighting raged over a wide area, and at the end of it the Ndwandwe were smashed. His kingdom shattered, Zwide himself escaped with part of the clan and settled in the eastern Transvaal district. Those who remained behind were killed by Shaka, or incorporated into the Zulu state; sections of the Ndwandwe army which survived in cohesive units fled to the north, where their commanders were able to carve out small empires of their own.

The destruction of the Ndwandwe removed the largest obstacle to Shaka's power. He turned his attention to clans living on his western and southern borders. In a series of campaigns between 1819 and 1824 he dislodged powerful groups living in the Drakensberg foothills and south of the Tugela River. Many were completely wiped out; others were driven over the mountains into the interior, or to the south. Some, chiefs like Mzilikazi of the Khumalo, and Matiwane of the Hlubi, became rootless marauders on the high veld, attacking all they came across. Others ended up as refugees amongst the Mpondo and Xhosa tribes on the fringes of the British Cape Colony. Large tracts of land were completely depopulated.

At the centre of it all, the new Zulu state went far beyond anything Zwide or Dingiswayo had envisaged. The clans incorporated into the Zulu state retained their identity but their chiefs were subordinate to Shaka, who often killed off the legitimate ruler and raised up a junior member of his family, who therefore owed his position directly to Shaka. Nguni chiefs were traditionally advised by a council called the *ibandla*, consisting of the *izikhulu*, or 'great ones' of the nation. Important clans within the Zulu state had representatives within the *ibandla*, but visitors to Shaka's court were horrified at the regularity with which Shaka had his advisers killed: they may not always have been men of the highest rank, but it was a brave man on the *ibandla* who would question the king's policies. The effect was to take power out of the hands of the traditional chiefs and invest it in the state. Military and civil state officials were called *izinduna* (sing. *induna*), and were appointed by Shaka himself. There was an element of meritocracy in this—even commoners could become *izinduna* if, for example, their skill in war brought them to Shaka's notice.

Army Organisation

The army was a crucial element in the system. It is difficult to arrive at reliable figures for the strength of Shaka's army, but if it was 400 in 1816, 4,000 in 1818, and a maximum of about 15,000 when the great phase of expansion ended in 1824, its rapid growth is evident. The *amabutho* continued to be organised on an age basis, with youths of the same age being recruited from all the clans across the country. This reduced the risk, in such a conglomerate kingdom, of too many men from the same clan dominating a regiment, and being a potential source of dissent. Each *ibutho* was between 600 and 1,500 strong, and they were quartered in barracks known as *amakhanda* (sing. *ikhanda*), literally 'heads', which were strategically placed about the kingdom to act as centres for the distribution of royal authority. The *amakhanda* themselves were civilian homesteads writ large: there was a circle of huts around a central open space which served both to contain the regiment's cattle and as a parade ground. They were surrounded by a stockade, sometimes a formidable barrier consisting of two rows of stakes leaning inwards so as to cross at the top, with the gap in between filled with thorn-bush. At the top of each *ikhanda* was a fenced-off section known as the *isigodlo*, where the king or his representatives would live when in residence. Each regiment had its own *induna* appointed by the king. In some cases female members of the king's family were placed in charge of *amakhanda*.

In Shaka's time the vast majority of warriors were unmarried. This had less to do with channelling warriors' frustrated sexual energies into military aggression (as the Victorians suggested) than with maintaining control over military resources. Whilst unmarried the warriors were, in effect, subject to whatever national service the king might dictate: when they married they were allowed to disperse, establish their own homesteads, and give their first allegiance to their families and clan chiefs. By prolonging bachelorhood artificially, Shaka kept his army at full strength. This was not as uncomfortable for the warriors as it may seem, as Zulu moral codes provided perfectly acceptable outlets for sex outside marriage.

As unmarried men with no resources of their own, the warriors were dependent on the king's bounty. The vast numbers of cattle looted in Zulu raids were the property of the state, but the king quartered them with his regiments, who were allowed to use their milk products. Morale within the Zulu army was extremely high: the common age of the warriors, their extremely successful record, and the terror this inspired among neighbouring

The only contemporary portrait of King Shaka kaSenzangakhona, sketched by one of the Europeans who first visited his court. His appearance has been somewhat romanticised—note the size of the spear, and its elaborate head—but does tally in basic particulars with other descriptions. (Killie Campbell Africana Library)

In a scene reconstructed with some accuracy for the TV drama series 'Shaka Zulu', Shaka trains members of Chief Dingiswayo's *iziCwe* regiment in the use of his newly-invented stabbing spear; note the combined use of the shield with an under-arm spear thrust. (SABC/Emil Wessels)

peoples, combined with the material benefits—in terms of gifts of cattle—which proceeded from a successful expedition, all led to a high *esprit de corps*. Since the *amabutho* looked to the king for patronage, this further strengthened the position of Shaka himself.

Organisationally each *ibutho* was divided into two wings, led by *izinduna*, and sub-divided into companies, *amaviyo*. Each *iviyo* numbered roughly 50 men. In addition, some regiments were partially divided into *isigaba*—groups of *amaviyo* who were particularly associated with each other for one reason or another. When the king established a new *ibutho* and granted it a herd of cattle, he would select beasts with a particular uniformity of hides. From these would be made the war shields, and each regiment therefore had its own distinctive shield colour. War shields were the property of the state, not the individual; kept in raised stores in each *ikhanda*, they were issued at the start of each campaign. The *isihlangu* shield might be as much as 50 in. long and 30 in. wide, individual warriors picking out shields which suited their personal height. In Shaka's time the shield colours were meticulously adhered to, the difference between particular colours often being quite subtle: e.g., an *ihwanqa* shield was black with white patches all over

it, while the *impunga* shield was the same, but the patches were less clearly distinct. In general the most senior regiments carried white shields, and the youngest black, with all grades for regiments in between, although dun-coloured, red and grey (black and white hairs intermixed) were also carried.

War regalia

Each regiment also had its own uniform of feathers and furs. The bushy parts of cows' tails (*amashoba*) were worn in such profusion as to almost cover the body completely. They were worn in dense bunches, suspended from a necklace, falling to the

Shaka's 'tactical edge': the Zulu stabbing spear, *iklwa*. The exact specifications varied, although these are typical. The tang fitted into the bored haft and was secured by glue and bindings. (Author's collection)

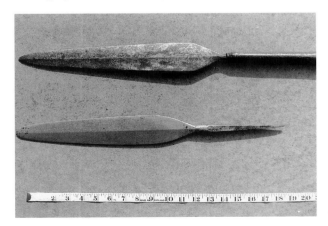

80

waist at the front and the knees at the back. They were worn around the elbows and knees, and sometimes from the wrists and ankles. A kilt made of golden civet and green samango monkey pelts, carefully twisted together to resemble tails, was worn over the ordinary *umutsha* by some senior regiments. A headband called *umqhele* was worn: made of leopardskin for junior regiments, and otterskin for senior ones, it was stitched into a tube, stuffed, and neatly tied at the back of the head. Oblong earflaps of samango skin for most warriors but occasionally of leopardskin, hung down either over the cheeks, or sometimes on either side of the back of the head. On to this basis were fixed the plumes granted to each individual *ibutho*.

There is very little direct surviving evidence relating to specific Shakan regiments, but certain conventions were followed. Young regiments, for example, usually wore the long grey tail feathers of the sakabuli bird. These were either worn in a dense bunch, attached to a plaited grass framework which fitted on to the top of the head; or in plumes on either side of the head, tied to quills and tucked inside the headband, so that the plumes pointed out and back. Blue crane feathers were a sign of seniority, worn either at the front of the head, or in ones and twos on either side. The young regiments often wore *amaphovela*, a grotesque headdress consisting of two stiff horns of cowhide standing upright above the temples, the bottoms sticking out below the headband, and with either small tufts or

King Dingane's residence, emGungundhlovu, partially reconstructed as a set for 'Shaka Zulu'. The original complex had a larger circumference and an inner palisade, but this does give a fair impression of the appearance of an *ikhanda*.

whole cowtails attached to the tips, the latter falling back down the head. Ostrich plumes were worn in great profusion at the front, back or sides, sometimes sticking out at all angles. The black/white imagery was continued, young regiments having more black ostrich feathers, senior ones more white. In addition, the king might grant particular plumes to regiments who distinguished themselves, and small bunches of the scarlet feathers of the lourie bird were given as rewards for bravery to individual warriors. Other similar symbols of bravery were a necklace of interlocking wooden beads, and *ingxotha*—a brass armband, rather like the cuff of a gauntlet, worn around the right forearm.

Theoretically, each warrior was supposed to provide his own uniform, and if it was not up to scratch he was likely to be mocked and thrashed by his fellows. In practice, however, the huge expansion of the army during the *mfecane* far outstripped the capacity of Zululand's wildlife to costume it, and feathers and pelts were obtained either as tribute or by trading with other parts of southern Africa, notably Thongaland in the northeast. There is a certain amount of evidence to suggest that in Shaka's time a good deal of this costume was worn into battle; the more expensive

81

and fragile items would probably have been left at home in the *ikhanda*, however.

Shaka's personal war dress is said to have consisted of a kilt of civet and monkey skins, with a collar of the same material, and white cow tails around the elbows and knees. Around his headring he wore a headband of otterskin into which were tucked bunches of lourie feathers tied to thorns. At the front he wore a single long crane feather. His shield was white, with one black spot on the centre right face.

A young Zulu warrior, photographed in the 19th century; the bulk of Shaka's warriors were unmarried men such as this. This man is probably not a member of the Zulu king's army, and wears no regimental regalia, although his shield is about the right size and is appropriately coloured black. (S. Bourquin)

The army on campaign

Before a regiment set out on campaign it was doctored by an *isangoma* who specialised in preparations for war. The warriors would be sprinkled with magic potions, and required to chew a piece of meat which had been specially prepared. Often they had to drink a potion which made them vomit. The intention was to bind them together and make them invulnerable to enemy weapons. The king might call up two regiments, and order them to challenge one another to see who would excel in the coming fight. Warriors would step out from the ranks and *giya*—proclaim their own virtues, act out their past deeds of valour, and challenge warriors known to them in the rival regiment; bets would even be laid. After the fight, Shaka would call up the same regiments, and the challenges would be recalled, though the bets were not called in. Those who had particularly distinguished themselves would be rewarded, and those accused of cowardice executed.

When an army set out on campaign it began in a single column, but then split into several columns. As it neared enemy territory it sent out an advance guard of men from each regiment, who made no attempt to conceal themselves but acted as aggressively as possible, hoping to convince the enemy that they were the main body. They were preceded by a screen of scouts who did conceal themselves, and who were expected to note every detail of the enemy's movements. Shaka's military intelligence system was renowned for its efficiency. Once the enemy was spotted, the army (or *impi*, the name for any body of armed men) was formed into an *umkhumbi*, or circle, and given final instructions for the attack. For most of his reign Shaka accompanied his armies in person, and was undoubtedly the most able commander of his generation. Once the attack had been launched the Zulu commanders watched the battle from high ground, issuing orders by runner or hand signals; by this stage, however, it was usually very difficult to recall an attacking force.

After the battle was over there were certain ceremonies to perform. Any man who killed another in battle was required to disembowel the corpse of his victim. This was not gratuitous mutilation: it was believed that the spirit of a dead warrior was in his stomach, and if it was not released he would haunt his slayer, visiting all manner of misfortune upon him until he eventually drove him mad. It must be admitted, however, that the tension of combat was sometimes vented on enemy dead. The victorious warrior was also supposed to dress himself in the clothing of his fallen opponent, and wear it until he had performed certain cleansing ceremonies at his personal *umuzi*. For this reason Zulu armies often disbanded after a successful battle, and there was a limit to the prolonged campaigning which even Shaka could make them endure.

Provisioning the army was another problem. At the start of the campaign the warriors were accompanied by *udibi*—boys too young to fight—who were allocated to individual warriors, often relatives, as personal servants to carry sleeping mats and food. These boys only accompanied the army on the first day of march, however, returning to their homes after that. In Shaka's day this was

An *induna* or military commander, painted by Angas. His shield is smaller than that of the warrior in the background and is probably for dancing rather than for war. He wears bunches of scarlet and green lourie feathers on either side of his head, a badge of rank or distinction. The beads around his neck suggest a festive occasion. (British Museum)

enough to see the *impi* beyond the Zulu borders, since Shaka expected his troops to cover up to 50 miles a day, and beyond that the *impi* had to forage for its own supplies. If Shaka rationalised this situation at all, he no doubt believed that it was another incentive for his *amabutho* to be successful in their raiding.

Both the Zulu state and the army were highly centralised, and needed a dynamic personality at their head to keep them functioning—especially in the early years, when there was no inherited weight of tradition. Shaka was certainly dynamic. Though many accounts of his bloodshed have been grotesquely exaggerated, there is no question that the lives of his individual subjects meant nothing to him, and that he drew no distinction between the interests of the state and his own personal wishes. He waged war to the death; and at his court a flick of his wrist would consign a man to the executioners for no more weighty crime than making him laugh when he wanted to be serious, or interrupting his speech with a sneeze. He maintained an iron grip on his empire, and as a general he was unsurpassed; only towards the end of his life did his judgement falter and his behaviour become increasingly psychotic.

The Coming of the Whites

On Christmas Day 1497 the Portuguese explorer Vasco de Gama noted in his log the existence of a stretch of African coastline which he named *Terra Natalis* in honour of the birth of the Lord; it was to be over 300 years before there was any further European interest in the area, but the area south of Zululand was to remain known as Natal.

The first whites to play a rôle in Zulu history arrived at the bay of Port Natal—later Durban—in 1824. They were a party of traders, hunters and adventurers led by two ex-Royal Navy lieutenants, James Saunders King and Francis George Farewell; their aims were to explore the commercial potential of links with the Zulu state. To reach Shaka's kingdom they had to travel through miles of depopulated countryside, and when they arrived the Zulu king took pains to impress them with the

One of a remarkable trio of photographs of Chief Ngoza ka Ludaba, taken in about 1865. Ngoza was chief of the Majozi, a section of the Chube clan, who broke away during the reign of King Mpande and settled in Natal. In this view he wears simple everyday costume limited to the *umutsha* groin-flap. (Africana Museum, Johannesburg)

power and wealth of his kingdom. It is true that the whites probably played only a very minor rôle in Shaka's affairs; none the less the Zulu king does seem to have been intrigued by them, granting them title to the land around the Port, and questioning them closely about the British colonies beyond the fringes of his own sphere.

Shaka was particularly interested in the European way of making war. He was fascinated by the 'Brown Bess' muskets carried by the party, and insisted on a demonstration; when a lucky shot fired by one of the sailors dropped an elephant, he was suitably impressed. He constantly demanded that the whites join him on his expeditions, and on several occasions they did so.

They also had the opportunity to witness Shaka's last clash with the Ndwandwe. In 1826 Zwide's successor moved down from the Transvaal in an attempt to regain his old lands. Shaka mustered his army and marched north-west, confronting the Ndwandwe at Ndolowane Hill. One of the whites' servants was ordered to fire several times into the Ndwandwe ranks, after which the Zulus charged. Twice they were repulsed; but at last the Ndwandwe gave way, and the Zulus slaughtered them.

In general, however, Shaka's policy looked increasingly southward. He moved his personal capital from kwaBulawayo ('the place of killing') to Dukuza in Natal, and established an *ikhanda* not far north of the Port. In 1828, much to the embarrassment of the whites, he sent a diplomatic mission to the Cape Colony. At the same time he sent his army on a raid which harried the Mpondo on the very fringe of British territory. His exact purpose is not clear; in any event the mission was coolly received, and Shaka was angry at its failure. When the army returned he sent it straightaway on a raid to the north.

It was a move that showed uncharacteristic lack of judgement. The army was exhausted, and Shaka was alienating his power-base. The majority of the Zulu people were weary of Shaka's increasingly erratic behaviour and the frequent summary killings. In September Shaka's half-brothers Dingane and Mhlangana seized their moment, and pounced on the king as he sat largely unattended, receiving a delegation from another tribe. They stabbed him to death with the spears of his own invention. Dingane immediately seized the throne. When the army returned—defeated for once—it was relieved to escape Shaka's wrath.

Dingane

King Dingane was very different in character from his predecessor, and had different problems to contend with. He lacked Shaka's zest for military expansion, and his reign was characterised by a need to keep together the state system which, under Shaka, had not had time to mature. The first problem was securing his own position. Personal favourites of Shaka were killed, and Dingane re-organised the army. Several of Shaka's *amabutho* were allowed to marry and disperse, and the remnants of others were re-organised into new regiments. Dingane then called up youths of an appropriate age and started enrolling new regiments dependent on his personal patronage. Initially he did not send his army on campaign; but the defection of a large section of the nation, the Qwabe clan of Chief Nqetho, who simply crossed the Tugela and fled to the south of Natal, persuaded him to adopt a more aggressive policy towards his neighbours. The Ndebele (Matabele)—an embryonic state under construction in the Transvaal under the leadership of Mzilikazi, a refugee from Shaka—particularly attracted Dingane's attention, although fighting was inconclusive.

Natal was another problem. The original European settlers had either died or moved on, but

Ngoza in full regalia, with young warriors. Although not the uniform of an *ibutho* of the Zulu king's army, since the clan had split away, this does show many characteristic items of Zulu 'full dress'—note the *amaphovela* and *isakabuli* feathers in the young warriors' headdresses. The size of the larger *isihlangu* shields is very evident here. (**Africana Museum, Johannesburg**)

they had been replaced by an increasing group—mostly elephant hunters—who proved quarrelsome and scheming. Dingane wished to remain on good terms with whites, but watched with apprehension as once-empty Natal began to fill up with blacks—survivors of Shaka's raids returning to their lands, and political refugees fleeing from Zululand. These people placed themselves under white protection, and formed the nucleus of a black population hostile to Zululand on its very borders. This was a situation which ultimately undermined the absolute authority of the Zulu monarch, since it sapped his army's strength and gave a safe refuge for dissidents.

Indeed, it was from Natal that the threat to Dingane's kingdom was to come, but it came from an unexpected source: the arrival of a new group of whites—the Boers.

The Boers, or Afrikaners, were descendants of Dutch, French and German settlers at the Cape who, in the 30 years following the British occupation in 1805, had become so disgruntled under British rule that they were prepared to leave. In 1834 a reconnaissance party had reported that

Natal was excellent cattle country and largely under-populated; in the mid-1830s Boer families packed their possessions into ox-wagons and began the movement known as the Great Trek. In 1836 they did what Dingane had failed to do—they drove Mzilikazi out of the Transvaal. In 1837 some of them crossed the Drakensberg and set up temporary camps in the Natal foothills.

Their arrival disturbed Dingane. There is little doubt that he felt their huge herds, military skill in African warfare, and lack of respect for native chiefs were a serious threat to the stability of his kingdom. Dingane entered into negotiations with the Trekker leader Piet Retief, and finally agreed to cede him part of Natal. But when Retief and 70 of his unarmed followers attended Dingane's residence at emGungundhlovu on 6 February 1838 for a celebratory dance, Dingane suddenly leapt to his feet and cried out 'Slay the wizards!' The Trekkers were overpowered and dragged to Dingane's place of execution, where they were clubbed and impaled.

The next day Dingane mustered his army and despatched it against the Boer encampments in Natal under the command of Ndlela kaSompisi of the Ntuli clan, one of the men who had risen through the ranks of Shaka's army. The subsequent campaign was a crucial test for the Zulu army: for

Ngoza in war dress, with members of a senior *ibutho*; note the headrings, padded otterskin headbands, and single crane feathers worn by these middle-aged warriors. These photos are probably virtually unique as a record of the appearance of authentic Zulu regimental costume of the period. (Radio Times Hulton Picture Library)

A fascinating photograph, apparently taken early in the 20th century; the original caption unfortunately does not record the occasion, but this may well be a group of surviving veterans of King Cetshwayo's army. The warriors in the centre have similar headdresses and shields, suggesting an old *ibutho* uniform. The two on the outside have bunches of *isakabuli* feathers on top of their heads; the rest have large bunches of lourie feathers on either side. The man in the centre is clearly a chief, and carries a staff, as well as a small bag of magical charms with his shield. (Brian Maggs)

the first time it would have to face firearms in large quantities. The Boers had perfected offensive tactics involving firing from horseback, and the defensive circle of wagons known as the *laager*. The Zulus, however, consistently refused to be overawed by guns, and commanders such as Ndlela showed great tactical ingenuity in countering Trekker tactics.

The Zulu attack fell upon the foremost encampments on the Bushmans and Bloukranz Rivers on the night of 16/17 February. Dawn was the traditional time for a Zulu attack—it caught the enemy unawares, when the spirits are lowest, yet gave sufficient light to direct the attack. On this occasion it is probable that this practice was abandoned in the hope of catching the Boers unprepared, when they could not use their guns effectively. The night attacks were partially successful: the leading Boer parties were wiped out, but survivors escaped in the confusion and were able to warn camps further back. Several put up a spirited defence and drove the Zulus off. Even so, the Boers lost nearly 300 of their men, women and children dead, and a further 200 of their servants. The Zulus also took most of their cattle.

Yet the attack had failed in its purpose of driving out the Trekkers, and Dingane no doubt realised a counter-attack was inevitable. When it came, however, it proved surprisingly easy to repulse. On 6 April a party of 347 mounted men led by Piet Uys and Hendrick Potgeiter set out towards emGungundhlovu; four days later they spotted a huge herd of cattle near eThaleni Mountain, and advanced to round it up. It was a trap: as many as 6,000 Zulus, concealed in long grass and on nearby heights, swept down, scattering the Boer forces and killing Uys himself.

For the British traders at Port Natal the war proved a dilemma. Dingane had sent them messages assuring them he meant no harm, but they felt morally obliged to side with fellow whites. They

Young warriors step out from the ranks of their regiment to *giya*—proclaim their own praises, and boast of the feats they will perform in the coming battle—part of the ceremony of mustering the Zulu army for war. (Author's collection)

were also tempted by the possibility of looting some of Dingane's cattle. In April, therefore, 18 of the settlers raised an army of around 4,000 Natal blacks, and crossed into Zululand in support of the Trekkers. They got as far as the *ikhanda* of 'Ndondakasuka on the Zulu side of the Tugela when, on 10 April, they ran into a Zulu *impi*. Many of the Natal levies were armed with rifles, and the battle raged back and forth; but at last one flank of the settler army collapsed, and the Zulus were able to complete their encircling movement and drive the settlers back, pinning them against the river. Only four settlers escaped, and hundreds of their levies were killed. The Zulus followed up their success with a raid which swept through Natal, destroying the whites' huts at the Port. So far, in their first conflict with whites, the Zulus were winning hands down.

The tide turned in August. Dingane made one more attempt to exterminate the Boer camps in the Drakensberg foothills. By now most of the Trekker families had collected in a large laager of over 200 wagons on the Bushmans River. Between 13 and 15 August as many as 10,000 Zulus repeatedly attacked the position. On one occasion they used the cover of a *donga*, a dry watercourse, to advance

within a few yards and fling throwing spears over the wagons into the laager. Shaka had outlawed throwing spears, but Dingane had re-introduced them apparently in an attempt to counter Boer firepower. Since a spear could be thrown with some accuracy for up to 50 yards, while an average rifle of the time was not very effective beyond 100 yards, there was some logic in this. On another occasion the Zulus tried to set fire to the wagons with spears wrapped in burning straw. These attempts were uniformly unsuccessful, however, and the Zulus were eventually forced to retreat.

Blood River

In November 1838 a new leader, Andries Pretorius, joined the Boer laagers, and the Trekkers went on to the offensive. Pretorius organised a 'commando' of around 470 whites and 340 black or Coloured servants, accompanied by 64 wagons and at least two small cannon, and set out on 3 December. On the 14th they ran into a Zulu advanced guard; on the 15th they drew up in a laager on the banks of the Ncome River. The site of the laager was carefully chosen, so that one side was protected by the river and another by a *donga* which flowed into it. Wooden gates were used to block the gaps between each wagon, and the horses and oxen were brought within the circle. Lanterns were tied to whip-stocks and raised over the wagons to hinder any Zulu attack under cover of darkness.

They attacked at dawn. In fact, daylight caught Ndlela with his force divided. He had to cross the Ncome to attack the laager, but while his left horn was in position, the chest and right horn were still drawn up on the hills overlooking the Zulu bank. The left horn was supposed to remain out of musket range until the rest of the army had crossed, but as soon as the light was clear they rose to their feet and charged. A few yards from the wagons they were met with a heavy volley, and forced to retire. They tried the same manoeuvre several times without success. Bodies of warriors then broke away to occupy the deep *donga*, where they could mass only a few yards from the wagons. Pretorius ordered a sally, which lined the lip of the *donga* and fired down into the Zulus, who were too cramped to reply with their spears. Ndlela finally managed to get his chest and right horn across the river; but it was impossible to control them, and the regiments frittered themselves away in unco-ordinated attacks. At last the Boers rode out and chased them from the field. The Zulu reserve tried to restore the situation, but the Boers caught them as they crossed the drifts. So many Zulus were forced into the river that it became choked with corpses and stained blood-red. The Ncome has been known as Blood River ever since.

The defeat at Blood River was a catastrophe for Dingane, but it did not destroy the Zulu state. Pretorius advanced to emGungundhlovu and

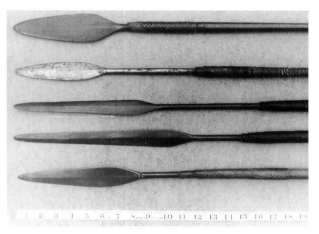

A selection of throwing spears. Outlawed by Shaka, these were re-introduced during the reign of Dingane, perhaps because they offered a potential counter—however inadequate—to Boer musketry. The three in the centre date from the 1879 war. (Author's collection)

found it in flames, the king fled. The bodies of Retief's men still lay on the hill of execution, and the treaty ceding Natal was found in Retief's wallet. When a party from the commando tried to round up cattle beyond the White Mfolozi on 27 December it walked into a repetition of the eThaleni trap, and only just escaped.

The Voortrekkers withdrew, and opened negotiations with Dingane to end the war. The Trekker terms were that Dingane should abandon southern Zululand and move north. This he agreed to do, and even sent his eMbelebele regiment to build a new homestead in what is now southern Swaziland; the Swazi, however, resisted, and Dingane's plan was frustrated. His final downfall came about when his half-brother Mpande defected to the Boers with a large section of the army. Mpande had been thought a harmless simpleton, but this facade hid a shrewd political mind. The Trekkers agreed to acknowledge Mpande king of the Zulus, and to provide military support, in return for peace and land in Natal.

In fact, the Boers took little part in the subsequent fighting. Mpande's army confronted Dingane in the Maqongqo Hills in northern Zululand. Though the Boers were hardly engaged, their presence was enough to give Mpande the edge, and Dingane was defeated. He fled with a few loyal retainers to the territory of Chief Sambane of the small Nyawo clan. In a fit of rage, he had Ndlela killed for losing the battle. Dingane did not long

survive him—Sambane conspired with the Swazis to have him killed. The exact details of his death are uncertain, but one story has it that he was set upon one morning as he crawled out of his hut. This was in March 1840; on 10 February Pretorious had already proclaimed Mpande king of the Zulus.

Mpande and Cetshwayo, 1840–1878

Both the personality and reign of King Mpande have been much misunderstood. It is true that he was vain, and enjoyed the pleasures of his court life, but Mpande's apparent indolence concealed the deep political perception of a born survivor. He had, after all, remained alive under both Shaka and Dingane, when so many of his family had been assassinated as potential rivals. He was to rule for over 30 years—longer than the other kings put together—and to die a natural death. He not only managed to hold the kingdom together in the

The arrival of the Boers in the 1830s brought a technological challenge which the Zulus were not equipped to meet. The combined use of horse and gun, and the defensive wagon laager, proved difficult to overcome. This is the reconstructed laager on the battlefield of Blood River. (Author's collection)

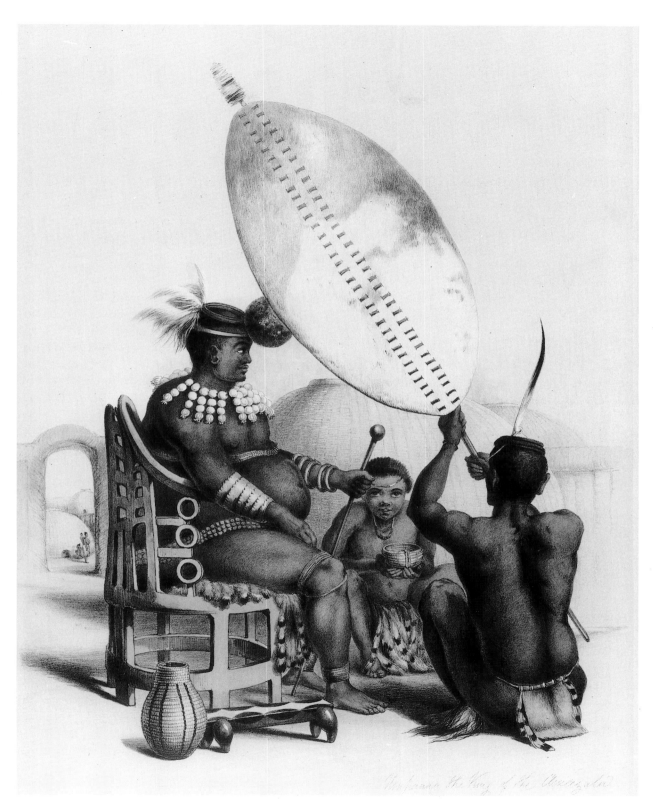

King Mpande kaSenzangakhona; a famous portrait by Angas which captures the king's deceptively indolent appearance. On hot days his attendants would hold a shield to protect him from the sun. Note the *ingxotha* on Mpande's right arm. (British Museum)

A group of warriors photographed at King Cetshwayo's 'coronation' in 1873. Several regiments are represented, and the men seem to be wearing war dress—a simplified form of ceremonial regalia—and carrying the *umbhumbhuluzo* shield. (Killie Campbell Africana Library)

aftermath of the Trekker and civil wars, but consolidated its position during years of menace from growing European colonies on its borders.

The two years of conflict between 1838 and 1840 were a disaster for the Zulu kingdom. The dead and wounded amounted to several thousands, and the army was shattered by the civil war. Individual chiefs had exacted a high price in personal power in exchange for supporting Mpande, and many who were dissatisfied with the state of affairs in Zululand moved to Natal. In addition, the Boers took 30,000 head of cattle as the price of their help in defeating Dingane, and laid claim to land as far as the Black Mfolozi—two-thirds of the kingdom itself. Fortunately, in 1842 Britain decided to exercise its claim to Natal; after a sharp fight at Port Natal the Trekkers withdrew for the most part to the Transvaal, and their claims to Zulu territory lapsed. The southern borders of the kingdom became accepted as the Tugela and Buffalo Rivers.

Nevertheless, the reign of Mpande, and to some extent that of his son Cetshwayo, were marked by an attempt to re-establish the central authority of the Zulu state. Mpande's position was precarious, since he needed the support of the *izikhulu*, the great chiefs who made up the *ibandla* council, and could no longer afford to intimidate them as Shaka had done. Although the king continued to exercise the power of life and death over his subjects, the more despotic elements of Zulu kingship were gone for good.

Natal posed an ever-increasing threat to Zulu security. From the depopulated wastelands witnessed by Farewell in Shaka's day, the black population of Natal had grown to 100,000 by 1845, and 305,000 by 1872. In the 1850s as many as 4,000 a year were leaving Zululand. When, in 1843, Mpande tried to consolidate his position by attacking rival members of his own household, an aunt, Mawa, simply fled to Natal with 3,000 of her followers. Why were they leaving? Some, like Mawa, were fleeing the king's justice; but many went because, with the increase in the numbers of whites in Natal seeking workers, life there offered more potential for cattle and wives than the Zulu army. In the 1850s one estimate put the total strength of Mpande's *amabutho* as low as 6,000. Nevertheless, the king patiently revised the state system and gradually rebuilt his authority.

This process suffered a set-back in the 1850s. Mpande, unlike his predecessors, had a number of sons, but was unwilling to weaken his own position by naming his successor. His eldest son, Cetshwayo, had considerable support amongst the *izikhulu*, but the king himself favoured his next eldest, Mbuyazi. Both princes had military experience, and were popular within their respective regiments. Each began courting chiefs and *izinduna*, and each developed a faction—the iziGqoza of Mbuyazi, and the uSuthu of Cetshwayo. The king tried to avoid conflict by keeping the princes at opposite ends of the country, but in November 1856 the iziGqoza fled to the Tugela River and Mbuyazi tried to appeal to the Natal authorities for support. It was not forthcoming, but the white hunter and trader John Dunn offered support in a private capacity. Cetshwayo called together his own supporters and, on 2 December 1856, attacked the iziGqoza at 'Ndondakasuka on the banks of the Tugela, not far from where the Port Natal settlers had been massacred in 1838. John Dunn's party fired volleys at the attacking uSuthu, and Mbuyazi's regiments put up a stiff fight; but the uSuthu numbers prevailed, and the iziGqoza were pinned against the river bank. When the fighting finished the victorious uSuthu massacred the iziGqoza; as many as 20,000 were slaughtered. Mbuyazi and several of Mpande's other sons were killed.

The victory at 'Ndondakasuka established Cetshwayo's claim to the throne beyond doubt. Mpande continued to rule, however, and the next decade and a half was marked by shifting internal allegiances. In September or October 1872 Mpande finally died and was buried at his royal *ikhanda* at Nodwengu on the Mahlabatini plain.

Cetshwayo persuaded the Colony of Natal to recognise his coronation the following August—support which would cost him dear in due course—but once enthroned he felt able to adopt a more rigorous policy than his father. He refused to negotiate with the Transvaal Boers over a border dispute which had been smouldering for ten years, and he tightened his control over the *amabutho*. The *izikhulu* remained powerful, however, and resisted attempts to re-centralise state power; it could, and did, veto the king's decisions, and the king's authority over several very powerful chiefs, like his half-brother Prince Hamu kaNzibe, and Zibhebhu kaMapitha of the Mandhlakazi section, remained tenuous. These divisions would come to the fore in the subsequent war of 1879.

The army had changed noticeably since Shaka's day. The majority of the warriors were no longer recruited from newly subject clans as in the days of military expansion, but through natural means. At the age of 14 or so each boy was expected to serve as an *udibi*; and at the age of 17 or 18 they would report to an *ikhanda* and *kleza*—drink milk direct from the udders of the king's cattle—accepting his bounty, and in return offering service to the state. They underwent a period of cadetship, looking after the king's herds and the royal homesteads. When there were sufficient numbers of them around the kingdom the king would call them together and form them into a new *ibutho*, ordering them to go and build their own *ikhanda* at a specified location. Occasionally a new regiment would be incorporated with an old one, or assigned to an existing barracks. The warriors were not, however, permanently mustered as they had been in Shaka's time: once the units had been established, warriors were allowed to spend long periods at home with their families while the *amakhanda* would be cared for by a skeleton staff. The king would call up a particular *ibutho* when he had need of it.

It is important to note that the duties of the

A watercolour by African artist Gerard Bhengu of one of the ceremonies of the *umkhosi* or 'first fruits' festival: the killing of a black bull by warriors of a young *ibutho*. (Killie Campbell Africana Library)

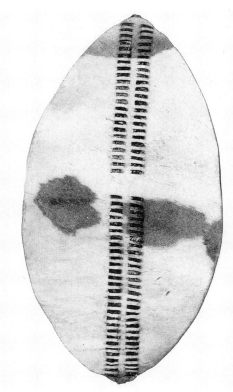

regiments were not, and never had been, purely military, although in Shaka's day there was more than enough campaigning to keep them busy. They were also the state workforce, and were required to work the king's fields, build new homesteads, organise hunts, and partake in the national ceremonies. The greatest of these was the *umkhosi*, the 'first fruits' or harvest festival, which took place every year in December or January. The king would give the order for his army to muster, and the *izinduna* at the various military centres would summon the warriors in their local areas. If an *ibutho* had its headquarters near the king's homestead—Cetshwayo established himself at oNdini, or Ulundi, on the other side of the plain from

A shield, white with red spots, from the Thulwana *ibutho*, taken from King Cetshwayo's residence at Ulundi after the battle of 1879. (Africana Museum, Johannesburg)

The two types of shield carried by the Zulu army from the 1850s: (left) the *umbhumbhuluzo* (here, 39½ × 19½ in.) and the *isihlangu* (here, 54 in. × 29 in.); the former lacks its fur crest, which has also been cropped off the edge of the photograph of the *isihlangu*. Both these examples date from 1879. (Author's collection)

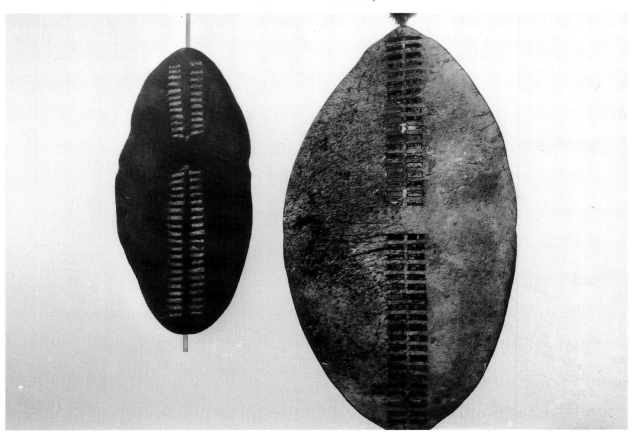

Nodwengu—it would be expected to muster within 24 hours. If not, the warriors would march to the capital by regimental companies from each district, and form up when there. The king would appoint them a place to camp. The ceremonies themselves included a binding together of the army, in which warriors of the youngest regiment present would have to kill a bull with their bare hands. The meat from the bull was then butchered and distributed amongst the *amabutho*.

Mpande had found it impractical to keep his young men unmarried for too long—they were tempted by the easy availability of wives in Natal—so the regiments married earlier. The prized white shields, once a symbol of élite unmarried regiments, became synonymous with married men. Indeed, both Mpande and Cetshwayo maintained *amabandhla amhlope*, 'white assemblies', who appear to have been a compromise between old and new systems, intended to prolong the active service of married men. These were married men permanently available to the king but who were allowed to live with their wives in an *ikhanda*, though even they were allowed to return to personal homesteads almost at will. The famous Thulwana regiment, Mpande's favourite—which had so many men of rank that it had a section known as the *inhlabamasoka*, 'the select ones'—was such a regiment in Cetshwayo's time, and lived at Ulundi itself.

Cetshwayo had some success in revitalising the *amabutho*, particularly the youngest regiments who owed him the greatest personal allegiance. The iNgobamakhosi, Cetshawyo's favourite, was a *palane* regiment of unusual size—perhaps as many as 6,000 strong. The uVe, formed shortly before the war in 1879, was 4,000 strong, and incorporated into the iNgobamakhosi. The flood of refugees had dwindled, and Cetshwayo cut down on the number of exceptions allowed to military service; he was therefore able to increase his army to about 40,000.

Tensions within the army sometimes reflected divisions within the state. At the first fruits ceremony in 1878 the Thulwana and iNgobamakhosi clashed, and some 60 warriors were killed. The fight had been sparked off by grievances over women taken as wives by a young section of the Thulwana, but it is no coincidence that the Thulwana were commanded by Hamu kaNzibe, who was widely thought to have resented Cetshwayo's ascendancy.

Another source of military manpower came from the abaQulusi, who were unusual in that they were essentially a regional, rather than age-grade regiment. They were descendants of an *ikhanda*, emaQulusini, established by Shaka near Hlobane Mountain in northern Zululand, who had settled in

A powder horn, apparently taken from a dead Zulu after Rorke's Drift; and (foreground) a wooden snuff container. (Keith Reeves)

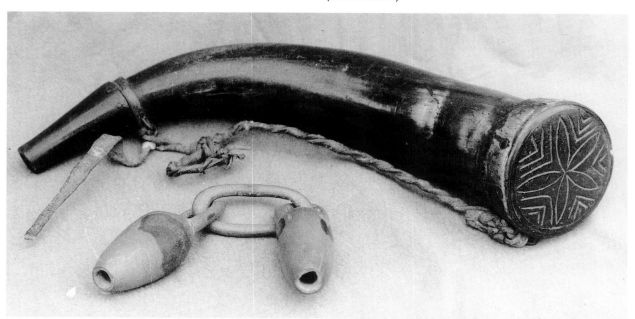

95

A remarkable pair of photographs, probably taken in 1873, showing a warrior in full regimental regalia. It is not possible to identify the *ibutho*, since sources for this period are incomplete and often contradictory. However, the components of full dress uniform are clearly visible: the extensive use of cow tails around the body, the earflaps and headband of leopardskin, and various plumes of the headdress. The shield is of the large *isihlangu* type. (S. Bourquin)

the same area when they dispersed and married. They mustered and fought as a state regiment, and were fiercely loyal to the king. There are references to an *ikhanda* still in use in the area in 1879.

There were differences, too, in the warriors' armament. In the 1850s Cetshwayo had introduced a new type of war shield amongst the uSuthu. Called *umbhumbuluzo*, it was about $3\frac{1}{2}$ft long by less than 2ft wide. Cetshwayo considered that this was lighter and easier to wield than the *isihlangu* type. Both types were carried, however, even within the same regiment. It is possible that the *umbhumbuluzo* type was more popular with the younger warriors. The colour-coding of the shields, so precise in Shaka's time, had become less so by the 1870s. The

overall equation of black with youth and white with experience remained the same, but the positioning of patches and spots was less exact, and there were fewer variations of type. Although our knowledge of shield colours in the 1870s is imprecise, there seem to have been no grey or dun colours, and some *amabutho* seem to have had different shield colours within the same regiment—these may have reflected particular sections or companies.

Guns, too, were available to the Zulu army in large quantities by Cetshwayo's reign. They had first been taken from the Voortrekkers in the 1830s, and Mpande had tried to obtain them to strengthen his position against Dingane. When he later became king he demanded guns from white traders in an attempt to compensate for the weakness of his army. Gun-running from Natal was officially frowned upon, but did take place. It was a common practice for European powers to dump obsolete arms on the unsophisticated native market, and Africa had an inexhaustible demand. In the aftermath of the

The youth of Shaka, c. 1805
1: Nandi
2: Shaka
3: Mthethwa chief

A

1

3

2

B

The Battle of Gqokli Hill 1818
1: Warrior, Isipezi regiment
2: Ndwandwe commander
3: King Shaka kaSenzangakhona
4: Warrior, Fasimba regiment
5: Young Ndwandwe warrior
6: Warrior, Ndabezibona unit
7: Senior Ndwandwe warrior

7

AngusMcBride

C

Meeting between Shaka and Europeans, 1824
1: Lt.Francis Farewell
2: *Imbongi*
3: King Shaka
4: Xhosa interpreter

D

The court of Dingane, 1830s
1: Youth, dancing dress
2: King Dingane
3: Ndlela kaSompisi

E

Skirmish between Boers and Zulus, 1838
1: Boer Voortrekker
2: Warrior, Mbelebele regiment
3: Warrior, Kokoti regiment

F

The Battle of 'Ndondakasuka, 1856
1: Warrior, uDhloko regiment
2: Prince Cetshwayo kaMpande
3: Warrior, Impisi regiment

G

Warriors muster, 1870s
1: Zulu girls
2: Warrior, Mtuyisazwe regiment
3: Warrior, uKhandempenvu corps
4: *Udibi boy*

H

The court of Mpande, 1870s
1: King Mpande kaSenzangakhona
2: Warrior, umXapho regiment
3: Warrior, iNdlu-yengwe regiment

Angus McBride

1

2

3

I

An *impi* is doctored for war, 1870s
1: *Isangoma*
2: Warrior, iNgobamakhosi regiment
3: Warrior, Thulwana regiment

J

The aftermath of Isandlwana, 1879
1: Warrior, Mbonambi regiment
2: Warrior, Indlondlo regiment
3: Warrior, iNgobamakhosi regiment

FOR NATAL

Angus McBride

3   2   1   K

The Battle of Mhome Gorge, 1906
1: Zulu rebel
2: Private,Durban Light Infantry
3: Constable,Zulu Native Police

Napoleonic Wars thousands of old 'Brown Bess' muskets bearing the Tower mark were sold cheaply in Africa, and with each new weapon that came into service the old makes would be sold off. The Zulus well appreciated their significance: after 'Ndondakasuka, John Dunn made his peace with Cetshwayo, who adopted him as his agent when dealing with whites. Cetshwayo wanted guns to secure his position within the kingdom, and Dunn purchased hundreds. Other important chiefs also had white traders who advised them, and who were a further source of supply. In addition, thousands of guns came into the Portuguese port of Delagoa Bay—as many as 20,000 in the 1870s alone. Most of these found their way into Zululand. Even rifles such as the Enfield, standard British issue in the 1850s and '60s, could be traded for as little as a sheep in the 1870s. If the quantity was sufficient, however, the quality was sadly lacking. Many of the guns were in poor condition, and the traders provided little back-up in terms of spare parts or even ammunition. Powder was of poor quality, percussion caps were in short supply, and pebbles were sometimes used in place of bullets. Nor was there anyone to train the warriors: individuals like Prince Dabulamanzi kaMpande and Chief Zibhebhu kaMaphita were recognised as good shots, but most warriors believed that the higher a gun was pointed, the further it would shoot, and many held the butt away from their shoulder to avoid the recoil. Battlefield accounts suggest the volume, not the accuracy, of Zulu fire.

The War of 1879

Lurid British accounts justifying the invasion of Zululand in 1879 portrayed it as a preventative campaign waged against a cruel and bloodthirsty despot and his army, a 'celibate man-destroying machine'. Most historians now accept this view as the propaganda it was, and suggest that the causes of the war lay rather in a British desire to simplify the complex political situation in southern Africa by joining the disparate British and Boer states together in a federation; a large independent Zulu state was seen as a threat to this scheme. In addition, many in the growing colony of Natal wanted to see Zululand opened to free trading and labour-recruitment, neither of which were possible when the king (in theory at least) controlled trade and Zulu manpower was fully utilised by the *amabutho* system. Minor border incidents which took place in 1878 were seized upon, and the British presented a stiff ultimatum to King Cetshwayo which demanded, among other things, the disbandment of the *amabutho*. The king himself and a number of his *izikhulu* were aware of the gravity of the situation; but feeling ran high within the army that the national honour was at stake, and the young regiments in particular refused to consider British demands. On 11 January 1879 the British crossed the border in three columns[1].

The king and his council considered their strategy carefully. It was not a war waged at their initiative, and Cetshwayo hoped to win political advantages by keeping the Zulu army within his borders: it would, therefore, be a defensive campaign. The British Centre Column, accompanied by Lt.Gen. Lord Chelmsford himself, was correctly identified as the most serious threat: the bulk of the army would be directed against this. Those men from the *amabutho* who lived in the coastal strip would report to the *amakhanda* there, and would be used to contest the progress of Col. Pearson's Right Column; the *abaQulusi* would try to check Col. Evelyn Wood's Left Column. The majority of the regiments were already at Ulundi, where they had gathered for the first fruits ceremony. They were doctored for war in the traditional way. A Sotho doctor from beyond the Drakensberg, renowned for his skill, was employed: he paid particular attention to guns. He burnt various medicines over a shard of pottery, and the warriors held their guns down so that the smoke wafted into the barrels, thus ensuring that they would fire straight and true. In the *giya* ceremonies, first the Khandempemvu (umCijo) and iNgobamakhosi *amabutho* vied against each other, then the Nokhenkhe and Mbonambi. Altogether this main striking arm totalled in excess of 20,000 warriors. Probably on 17 January, it marched off to confront Lord Chelmsford's army; and it encountered the British camped beneath a rocky outcrop known as Isandlwana.

[1]For a fuller account of the battles of 1879 see MAA 57, *The Zulu War*.

Isandlwana and Rorke's Drift

The king himself had not accompanied the army, which was entrusted to Chief Ntshingwayo kaMahole Khoza, who had a great reputation as a general, and Chief Mavumengwana, the son of Dingane's commander Ndlela. The army was in good spirits, but it should be noted that neither the *izinduna* nor the warriors had much combat experience, and there were few who remembered Blood River 40 years earlier. Nevertheless, the commanders managed to lead the army undetected to within a few miles of the British camp where, on 22 January, it was discovered by a British patrol. The young regiments, particularly the Khandempemvu, immediately launched an attack without waiting for instructions. The battle which followed took place with very little direction from the Zulu high command.

The battle caught Chelmsford's force divided. Early that morning, in response to the increase in Zulu activity in the area, the general had taken roughly half his forces away from the camp at Isandlwana to search for the *impi*. He had left behind six companies of the 24th Regt., two guns, and a number of mounted volunteers and levies. The Zulu advance developed from some hills to the left of the camp, and caught the defenders scattered over a wide plain in front of the camp. The 24th opened up a heavy fire, and the Zulus facing them were pinned down; but as the traditional 'chest and horns' attack developed, the British were outflanked. They began to fall back on the camp and, encouraged by the shouts of their *izinduna*, the Zulus rose and charged after them. The fighting raged at close quarters among the tents and transport wagons and on towards the Natal border, the British standing back to back while their ammu-

Zulu smiths do not seem to have manufactured battle-axes, but they were acquired from tribes renowned for making them by trade, like the Pedi of north-eastern Transvaal. These typical examples are decorated with metal wire, introduced by European traders in the mid-19th century. (Author's collection)

nition held out, until at last they were overcome. Elements of the Zulu reserve pursued the few survivors; and about 4,000 men of the Thulwana, Dhloko, iNdhlondhlo and inDlu-yengwe *amabutho*, led by Prince Dabulamanzi, crossed into Natal and went on to attack the supply depot at Rorke's Drift.

The garrison there—B Company, 2/24th—had been warned of the Zulu approach by survivors of Isandlwana, and were able to barricade the two mission buildings with biscuit boxes and mealie bags from the supplies. Dabulamanzi's men assaulted the post from five in the afternoon until after midnight but, although they stormed one of the buildings, they could not dislodge the defenders. At dawn on the 23rd they called the attack off.

Isandlwana was a disaster of the greatest magnitude for Chelmsford, killing 850 of his white troops and 400 Natal blacks who had been recruited to fight their traditional enemy, and scotching his invasion plan. Hundreds of rifles fell into Zulu hands, with thousands of rounds of ammunition. Yet it had been a costly victory for the *amabutho*. Over 1,000 warriors lay dead around Isandlwana, with a further 400 at Rorke's Drift. The survivors tried to bury the bodies in *dongas*, ant-bear holes, or in the grain pits of nearby homesteads, but the numbers were so great that many had to be left on the field with just a shield to cover them. Warriors took rifles from the men they had killed, and stripped and disembowelled the dead. They then dispersed to their homes, taking their wounded with them—hundreds of men suffering injuries from heavy calibre bullets, which were beyond the skills of the *izinyanga*. The king was angry that many of the warriors did not report to Ulundi for the purification ceremonies, and appalled by news of the casualties. 'An assegai has been thrust into the belly of the nation,' he said; 'there are not enough tears to mourn for the dead'.

There was other fighting on the 22nd; an *impi* of between 4,000 and 6,000 warriors attacked Col. Pearson's coastal column on the march at Nyezane. The Zulu attack was premature however, and despite the vulnerability of the British columns when on the march, the warriors were unable to press home their attack. Over 300 Zulu bodies were found on the field. Pearson's column continued its advance to the deserted mission station at Eshowe, where it received news of Isandlwana and

King Cetshwayo kaMpande, photographed during his visit to Britain.

entrenched itself. The local *amabutho* contingents besieged it.

The first phase of the war had gone Cetshwayo's way, although his inability to keep his army in the field made it difficult for him to exploit his advantage. It was March by the time he was able to collect together his army at Ulundi and, after careful discussion with his *izinduna*, decided to launch an attack against Evelyn Wood's Left Column. Since it had crossed into Zululand this had been engaged in constant cattle-raiding and skirmishing with the abaQulusi, and the followers of a renegade Swazi prince named Mbiline. It was undoubtedly the most dangerous of Chelmsford's surviving columns.

Hlobane, Khambula and Gingindhlovu
The new Zulu offensive coincided with fresh British activity. On 28 March Chelmsford had crossed the Tugela with a column intending to relieve Eshowe.

111

Artist's impression of the defence of the mission station at Rorke's Drift by B Co., 2/24th Foot on the night of 22/23 January 1879: engraving after Wollen. A sound defensive position and readily available ammunition negated superior Zulu numbers. (Author's collection)

A trophy of Zulu weapons and regalia taken by the 91st Highlanders from the field of Gingindhlovu, 1879. Note cow tail necklaces either side of the shield; the full kilt of different furs beneath it; and the percussion rifles. It seems likely that the warriors defending the coastal sector wore more regalia into battle than did the main *impi* directed from Ulundi. (National Army Museum)

He gave orders to other British commanders along the frontier to make demonstrations to draw off the Zulus. On the same day Wood tried to clear the abaQulusi from their stronghold on Hlobane Mountain. Several parties of mounted volunteers scaled the summit, where a running fight ensued. At the height of the action, however, the main Zulu army from Ulundi came into sight. Such bad luck

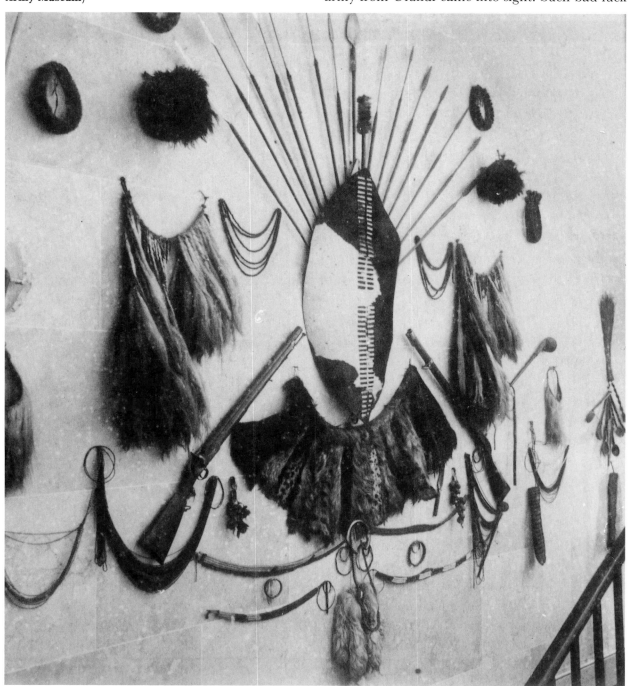

was appalling timing for the British, and it turned Hlobane into a débâcle as Wood struggled to extricate his troops. Those on the summit could only escape via a steep rocky staircase known as the Devil's Pass—over a hundred were killed. Wood fell back on his fortified base at Khambula Hill; the Zulus camped a few miles away that night, and the next morning advanced to attack Khambula.

The battle of Khambula was the most decisive of the war. Cetshwayo had learned from the stories of Isandlwana, and issued strict instructions that the *amabutho* were not to attack fortified positions, but to try to draw the British out from their earthworks. In the event, the Zulu right horn was in position before the chest and left, and a mounted British sortie was able to goad them into attacking. Wood's position consisted of a wagon laager and an earthwork redoubt; for over four hours the Zulus launched

fierce but unco-ordinated attacks which several times penetrated the defences, but were unable to overrun them. At last they were chased from the field by mounted volunteers in a particularly savage pursuit.

Zulu losses at Khambula were comparable to those at Isandlwana, probably considerably greater. British burial parties noted that the young *amabutho* had suffered particularly heavily, and many *izinduna* and chiefs had died because they had exposed themselves to encourage their men. Border patrols noted the lamentations from homesteads across the river as word of the casualties spread to the civilian population. And there was more bad news for Cetshwayo: on 2 April Chelmsford's Eshowe Relief Column had been attacked by 12,000 warriors at Gingindhlovu.

Local elements of most of the main *amabutho* made up the *impi*, which was led by Somopho kaSikhala and accompanied by veterans of Isandlwana like Prince Dabulamanzi and Sigcwelegcwele kaMhlekehleke, fiery commander of the iNgobamakhosi regiment. Chelmsford had drawn his forces up in a square, protected by a ditch and

Members of the Natal Native Contingent 'mopping up' after the battle of Ulundi. The artist has captured the appearance of the different African groups well: the man on the left is a Swazi, who seem to have worn full regalia into battle. In the centre is a Natal African, wearing some items of European clothing and with a distinguishing red rag just visible tied round his head. The Zulu wears no regimental regalia. (Author's collection)

earth rampart, and the combined volley, cannon and Gatling fire cut the warriors down before their charges could strike home. The *impi* was scattered. Chelmsford relieved Eshowe and retired to Natal to prepare a new invasion.

Ulundi

The twin blows of Khambula and Gingindhlovu shattered Cetshwayo's strategic plans. The morale of the army was shaken, and it was clear that military victory was impossible. As Chelmsford began his new invasion in June the Zulu king stepped up his attempts to reach a diplomatic solution. It was hopeless: the British were masters of the field, and were interested in peace only after Isandlwana had been avenged. Not that the Zulus had lost the will to resist: on one occasion a young *ibutho* refused to allow Cetshwayo's peace emissaries to pass, and Chelmsford's advance was accomplished in the face of constant skirmishing. Among the casualties was the young Prince Imperial of France, exiled heir to the Bonapartist throne; in Zululand as an observer, he was out on patrol one day when ambushed by a Zulu scouting party.

At last, however, Chelmsford reached the vicinity of Ulundi and the complex of *amakhanda* on the Mahlabatini plain. Cetshwayo once more summoned his army, and the warriors dutifully mustered. The king and his *izinduna* made careful plans to attack the British. On the morning of 4 July Chelmsford crossed the White Mfolozi, and formed his troops up in a large rectangle opposite Ulundi. The *amabutho* appeared on the surrounding heights and advanced slowly to attack, greeted by the roll of volley fire, the boom of the guns, and the chatter of the Gatlings. For nearly an hour the Zulu commanders tried to direct their men against the British weak points; one charge, on the rear face of the rectangle, was sustained to within a few yards of the line. But the 'beast's horns' were of no use against an unbroken wall of defenders, and the Zulus faltered. Lord Chelmsford ordered the 17th Lancers to charge the broken enemy, and the Zulus were driven from the field.

The war was a calamity for the Zulus: battlefield casualties amounted to about 6,000 dead, and many more injured. Thousands of cattle were taken by the British, and not only the *amakhanda* but hundreds of civilian homesteads were destroyed.

King Dinuzulu kaCetshwayo, photographed at about the time of the rebellion in 1888. He wears European clothes, but also a variation of the 'bravery bead' necklace. (Author's collection)

The political, military, social and economic structure of the greater Zulu state was shattered. The king was a fugitive; on 28 August he was run to ground, captured by a British patrol, and began the long road to exile in Cape Town.

The army had gone to war in the traditional way, infused with the spirit of Shaka. True, many had not worn their ceremonial regalia; the evidence is patchy, but it seems that the majority of the main *impi* left behind the more complex and constricting items, and wore only loin coverings and perhaps a headband and a few cow tails—the younger *amabutho* seem to have worn very little. The *impi*

115

The Ruin of Zululand

The pacification and post-war settlement of Zululand was left to Lord Chelmsford's successor, Sir Garnet Wolseley. He tackled it with much vigour and little insight. The country was divided up into 13 small kingdoms. There was some attempt to dismantle the Zulu state—pre-Shakan clans were returned to prominence—and to exploit the divisions within the kingdom which had become apparent in 1879. Prince Hamu kaNzibe, who had defected to the British during the war—the only member of the royal house to do so—was given a kingdom, as was John Dunn, who had abandoned his protector Cetshwayo to serve as a scout for Chelmsford. Also honoured was Zibhebhu kaMaphita of the Mandhlakazi section. He was known to be a shrewd and ambitious leader, and favourable to the whites; he was no friend of Cetshwayo's, but had loyally fought in the war as an able commander. He was given a tract in northern Zululand which contained many of the clans most loyal to Cetshwayo.

Trouble started almost as soon as the British troops withdrew. Hamu, Zibhebhu and Dunn raided Cetshwayo's supporters—who called themselves the uSuthu, after the king's faction in 1856—in a deliberate attempt to destroy their authority. They retaliated, and appealed to Britain to restore the king.

Cetshwayo was imprisoned in reasonable comfort at Cape Town, where he petitioned to be allowed to return to his kingdom. The British had long since abandoned the Confederation scheme, and watched glumly as Zululand slid towards civil war. In September 1881 the king was allowed to visit London to state his case: he dined with Queen Victoria at Osborne House, and was a great success with the British public. The Foreign Office cautiously gave him permission to return home. In January 1883 he landed on the coast of Zululand.

He was given a small tract of land and no real power. Zibhebhu and Dunn were allowed to keep their lands and, though the king built a new homestead at Ulundi and formed new age-regiments, they were shorn of their military function and regalia and allowed to give ceremonial service only. It was made quite clear that no revival

A sketch by Baden-Powell—who fought against Dinuzulu in 1888—of a warrior wearing the *ubushokobezi* badge, the symbol of the uSuthu faction in the 1880s, later adopted by the rebels in 1906. (Author's collection)

which fought in the coastal region did not muster at Ulundi; it operated closer to the individual warriors' homes, and so seems to have retained more regalia in action. Yet the army remained committed to the old tactics of frontal assault, and did not exploit the full potential of its firepower; only towards the end of the campaign was there any reluctance to face the British in the open, and sniping increased. On at least two occasions—Isandlwana and Khambula—the young *amabutho* showed a serious lack of discipline by allowing themselves to be goaded into an attack against the wishes of their *izinduna*. This in turn reflected a lack of strong direction and control at the top. Wedded to an inappropriate tactical outlook which condemned them to waste their lives in open assault, the Zulus had taken to the field time and again, even when it became clear that there was no hope of victory. In the end, desperate courage was not enough: but the nation could ask no more of them.

of the old state system would be tolerated. The uSuthu leaders greeted him with delight, but Cetshwayo could neither succour them nor control them. He was powerless when the uSuthu in Zibhebhu's district rose up and attacked their tormenter. But Zibhebhu was too good a general for them; he abandoned his homestead to them and fell back to the Msebe valley, where he positioned his warriors in long grass in ambush. On 30 March they walked into the trap; the Mandhlakazi charged down on them, and in the subsequent rout as many as 4,000 uSuthu warriors were killed.

Cetshwayo watched in helpless misery as violence erupted across the country. The British blamed him for provoking it, but did nothing to stop it. Zibhebhu took matters into his own hands. On the morning of 21 July Cetshwayo awoke to find a Mandhlakazi *impi* bearing down on Ulundi. He still had *amabutho* at his disposal, but any weapons they carried were their own and they were hopelessly outclassed. The uSuthu were smashed and Zibhebhu sacked Ulundi, killing the *izinduna* he found there, the majority being *izikhulu* from the old days. Fifty-nine of them were killed in a slaughter which marked the real end of the old Zulu state.

The king himself was wounded in his flight from Ulundi, and took refuge in the remote Mhome Gorge, in the territory of Chief Sigananda of the Chube clan in the rugged hill country above the Tugela. When he had recovered he went to the British magistracy at Eshowe, from where he tried to salvage something of the uSuthu fortunes. Here, on 8 February 1884, he died suddenly, officially of heart disease, though it was rumoured that he had been poisoned. His supporters took him back to the Chube territory, far away from the Mandhlakazi and British, and buried him.

Dinuzulu

His heir as leader of the luckless uSuthu and rightful king was his son Dinuzulu, who was not yet a teenager. Cetshwayo's full brother Prince Ndabuko kaMpande, and Chief Mnyamana of the Buthelezi clan, formerly head of Cetshwayo's *ibandla*, acted as regents. They turned to the British for help, and when that was not forthcoming accepted an offer from the Transvaal Boers, who promised military support against the Mandhlakazi. On 21 May 1884 the Boers proclaimed Dinuzulu king—a title the British refused to acknowledge—and then set out to attack Zibhebhu. They caught up with him on 5 June in a natural amphitheatre formed between the Gaza and Etshaneni mountains. As at Msebe, Zibhebhu prepared an elaborate ambush, but the trap sprung prematurely, and his warriors had to move into the open to attack. The Boers, firing from the saddle over the heads of the attacking uSuthu, cut the Mandhlakazi warriors down. Zibhebhu fled to Natal, and the Boers presented the bill: they claimed farms from Dinuzulu stretched across most of Zululand.

This was not what the uSuthu leaders had had in mind, and once more they appealed to Britain. This time the British listened, if only because the prospect of a Boer route to the sea, which would open communication with Germany, was held to be a direct challenge to British strategic interests in southern Africa. Negotiations with the Boers forced

Chief Bhambatha kaMancinza of the Zondi clan, the leader of the 1906 rebellion. (Africana Museum, Johannesburg)

them to restrict their claims, and on 9 May 1887 Zululand was finally annexed by Britain.

The annexation brought Zululand under the control of Natal's Native Law, and magistracies were established across the country. Dinuzulu, however, free of the Mandhlakazi challenge, set about restoring his authority. When he tried to have a man executed for witchcraft the magistrate summoned him to explain himself. He refused to attend and was promptly fined, and told that Zibhebhu would be allowed to return to his old lands. This was intended as a check to balance Dinuzulu's power, but it provoked a violent explosion. When Zibhebhu and a number of his adherents turned up to claim their old lands they found the uSuthu in possession. The local magistrate used his small force of native police (the *Nongqayi*) to evict the uSuthu; but in March 1888 an uSuthu chief refused to vacate his homestead, and called out his warriors. Dinuzulu was blamed for inciting rebellion, but when a party of soldiers went to arrest him they found him entrenched in a rocky outcrop known as Ceza Mountain, accompanied by 1,800 armed warriors recruited from the loyal uSuthu clans. A sharp fight ensued, and the troops had to withdraw leaving two dead on the field. All over the country the jubilant uSuthu rose up, raiding the homesteads of their enemies.

The magistracy at Nongoma in the centre of the country was seriously threatened. A refuge for white traders and farmers, it was defended by a small party of *Nongqayi*. Orders were sent to Zibhebhu asking him to reinforce the post, and he arrived with about 800 warriors and camped on a nearby hill. On the morning of 23 June about 4,000 uSuthu, led by Dinuzulu himself, attacked the post. The uSuthu *impi* divided in two, one portion attacking the magistracy, the greater portion falling on the Mandhlakazi. The Nongqayi drove their attackers off, but the uSuthu onslaught broke the Mandhlakazi, and once more Zibhebhu fled. It was to be his last military campaign—he lived quietly near Eshowe for a while before returning to his hereditary lands, where he died in 1905.

The attack on Nongoma was the uSuthu high-water mark. The British collected together a larger force, and on 2 July defeated the uSuthu at Hlopekulu Mountain, near Ulundi. Dinuzulu, Ndabuko and Prince Shingana kaMpande attempted to flee to the Transvaal, but they were turned away and went instead to Natal, where they surrendered. They were tried for treason and sentenced to exile on St. Helena.

The 1888 rebellion proved to be the last time the Zulu royal house went to war—a ghost of 1879, with Zulus once more meeting British soldiers in the field. There was to be one last tragic uprising; but, though the rebels tried to draw on the prestige of the old military system and the Zulu kings, its causes and supporters lay, for the most part, outside the traditions of the old Zulu state.

Rebel dead on the battlefield, July 1906. The amount of European clothing suggests that they are Natal rebels. Note the small size of the shield, typical of this period. (Africana Museum, Johannesburg)

Bhambatha

With the exile of Dinuzulu, Zululand became peaceful at last. In 1897 Britain handed it over to the Colony of Natal, and areas were opened up for European settlement. Dinuzulu was allowed to return to his old homestead, though the Government recognised him as a chief and not a king. Despite the heavy fighting in Natal the Boer War did not affect Zululand much—although one Boer commando angered the abaQulusi, as aggressive as ever, and was attacked one night at Holkranz, losing 56 of 59 of their number.

Nevertheless, the 1890s were not kind to the African population of Natal and Zululand. The

The entrance to Mhome Gorge, the site of the decisive battle of the 1906 rebellion. The rebel overnight camp was where the homestead now stands, at centre right. The Colonial forces ringed the surrounding heights. (Author's collection)

land reserved for them was cramped, and over-grazing brought about soil erosion. Cattle herds were decimated by rinderpest, and locusts ate their crops. When the Natal authorities, seeking to balance their budget in the post-Boer War recession, imposed a poll tax, it was the last straw. Many chiefs refused to pay; others sent to Dinuzulu, whom they still regarded as their king, for advice. He advised them to pay. Still some would not, and parties of police sent to collect the tax were driven off.

The country seemed to be ripe for rebellion; and a leader emerged in Bhambatha kaMancinza of the Zondi clan, who lived in the spectacular Mpanza valley on the Natal side of the Tugela. Bhambatha was in his mid-forties, a chief of no great rank, who had a reputation for faction fights. When he refused to pay the tax and police were sent to arrest him, he slipped across the border to consult Dinuzulu.

Privately Dinuzulu may have sympathised with Bhambatha, but he would not countenance rebellion: he did, however, allow Bhambatha to leave his family at his homestead. Buoyed up by what he took as tacit approval, Bhambatha returned to Natal, gathered his fighting men and, on the night of 4 April 1906 attacked a police patrol. In a stiff fight four whites were killed, and the body of one was used by Bhambatha's war-doctor to make medicine. He and his warriors then crossed into Zululand and made for the territory of Chief Sigananda of the Chube. Sigananda was in his nineties, and had served under Shaka as an *udibi*. He was steadfastly loyal to the Zulu royal house, and asked Dinuzulu whether he should join the rebels. Dinuzulu was evasive and Sigananda threw in his lot with Bhambatha.

In Natal, meanwhile, a state of emergency had been declared, and the militia called out. A force was put together under the command of Col. (later Sir) Duncan McKenzie, and marched out from Eshowe into the jumble of steep ridges and bush-choked valleys which comprised the Chube district.

The rebels had made the grave of King Cetshwayo their rallying point, and towards this the Colonial forces advanced. On 5 May they were descending a steep ridge known as Bope, when about 1,000 rebels burst from the bush and charged on them. The rebels were wearing a distinctive badge known as the *uboshokobezi*, a stiff piece of white cowhide or cow tail worn upright on the headdress; this was a deliberate identification with the Zulu kings, as the uSuthu had adopted this badge in the 1880s. Several had guns, but most carried spears and small shields which they held up before their faces as they ran—Bhambatha's doctors had told him that the white man's bullets would turn to water. They did not: and the rebels were driven off with heavy losses.

Mhome Gorge

The fight at Bope ushered in several weeks of sweeps and skirmishes. Bhambatha at least, had learnt something from the past: his men did not try the massed assaults of old, but tried to lure the whites on to disadvantageous ground to ambush them. Several times they gave McKenzie a run for his money. Then, on the night of 9–10 June 1906, McKenzie received an intelligence report that several rebel *impis*—including Bhambatha's—had converged on Sigananda's stronghold, the Mhome Gorge, and were camped at the entrance. McKenzie issued orders for his own scattered forces to advance upon the gorge.

The gorge itself is narrow and steep, the sides falling almost sheer for 1,000 feet in places. At the far end was a waterfall, a spot so inaccessible that Cetshwayo had hidden there after his defeat by Zibhebhu. The rebels believed that once they had entered the gorge they would be impregnable. This had made them careless: they spent the night at the

Chief Sigananda of the Chube (with bandaged ankles) photographed with Col. McKenzie (second from right) after his surrender. The old chief had been an *udibi* servant in Shaka's army, and was the most important Zulu leader to support Bhambatha in 1906; his career thus spanned the rise and fall of the Zulu nation. (Killie Campbell Library)

A detail from a famous study by Angas of a warrior of the *amaShishi* (*isaNqu*) regiment in the 1840s, showing the construction of the headdress. This man is not wearing a headband, so the shape of the *amaphovela*, and the way the 'earflaps' of this example fall down each side of the back of the head, are clearly shown. Note how the *isakabuli* feathers are tied to quills and thrust into the sides of the headdress. (Author's collection)

entrance and their sentries failed to notice McKenzie's approach. This had been a remarkable feat in itself, co-ordinating an advance over such impossible ground in the dark; but as dawn broke the rebels found themselves surrounded by troops on all the overlooking heights. The rebels' strength was estimated at about 20 *amaviyo*, or companies—perhaps 1,500 men. The Colonial force included 15pdr. artillery and Colt machine-guns.

As soon as the rebels realised their predicament, they formed a circle to receive instructions; seeing this, the Colonial troops opened fire. It was a massacre. Shot and shell rained down on the rebels from all sides. They broke, and fled back into the gorge. This proved to be no more than a trap, and for several hours the troops shot them down at leisure. At last they descended from the heights and swept the bush, flushing out survivors. The official report spoke of 600 rebel dead, but the real total was much higher. Among them was Bhambatha. He had been killed in a mêlée with Natal levies in the bottom of the gorge, but it was several days before he was recognised. It was imperative that proof of his death be made known; since it was impossible to recover his body, his head was cut off and taken to Natal for identification.

The battle at Mhome Gorge ended the rebellion in Zululand. Sigananda surrendered, and died later in prison. There was to be a further uprising in June across the Tugela in the Natal district of Mapumulo. Several battles occurred in the rugged country around the trading station of Thring's Post, but in the end machine guns prevailed over assegais. Nearly 5,000 rebels were brought to trial, the ringleaders exiled and the rest imprisoned. Among them was Dinuzulu kaMpande, who many believed was behind the uprising. That he had sheltered Bhambatha's wife told against him; he was convicted and sentenced to four years' imprisonment. He was not allowed to return to Zululand, and died in 1913 in the Transvaal, the last of the Zulu warrior kings. His followers took his body back to Zululand, and buried him in the heart of Zulu country, not far from where Shaka had begun his conquests.

*　　　*　　　*

Today there are over six million Zulus in South Africa, and they acknowledge Dinuzulu's great-grandson, Goodwill Zwelithini, as their hereditary king. Their principal political leader, Chief Mangosutho Buthelezi, is internationally renowned, and the memories of the warrior past are a significant source of national pride. Archaeologists have reconstructed part of King Cetshwayo's Ulundi homestead: it stands opposite the Legislative Assembly of modern KwaZulu on Mahlabatini plain.

The Plates

A: The youth of Shaka
A1: Nandi bids farewell to her son as he sets off to join the Mthethwa army in about 1805. The dress of a married woman at that time was very simple: the characteristic top-knot coloured with red ochre,

and a leather skirt. Nandi was renowned for her beauty and her fiery temperament, and so would probably have liked to wear beads (then scarce, and something of a luxury) and brass bangles.

A2: Shaka. This reconstruction is largely speculative; he is shown wearing the typical dress of a young warrior of the period—a leopardskin headband and sakabuli feathers. The cords around the body were made of twisted strips of lambskin, and were worn on festive occasions. At this stage the war shields were small and probably not uniform in colour. Sandals would have been worn.

A3: Mthethwa chief. He wears a leopardskin collar, to which only men of rank were entitled; the necklace of leopard claws and the bunch of lourie feathers in the headdress are also marks of distinction. He has a typical snuff-spoon tucked into his *isicoco* (headring) and carries a wooden staff, which also seems to have

been a symbol of chief's rank. All of these items were essentially 'civilian' in their significance, but were often carried over into the military sphere.

B/C: The Battle of Gqokli Hill, 1818
B/C 1: Warrior of the Isipezi ibutho or age group regiment. There is very little direct evidence relating to the uniforms of Shaka's regiments, so these tentative reconstructions are necessarily based on comparisons of fragmentary Zulu and European sources. The Isipezi seem to have carried white shields patterned across the middle with black spots, and to have worn crane feathers in their headdress.

B/C 2: Ndwandwe commander, based on a description by a British naval officer who encountered a party

A modern reconstruction—ignore the metal buckles—of a pair of cow tail leg ornaments, basically similar in appearance to the 19th-century originals. (Africana Museum, Johannesburg)

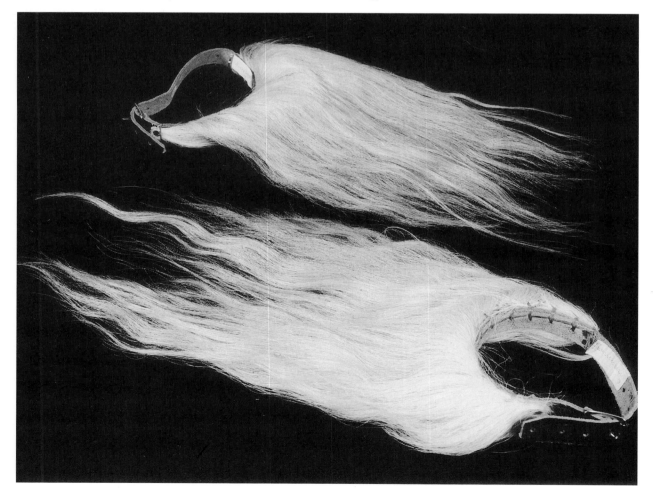

A modern reconstruction of the *umqhele* or leopardskin headband; the earflaps—*amabheqe*—appear considerably larger in early sketches and photographs. (Africana Museum, Johannesburg)

body. There is evidence to suggest that in this early period strips of civet or monkey skin were sewn into old spear-slits in the shield to draw attention to the warrior's prowess.

B/C 5: Young Ndwandwe warrior. There is even less information on the Ndwandwe than on the Zulus of this period; but a number of Zulu-style features remained in the dress of the Ndwandwe splinter groups—the Ngoni and Shangane—which presumably originated in Zululand, and which confirm what one would expect: that Ndwandwe and Zulu dress were similar. This warrior wears a headdress of sakabuli feathers, typical of a young man's costume.

A bunch of *isakabuli* feathers, as worn by young warriors, here mounted on a base for wearing on top of the head. Note too the *umqhele* at bottom right, here of cheetah fur. (Natal Museum, Pietermaritzburg)

of Ndwandwe wandering north after their defeat by Shaka in 1819. He wears a single crane feather in his headdress, and a kilt of civet and samango tails around his waist and body. Like the Zulus, the Ndwandwe would also have used cow tails as part of their war dress. At the time of Gqokli Hill the Ndwandwe would have been carrying small shields and throwing-spears, and wearing sandals.

B/C 3: King Shaka kaSenzangakhona. We have a detailed description of Shaka's war dress from *The Diary of Henry Francis Fynn*, one of the British traders who visited his court. He wore a collar and kilt of twisted tails, cow tails around his arms and legs, and a headdress with bunches of lourie feathers and one crane feather. His shield was white with one black spot.

B/C 4: Warrior of the Fasimba, Shaka's favourite regiment, who carried white shields and probably wore sakabuli feathers in the headdress. This man wears the marks of distinction of a brave veteran: a bunch of lourie feathers in the headdress, a brass *ingxotha* armband, and bravery beads around the

B/C 6: *Warrior of the Ndabezibona*, a section of the Fasimba, who carried black shields with a white spot in the centre. The full dress of the Fasimba is not known, but would have included all the elements usual for a young *ibutho*. This man has a porcupine quill in his headband, which was not purely decorative—it was used for removing thorns from the feet.

B/C 7: *Senior Ndwandwe warrior*, wearing a single ostrich feather in his headdress. The names of several of Chief Zwide's *amabutho* survive, suggesting that his army was well organised, albeit not to the Zulu standard. This may well have been a regimental uniform, although it seems unlikely that the shield colour was consistent or significant.

D: *The first meeting between Europeans and King Shaka, 1824*

D1: *Lt. Francis Farewell* had served in the Royal Navy until the end of the Napoleonic Wars. He wore at least part of his uniform on his first meeting with the king, and we show him here with an 1815 lieutenant's coat. Since he rode part of the way to Bulawayo, we have shown him in civilian riding breeches and boots.

D2: *Imbongi*, or praise-singer (pl. *izimbongi*). A feature of the Zulu court, such men wore fantastic costumes of their own devising, and danced and capered before the king calling out the praise-poems which recalled his heroic deeds. This man is shown wearing items recorded as typical of an *imbongi*—long braided hair coloured with ochre, a headring, antelope horns as a headdress, and cow tails and leopardskin around the body.

D3: *King Shaka*. There is some dispute as to whether Shaka was married; however, there are a number of references to his barber trimming his hair around his *isicoco*, so we have shown him wearing the headring. He would, of course, have worn different costumes for different occasions, but this seems to have been his most frequent 'official' dress. At this time the king was about 38 years old.

D4: *Shaka's interpreter*. A Xhosa from the eastern Cape frontier, captured by the British in one of the many 'Kaffir' Wars, he accompanied one of the exploratory missions to Natal, where he escaped and made his way to kwaBulawayo. The king was quick to appreciate the value of his talents. His Xhosa name was Msimbiti, but the whites called him Jacob or Jakot, and the Zulus, Hlambamanzi—'the swimmer'—since he had swum ashore from a boat to escape. He wears a blanket in the Xhosa fashion.

E: The court of Dingane, 1830s
E1: Youth in dancing dress. Dancing was a very important social activity, both as part of national festivals and simply for pleasure. Kings Dingane and Mpande were particularly fond of organising and taking part in dances in which hundreds or even thousands participated. This youth in festive dress is based on a sketch by George French Angas; the coloured fringes are of beadwork.

E2: King Dingane in dancing dress, based on sketches from life by the missionary Capt. Allen Gardiner. Dingane took a great personal interest in his own dancing costume and that of his female attendants, and liked to experiment with different combinations of beads, bangles and feathers. His chair, carved from a single block of wood, still exists. His shield was black with one white spot.

E3: Ndlela kaSompisi, Dingane's chief *induna* and most talented general, carries his war shield and wears the full kilt. The brass rings would have been given to him by the king, who distributed them to his favourites. In battle he would probably have

A pair of *izingxotha*, the brass armbands distributed by Zulu kings to warriors who had shown particular daring in battle; the exact design varied slightly over the years—these date from Cetshwayo's reign. (RRW Museum, Brecon)

worn an otter-skin headband, a crane feather, and perhaps lourie feathers.

F: Skirmish between Boers and Zulus, December 1838
F1: Boer Voortrekker ('those who trek to the fore'). The Boers fought in their everyday clothes, which at this time included short jackets or waistcoats, wide-brimmed hats and *veldschoen*—light home-made shoes of hide. Their weapons were flintlock or percussion muskets; ammunition was carried in leather bags slung over the shoulder, though powderhorns were sometimes attached to the waistbelt.

F2: Warrior, probably of the Mbelebele, Dingane's favourite regiment, based on a sketch by Gardiner. There is surprisingly little information on Dingane's *amabutho*. Gardiner's original sketch describes the warrior as 'partly panoplied', presumably meaning war dress. The cow tail necklace is a lighter variant of the full-dress type. The Mbelebele were quartered at King Dingane's personal residence, emGungundhlovu.

F3: Warrior of the Kokoti regiment in war dress. The Kokoti were ordered by the king to carry only knobkerries, and these were apparently slung— bizarrely enough—down the back, from a neck thong. This unusual dictate was reportedly a punishment for the regiment having mocked other *amabutho* for having failed to defeat the Boers and boasting that they could do so even without spears.

G: The Battle of 'Ndondakasuka, December 1856
G1: Warrior of the uDhloko regiment. This *ibutho* apparently wore most of their ceremonial regalia into action at this battle, where they formed part of the uSuthu forces. At this date they were unmarried, and wore a spectacular headdress of black and white ostrich feathers intermixed. The same regiment later took part in the Zulu War of 1879, wearing a costume modified to reflect their more senior status. Note the smaller *umbhumbuluzo* shield.

G2: Prince Cetshwayo kaMpande, in the costume he wore at this battle; he took an active part in the engagement, leading the centre of the uSuthu forces. He is wearing an *umutsha* of black lambskin, and an *ibeshu* of samango monkey skin. He carries the shield of the Thulwana regiment—at this date unmarried—and wears a single crane feather reflecting his royal status, despite his lack of the headring. He is also wearing a necklace of magical charms, and carrying a civilian percussion shotgun.

G3: Warrior of the Impisi regiment, which formed part of Prince Mbuyazi's iziGqoza faction. The iziGqoza apparently adopted a headdress similar to the *amaphovela* as its badge.

H: Warriors on their way to muster, 1870s
H1: Zulu girls. Unmarried girls were also organised into age group guilds, but they were not required to live barracked together like the youths. They had no military function, but particular age groups would be allocated to male regiments, and the warriors would choose their brides from among them. Basic dress consisted of nothing more than a short skirt, though beads were extremely popular as ornamentation.

A particularly fine example of a charm necklace, consisting of snake- and animal-skin pouches of magical medicine, teeth, and various selected blocks of wood, some of them ritually burnt at the edges. This example was acquired from one of Cetshwayo's war doctors by Lt.Col. A. W. Durnford, who was later killed at Isandlwana. (Royal Engineers Museum)

H2: Warrior of the Mtuyisazwe, a regiment incorporated into the outsize corps named uKhandempemvu or umCijo. The Mtuyisazwe wore *amaphovela* headdress, and carried black shields with a white spot across the centre; they also wore a wide cowhide waist belt.

H3: Warrior of the uKhandempemvu; his costume is quite distinct from that of H2, even though they were considered to be part of the same unit. He wears a bunch of sakabuli feathers on top of his head, and carries a red shield; other companies of the same regiment carried black shields. Both H2 and H3 are of the same age group. The uKhandempemvu played a significant part in the battle of Isandlwana; the full regalia shown here would not, however, have been worn in action.

H4: Udibi boy. These were boys of pre-cadet age who acted as servants for individual warriors, carrying their food or, as here, sleeping mats and other possessions.

I: The court of Mpande, 1870s
I1: King Mpande kaSenzangakhona dancing with his warriors at an *umkhosi* ceremony, c.1870. Although obese, the king was said to have been a graceful

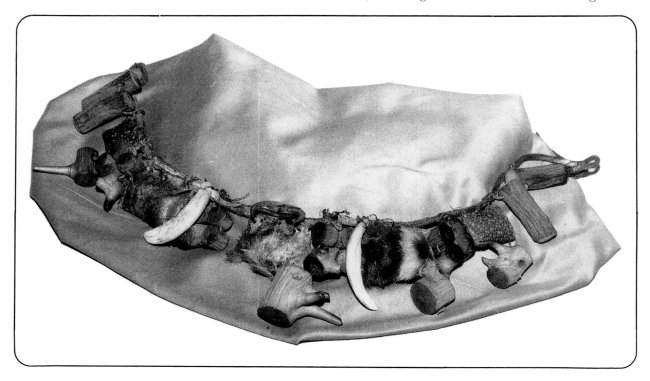

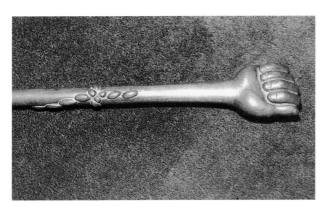

The beautifully carved head of King Cetshwayo's staff. (S. Bourquin)

dancer even at the end of his life. His festive costume was extremely lavish: his body was covered with monkey skin and cow tails, and his headdress consisted of black ostrich feathers, large bunches of lourie feathers, and a crane feather. His shield was white with a small mark, and he carried a black-wood dancing stick.

I2: Warrior of the umXapho regiment. In the 1870s differences between full ceremonial uniforms were slight. The umXapho wore ostrich feathers all over their heads, and carried black shields.

I3: Warrior of the iNdlu-yengwe regiment; note the similarity with the costume of I2. The differences lie mainly in the arrangement of the ostrich feathers, and the fact that the iNdlu-yengwe have sakabuli feathers. They also have white spots low down on their shields. On festive occasions the warriors would not have carried spears.

J: An impi being doctored for war, 1870s
J1: Isangoma. Braided hair and a plethora of magical charms distinguish the dress of the diviner; he also wears rattles made from insect cocoons around his ankles. As part of the ceremony the *isangoma* cut strips of meat from a slaughtered bull, treated them with magical potions, and threw them to the warriors, who were each expected to take a bite.

J2: Warrior of the iNgobamakhosi regiment in full dress. He wears an *amaphovela* headdress with feathers of the black-tailed finch (*isakabuli*); and an *ingxotha* armlet of the type favoured by King Cetshwayo on

his right arm. His shield is red and white, although other companies of the regiment almost certainly carried black, or black and white shields. The iNgobamakhosi was a very large regiment, and a favourite of the king's.

J3: Warrior of the Thulwana regiment. Compare with Plate G2. The Thulwana had many men of high status within their ranks, and their uniform was correspondingly lavish. They wore the full kilt, and several brass bands on the right arm. Their shields—here an *isihlangu*, but both types were carried—were white with small red or black marks. Both the iNgobamakhosi and the Thulwana were members of the Undi corps—quartered at Ulundi—but there was a fierce rivalry between them, and they could not in fact live together. Both regiments played a prominent part in the fighting of 1879.

K: The aftermath of Isandlwana, 22 January 1879
K1: Warrior of the Mbonambi regiment. He moves with his comrades through the wreckage of the camp at Isandlwana, looting, stripping and disembowelling the enemy dead in accordance with custom. This regiment seems to have been formed and re-formed several times, but in 1879 it comprised unmarried men in their early thirties. There are conflicting descriptions of the headdress, but little of this was worn into action beyond, perhaps, a headband and bunch of lourie feathers. This man has a charm necklace, which were very popular at this time. It seems to have been up to individuals how much of their costume they retained on campaign.

K2: Warrior of the iNdlondlo regiment, a 900-strong unit incorporated into the Thulwana. The full dress uniform was similar to that of the Thulwana, but nothing so lavish would have been worn into action.

K3: Warrior of the iNgobamakhosi regiment. The young regiments in 1879 seem to have worn very little regalia into action: perhaps the *umqhele*, a charm necklace, and sometimes cow tails around the arms and legs, but little else apart from the loin covering. He has put on the tunic of a soldier of the 24th Regiment whom he killed, in accordance with ritual. Large numbers of breach-loading rifles fell into Zulu hands after the battle.

L: The Battle of Mhome Gorge, 10 June 1906
L1: Zulu rebel, wearing the *ubushokobezi* badge and cast-off European clothing, and carrying a small shield typical of the period. Eyewitness accounts mention that some rebels still wore the working overalls of the Castle brewery.

L2: Private, Durban Light Infantry, the principal Colonial infantry unit to see action in the 1906 rebellion. The DLI wore khaki tropical field service uniforms similar to those of the British regulars in the Boer War, although the sun helmet was of a slightly different shape. Equipment was of the Slade-Wallace pattern.

L3: Constable of the Nongqayi, the Zululand Native Police. The Nongqayi were raised in the 1880s; despite the distinguished service they rendered during the 1888 uprising they were disbanded shortly afterwards in deference to the fears of many Colonists about arming Africans. They were, however, re-formed at the outbreak of Bhambatha's rebellion in 1906, and proved tenacious fighters. Their uniform consisted of a blue jacket with breast pockets, and blue trousers cut off below the knee. They carried Martini-Henry rifles and had black Slade-Wallace equipment. At Mhome Gorge they seem to have worn blue jerseys.

The present king of the Zulus, HM King Goodwill Zwelithini kaCyprian, dressed in ceremonial regalia which has changed only slightly since King Shaka's day. (Author's collection)

Zulu War Campaign

Origins of the War

When the final shot had been fired at the battle of Ulundi on 4 July 1879, the Zulu army, which had been buoyed up by the great victory at Isandlwana at the start of the war, but then demoralized by the crushing defeat at Khambula, finally accepted that it was beaten, and that the war was over. That final shot was also the culmination of two years of hectic political activity aimed at clearing a major obstacle in the path of advancing British Imperialism in southern Africa.

Zululand had emerged as a strong and aggressive kingdom during the reign of King Shaka kaSenzangakhona, early in the nineteenth century. The first white settlers had arrived during Shaka's reign, however, and by the 1870s, Zululand had been hemmed in on two sides by the rapid expansion of European colonial communities; the British in Natal to the south, and the Boers of the republic of the Transvaal to the west. The coming of the whites had not always been peaceful, and the Zulu state had suffered from a number of ruinous wars which sapped its economic and military strength. In 1873, however, a new Zulu king, Cetshwayo kaMpande, initiated a programme of internal reforms aimed at revitalizing the state apparatus. The timing was unfortunate: at the same time his neighbours were coming to regard the existence of his kingdom as a threat to their own interests in the region. It was, therefore, only a matter of time before the different aspirations of the two nations, British and Zulu, brought them to contention, and ultimately confrontation.

The British, who had taken control of the Cape in 1806 for strategic reasons during the Napoleonic Wars, had found it an expensive possession. The constant squabbles between the British, Boers (the descendants of the original Dutch settlers), and various African groups had led to incessant petty warfare which had proved a drain on both the Treasury and the War Department. In the 1870s,

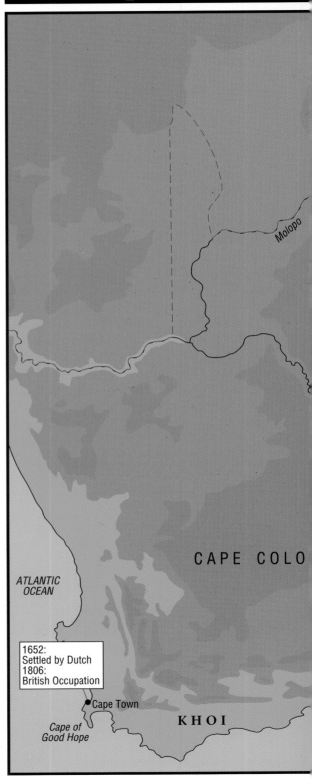

Molopo

ATLANTIC
OCEAN

CAPE COLO

1652:
Settled by Dutch
1806:
British Occupation

Cape Town

Cape of
Good Hope

K H O I

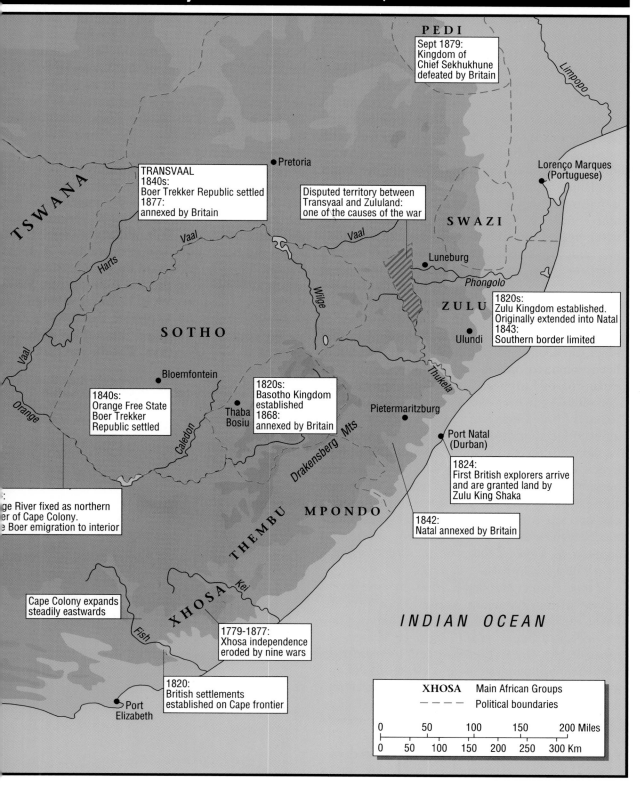

PEDI

Sept 1879:
Kingdom of
Chief Sekhukhune
defeated by Britain

Limpopo

TRANSVAAL
1840s:
Boer Trekker Republic settled
1877:
annexed by Britain

•Pretoria

Lorenço Marques
(Portuguese)

TSWANA

Harts

Vaal

Disputed territory between
Transvaal and Zululand:
one of the causes of the war

Vaal

SWAZI

•Luneburg

Phongolo

ZULU

1820s:
Zulu Kingdom established.
Originally extended into Natal
1843:
Southern border limited

Wilge

SOTHO

•Ulundi

Thukela

•Bloemfontein

1820s:
Basotho Kingdom
established
1868:
annexed by Britain

Pietermaritzburg•

1840s:
Orange Free State
Boer Trekker
Republic settled

Thaba
Bosiu

Caledon

Port Natal
(Durban)

Orange

1824:
First British explorers arrive
and are granted land by
Zulu King Shaka

Drakensberg Mts

MPONDO

THEMBU

1842:
Natal annexed by Britain

:
ge River fixed as northern
er of Cape Colony.
e Boer emigration to interior

Kei

XHOSA

Cape Colony expands
steadily eastwards

INDIAN OCEAN

Fish

1779-1877:
Xhosa independence
eroded by nine wars

1820:
British settlements
established on Cape frontier

•Port
Elizabeth

XHOSA Main African Groups
- - - - Political boundaries

0   50   100   150   200 Miles

0   50   100   150   200   250   300 Km

they attempted to resolve these conflicts by adopting a policy known as Confederation, which proposed to unite the various rival black and white groups under a single – British – authority.

In 1877 Sir Henry Bartle Frere was installed as the new High Commissioner for South Africa, with the express intention of implementing Confederation. Frere very quickly became convinced that the Zulu kingdom posed the greatest single threat to the scheme. He became obsessed with the idea that Cetshwayo was behind a wave of unrest which was sweeping through the black population across South Africa, and began a propaganda campaign to pave the way for military intervention. Cetshwayo was described as an 'irresponsible, bloodthirsty and treacherous despot', and his warriors as 'celibate, man-slaying machines'. By this time, however, the home goverment was entangled in a crisis in the Balkans and a serious war in Afghanistan, and it was opposed to a new war in Africa. Frere was told to treat the Zulus with 'a spirit of forbearance'. His policy was too far advanced for him to abandon it, however, and he pressed on with his plans.

In March 1878 Lieutenant-General the Honourable Sir Frederic Thesiger – who was to become Lord Chelmsford on the death of his father in October of that year – took command of the Imperial forces in South Africa. Chelmsford agreed with Frere that a war with the Zulus was inevitable. Frere now had the means of prosecuting a war against the Zulus, and all he needed was an excuse. By manipulating the poor communications system between Cape Town and London, he hoped to present the home government with a *fait accompli*.

Frere found the justification he sought in reports of several minor border infringements. These incidents were of themselves innocuous – on one occasion a small party of Zulus had pursued some fugitives across the Mzinyathi river into Natal and dragged them back into Zululand; on another Colonial officials who had strayed into Zululand were temporarily detained as spies. Frere, however, siezed on these incidents as proof of the aggressive intentions of the Zulu king.

On 11 December 1878 King Cetshwayo's representatives were summoned to a meeting at the Lower Drift on the Thukela river, to receive the findings of a Boundary Comission, which had been arbitrating in a dispute concerning rival Boer and Zulu claims to a slice of territory along the Ncome (Blood) River. Britain had annexed the bankrupt Boer republic of the Transvaal in 1877 – much to the disgust of many of its inhabitants – and this dispute had been instrumental in shaping Frere's attitude towards the Zulu 'threat'. Contrary to his expectations, the Commission had found in favour of the Zulus, but the High Commissioner had taken the opportunity to make their findings conditional upon the Zulu acceptance of his demands. These included compensation for the border incidents, and, more seriously, the abandonment of the Zulu military system. If the Zulus did not comply within thirty days, it would be war. The demands were impossible, since they struck at the core of the Zulu way of life. Frere knew this; he counted on it. However willing King Cetshwayo might be to placate the British, Zulu society could not withstand the sudden disbandment of the military system. The die was cast.

▼*A water-colour by Orlando Norie of the 1st Battalion, 13th Light Infantry, on the march during the Zulu War. The 1/13th were part of Wood's Column. (Somerset L. I. Museum, Taunton)*

Opposing Strategies

The British Plan

Lord Chelmsford's strategy was shaped by his need to protect Natal and the Transvaal from a possible Zulu invasion, while at the same time confronting the Zulu army with sufficient force to destroy it. Since the home government had not sanctioned an offensive campaign, the forces at his disposal were limited. He distributed them at five points along the Natal and Transvaal borders, which were marked by the Thukela, Mzinyathi and Ncome rivers. He had originally intended all five columns to converge on the Zulu capital, Ulundi, but this plan resulted in a logistical nightmare which he lacked the facilities to resolve. In the end, only three of the columns were used offensively, the remaining two being intended to guard against Zulu counter-strikes.

The Right Flank Column (No. 1) was to cross into Zululand at the Lower Drift on the Thukela, under the command of Colonel C. K. Pearson, 3rd Buffs. No. 2 Column, under Colonel A. Durnford, R. E., was stationed in the difficult country above the Middle Drift of the Thukela. The Centre Column, No. 3., commanded by Colonel R. Glyn, 24th Regiment, was to cross into Zululand at Rorke's Drift on the Mzinyathi, while the Left Flank Column (No. 4), under Colonel H. E. Wood, VC, 90th L.I., would invade from a point known as Bemba's Kop on the Ncome. The remaining Column, No. 5, commanded by Colonel H. Rowlands, VC, was to be based at Luneburg in the Transvaal to keep an eye on both the Zulus and sullen republican elements in the Transvaal. Chelmsford himself accompanied the Centre Column.

The plan was essentially a sound one. The three invading columns were each thought to be

The First Invasion of Zululand, January to April 1879

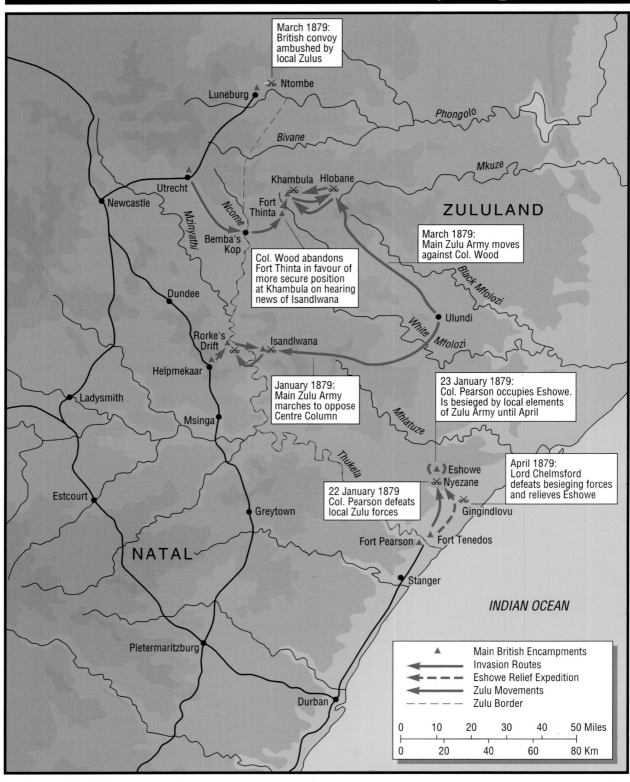

March 1879:
British convoy
ambushed by
local Zulus

Ntombe

Luneburg

Phongolo

Bivane

Mkuze

Khambula Hlobane

Utrecht

Fort
Thinta

ZULULAND

Newcastle

Ncome

Bemba's
Kop

March 1879:
Main Zulu Army moves
against Col. Wood

Col. Wood abandons
Fort Thinta in favour of
more secure position
at Khambula on hearing
news of Isandlwana

Mzinyathi

Black Mfolozi

Dundee

Ulundi

Rorke's
Drift

Isandlwana

White Mfolozi

Helpmekaar

January 1879:
Main Zulu Army
marches to oppose
Centre Column

23 January 1879:
Col. Pearson occupies Eshowe.
Is besieged by local elements
of Zulu Army until April

Ladysmith

Msinga

Mhlatuze

April 1879:
Lord Chelmsford
defeats besieging forces
and relieves Eshowe

Eshowe
Nyezane

Thukela

22 January 1879
Col. Pearson defeats
local Zulu forces

Gingindlovu

Estcourt

Greytown

Fort Pearson

Fort Tenedos

NATAL

Stanger

INDIAN OCEAN

Pietermaritzburg

▲   Main British Encampments
⟵   Invasion Routes
⟵ - -   Eshowe Relief Expedition
⟵   Zulu Movements
- - -   Zulu Border

Durban

0	10	20	30	40	50 Miles
0	20	40	60	80 Km	

strong enough to defeat the Zulu army on its own, while the two reserve columns considerably reduced the risk of a Zulu raid against vulnerable settler communities. No message having been received from Cetshwayo by 11 January 1879, the columns began to cross into Zulu territory.

▲King Cetshwayo kaMpande. He became king in 1873, and attempted to revitalize the Zulu kingdom at a time when it was under threat from European encroachment. This brought him into conflict with the British and led to the disastrous Anglo–Zulu War of 1879. (Killie Campbell Collection)

The Zulu Plan

King Cetshwayo had not wanted the war. Once British troops were on Zulu soil and attacking Zulu homesteads, his young warriors clamoured to be allowed to fight, but he forbade them to cross into Natal, hoping that a purely defensive war would win him political advantages.

The king correctly identified the Centre Column as the strongest among the invading forces. His strategy was to use warriors living in the country covered by the flanking columns to try to disrupt their advance, while the main Zulu Army was directed against the Centre Column. In the middle of January the king summoned the main army of more than 20,000 warriors to Ulundi. Cetshwayo did not take to the field himself, leaving command to his most senior general, Chief Ntshingwayo kaMahole Khoza, but in a final review he gave his warriors their overall instructions: he told them to march slowly and not tire themselves, and to avoid attacking entrenched positions. They were to drive the enemy back across the border, but on no account to follow them up. The great army marched off in high spirits, convinced of its invulnerability, and determined to wash its spears in the blood of the *abeLungu*, the White Men.

The Commanders

The British

The British commander, Lord Chelmsford, was in many ways a typical Victorian career soldier. He had joined the army in 1844, in time to see action in a number of Colonial campaigns. He had been present in Abyssinia in 1868, when the arid mountain landscape, the heat and thirst, and the insuperable problems of transport, had been as much the enemy as 'mad' King Theodore. He had also served in the Indian Mutiny, and when he succeeded Sir Arthur Cunynghame as Commander of British Forces in South Africa the Ninth Cape Frontier War, against the Xhosa people, was just drawing to a close. The Cape Frontier was a notoriously difficult theatre of operations, as the Xhosa traditionally employed elusive guerrilla tactics from wooded mountain strongholds or deep, bush-choked valleys. Chelmsford had a hotch-potch array of troops at his disposal, including local Volunteers, Irregulars, and African levies, stiffened by regular Imperial troops. With these he had successfully combed the bush and crushed the Xhosa. Chelmsford had earned some praise for the way he had handled his motley command, often under the most trying circumstances, but the lessons he learned seem to have left him ill-equipped for a war against the Zulus. He had seen rare Xhosa massed attacks collapse in the face of disciplined volley-fire, and he was convinced that African warriors could not sustain a heavy attack in the face of concentrated fire-power. The impeccable manners of this tall, Victorian gentleman masked his lack of respect for the military capabilities of Colonials. Confidant that Imperial troops could win the day, he consistently disregarded the advice of those who knew the country and the Zulus. But the Zulus fought a different type of war from the Xhosa, and nothing in Chelmsford's experience had prepared him for it. His main worry, expressed on a number of occasions, was that he might have difficulty in bringing them to battle.

The campaign had not been long under way when Chelmsford ordered No. 2 Column, under the command of Colonel Anthony Durnford, R.E., up to support him. Durnford was a controversial character. He had been stationed in Natal for a number of years as the Colony's chief Engineer, and he admired and respected the black population. In 1873 he had been placed in command of a party of Volunteers who had been directed to stop Chief Langalibalele from fleeing across the Drakensberg mountains during a minor rebellion. Durnford had intercepted Langalibalele at Bushman's Pass, but in the ensuing skirmish was forced to retreat. Three Volunteers were killed and

1 *Sir Henry Bartle Edward Frere, the British High Comissioner for Southern Africa. Frere was charged with the introduction of a policy of Confederation, to facilitate British rule. He quickly became convinced that the Zulus were a major obstacle to the scheme. (S. Bourquin)*

2 *Lieutenant-General Frederic Thesiger, 2nd Baron Chelmsford. He was the senior British commander in South Africa. He was experienced in Colonial warfare, but under-estimated the Zulu strength. (S. Bourquin)*

3 *Colonel Richard Glyn, 24th Regiment. Glyn was the commander of No. 3 Column, but Lord*

Chelmsford's decision to accompany the Column effectively took the command out of his hands. Glyn suggested the laagering of the camp at Isandlwana, but was over-ruled by Chelmsford. (National Army Museum)

4 *Brevet Colonel A. W. Durnford, RE, who commanded No. 2 Column. Durnford was an advocate of the use of black troops, and his own command largely consisted of Africans. Chelmsford considered him impetous, and many have since blamed him for the Isandlwana disaster. (Ian Knight Collection)*

Durnford himself lost the use of his left arm, which thereafter he habitually wore thrust into the front of his tunic. Although Durnford's personal courage was never doubted, many considered the incident a fiasco, and held him to blame. At the outset of the Zulu campaign, Durnford had argued for a properly uniformed and organized force to be raised from among Natal's black population, most of whom were hostile to the Zulus. Lack of funds and Colonial nervousness had curtailed the raising of anything more than an unsophisticated Levy,

◀Colonel Henry Evelyn Wood, 90th Light Infantry, who commanded No. 4 Column. Wood was an energetic and capable officer with a flair for Colonial warfare. He wore this uniform throughout the Zulu War, apart from the helmet which he apparently replaced with a plain foreign service pattern. (Ian Knight Collection)

▼Lieutenant-Colonel Redvers Buller, Wood's dynamic cavalry commander. Wood was one of the few Imperial officers who realized the potential of locally raised irregular cavalry: this sketch shows the practical kit he wore in the field. (National Army Museum)

but Durnford's personal command was made up largely of black troops, who held him in high regard. His relationship with Chelmsford was strained, however, as Chelmsford considered him impetuous, and on one occasion had felt it necessary to censure him for disobeying orders and acting on his own initiative.

Of the remaining columns, the most important was the Left Flank Column, commanded by Colonel Henry Evelyn Wood. He, too, had seen a good deal of active service, and his interesting career was to take him from Midshipman in the Navy to Field Marshal in the Army! He had been a member of a group of promising officers gathered together by the *enfant terrible* of the military establishment, General Sir Garnet Wolseley, and known as the 'Ashanti Ring' after their service in West Africa in 1873. Wood was slightly vain and had a reputation for being accident-prone – he was once trampled by a giraffe – but he was a thorough and energetic officer with a rare flair for Colonial warfare, and he had served under Chelmsford on the Cape Frontier.

Wood's commander of cavalry, and very much

▲ *Chief Zibhebhu kaMapitha, a Zulu regimental commander and perhaps the most talented Zulu general of his generation. He fought at Isandlwana, where he was wounded in the hand, and later at Khambula and Ulundi. (S. Bourquin)*

his right-hand man, was Lieutenant-Colonel Redvers Buller. He had seen action in China, and was another member of the 'Ashanti Ring'. He had commanded Irregulars on the Cape Frontier, and was one of the few Imperial officers to recognize their worth. He was a dynamic and charismatic leader, and a tough and tenacious fighter. His personal courage was legendary, and this, combined with his habitual care for his men's welfare, had earned him their devotion. In the coming campaign, Wood and Buller would prove a deadly combination.

The Zulus

Since, with the exception of Shaka, it was not customary for a Zulu king to command his army in person, it was left to his senior representatives to lead them into battle. In 1879 the main Zulu

army was comanded by the Chiefs Mnyamana kaNgqengelele and Ntshingwayo kaMahole.

Chief Mnyamana was an immensely powerful figure. He was leader of the Buthelezi clan, one of the most important in the kingdom, and he had been Cetshwayo's principal *induna* since his coronation. As such, he was effectively the nation's prime minister, and it was in that capacity, rather than as a military commander, that he accompanied the army. He was in his mid-sixties, a tall, spare man with a peaked beard and greying hair, a deep voice and an imposing manner.

The man appointed to direct the troops was Chief Ntshingwayo kaMahole. He was also a man of great renown and considerable military ability, and he and Mnyamana were close personal friends. He was shorter and fatter than Mnyamana, but a greater orator.

There were a number of other talented commanders in the Zulu forces. Chief Zibhebhu kaMapitha was head of the Mandlakazi, a section of the Zulu Royal House, and a cousin of the king's. Again, he was a very powerful man within the kingdom, who had fostered close links with white traders, and grown wealthy as a result. In the prime of life, he was known to be discontented with his role as a provincial Chief. He had opposed the war, but once the fighting began he threw himself wholeheartedly into it. He was perhaps the most inspired Zulu tactician of his generation, but circumstances would remove him from the field for much of the war. The king's half-brother, Prince Dabulamanzi kaMpande, was another younger leader, reckless and headstrong, a fierce royalist and a supporter of the war. He was to be one of the few commanders to achieve reknown amongst the British, who attributed many deeds to him that had been performed by other commanders. Nevertheless, he was personally courageous, a good shot, and a daring leader.

There were other Zulu *indunas* who would distinguish themselves during the war, both high and low. Sigcwelegcwele kaMhlekehleke was the dynamic leader of the iNgobamakhosi, the largest and perhaps most aggressive of the younger regiments in the army. Serving as a junior commander in the same regiment was Mehlokazulu kaSihayo, who had been named by the British in the Ultimatum as one of those who had violated the Natal border. Like many of his generation, he resented European influence in Zulu affairs, and had no great respect for white culture or methods of fighting. And therein lay the great Zulu weakness: their commanders were able men who had grown up in an environment which had honoured the military virtues of courage and discipline, but very few of them had ever experienced the devastating effect of European firepower, and many of the younger warriors had not yet been tested in any battle.

◀ Prince Dabulamanzi kaMpande, photographed after the end of the Zulu War. He commanded the uNdi corps during its unsuccessful attack against Rorke's Drift, and later fought in the Eshowe sector. (National Army Museum)

▶ Chief Sigcwelegcwele kaMhlekehleke, commander of the iNgobamakhosi ibutho. The iNgobamakhosi was one of the youngest regiments in the Zulu army and a favourite of the king's. It played a prominent part at Isandlwana, Khambula and Ulundi. Sigcwelegcwele himself fought at Isandlwana and Gingindlovu. (S. Bourquin)

The Armies:
Isandlwana Campaign

Chelmsford's Centre Column

Chelmsford's No. 3 or Centre Column was both his strongest and his most experienced. Nominally it was under the command of Colonel Richard Glyn, 24th Regiment, but the presence of Chelmsford himself effectively reduced Glyn's role to that of a cipher. The Column's backbone consisted of the two battalions of the 24th Regiment (2nd Warwickshires). It was unusual for two infantry battalions of the same regiment to be serving together, because the reforms instituted by Minister of War Edward Cardwell, when introducing the system of two linked battalions, had intended that one should always remain at the home depot while the other served overseas. In fact, the demands of policing an expanding empire meant that at any given time more battalions were overseas than were at home. The 1/24th had been overseas for a number of years, and had been in South Africa since 1875. It had played a prominent part in the Cape Frontier War, and its massed rifle-fire had broken a Xhosa charge at the battle of Centane in February 1878. Each Imperial infantry battalion had a theoretical strength of eight companies of 100 men each, but sickness and detached duty meant that they were seldom up to strength. The 1/24th mustered less than 700 men, but most of its NCOs and many of the Other Ranks were long-service men, and the battalion as a whole was composed of mature, seasoned, acclimatized veterans who were used to serving together and with their officers.

The 2/24th, by contrast, had been raised under the recently introduced Short Service system – whereby a man enlisted for six years' active service, rather than twelve as before – and many had been recruited at Brecon, in South Wales, where the regimental depot had been established in 1873. As a result, most of its men were younger, and there was a higher proportion of Welsh accents. The 2nd Battalion had arrived in South Africa in 1878, and had been employed to mop up the last Xhosa resistance in the bush country. They were therefore less experienced than the men of their sister battalion, but were nonetheless fast becoming acclimatized to South African conditions. If there was any rivalry between the two battalions, it seems to have been friendly, and the officers were apparently delighted to be working together.

In 1879 the British Army was undergoing a period of increased professionalism. The long tradition of parade-ground manoeuvres and conspicuous uniforms was at last giving way to more fluid tactical theories and an appreciation of camouflage. None the less, British troops still went to war in Zululand wearing scarlet jackets, blue trousers and white foreign service helmets – one of the last major campaigns in which they did so. At the same time, half a world away, troops fighting in Afghanistan were wearing khaki. Each regiment was distinguished by coloured patches on the collar and cuffs, and by regimental badges on the collar and helmet. The 24th's facings were green, and their collar badge was a sphinx. Surprisingly, the red jacket was not always conspicuous in the sometimes harsh browns and greens of the African landscape, but the white helmet was a gleaming and tempting target. Veterans soon learned to remove the brass badge and tone down the helmet with dye improvised from tea, coffee or tree-bark.

Infantry equipment consisted of the integrated Valise Pattern system. This included a waist-belt with ammunition pouches on each side of the buckle, containing a total of forty rounds, and a black leather 'expense pouch' containing a further thirty rounds. A rolled greatcoat, mess-tin and the valise were supported by braces, although the

►*Gunner, Royal Artillery, Zulu War. Most RA other ranks seem to have prefered the undress frock coat on active service, rather than the more ornate tunic, while officers usually wore the braided dark blue patrol jacket.*

W.O. LANG

◀ *The 1/24th on the march from the Cape Frontier, where they had played an active part in suppressing the Xhosa, to Zululand. The Irregulars seated on the right are probably from Buller's unit, the Frontier Light Horse. (Ian Knight Collection)*

▲ *The 1/24th in South Africa. This particular company remained on outpost duty in southern Natal during the Zulu War and so missed the disaster at Isandlwana. Nevertheless it presents an excellent picture of the mature veterans who made up the battalion. (RRW Museum, Brecon)*

valise was usually carried in transport wagons on campaign. A wooden water-bottle over one shoulder, and a canvas haversack over the other, completed the equipment. Infantry weapons consisted of the 1871 pattern Martini-Henry rifle, a single-shot breech-loader which fired a heavy .450 bullet. It was sighted up to 1,450 yards, but its most effective battle range was 350 yards. It was topped by a socket bayonet which the troops nicknamed 'the lunger'.

Officers wore either a scarlet or blue braided patrol jacket, and carried swords and revolvers.

In addition to his infantry, Chelmsford had N/5 Battery, Royal Artillery, which consisted of six 7pdr Rifled Muzzle-Loading guns. The 7pdr had originally been designed as a mountain gun, but its narrow carriage had proved unsuitable for South Africa, where it was mounted instead on 'Kaffrarian' carriages, modified versions of the larger 9pdr gun carriage. The 7pdr had a maximum range of 3,100 yards, but it suffered from a low muzzle velocity which reduced the effectiveness of shrapnel and shell. The Royal Artillery wore a blue uniform with yellow piping.

Chelmsford's force was singularly lacking in regular cavalry. To make up for this deficiency, several squadrons of Mounted Infantry had been raised. These consisted of men from Infantry Battalions who could ride. They wore their regimental jackets with buff cord riding-breeches, and were armed with Swinburne-Henry Carbines. They were augmented by men from the Natal Volunteer Corps. These were men from the Natal settler population, who had formed Volunteer units once it became clear that the British Government was not prepared to maintain a large garrison in the Colony during peacetime. The government provided uniforms and weapons, the men provided their own horses. The men knew the country and were often good riders and shots, but their numbers were small, and only the quasi-military Natal Mounted Police approached the disciplinary standards of regular troops. Most Volunteer units adopted black or blue uniforms with white helmets. The Centre Column included detachments of the Natal Mounted Police, Natal Carbineers, Buffalo Border Guard and Newcastle Mounted Rifles.

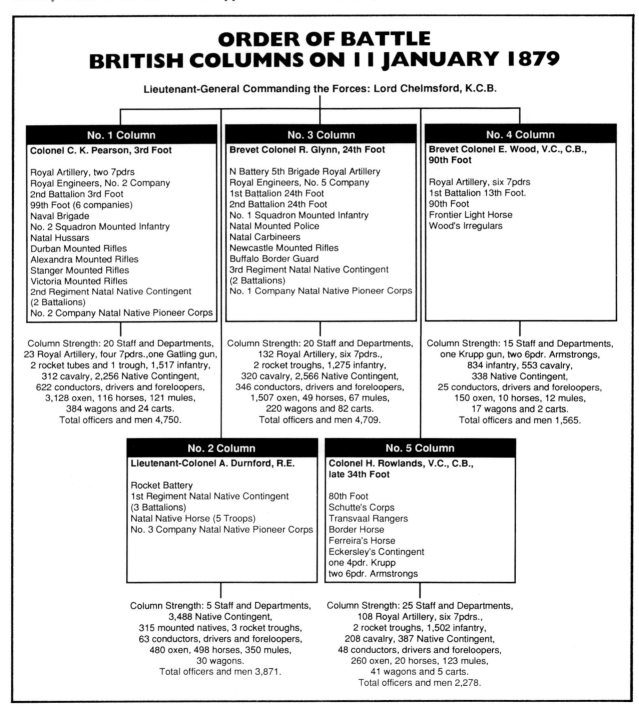

ORDER OF BATTLE
BRITISH COLUMNS ON 11 JANUARY 1879

Lieutenant-General Commanding the Forces: Lord Chelmsford, K.C.B.

No. 1 Column

Colonel C. K. Pearson, 3rd Foot

Royal Artillery, two 7pdrs
Royal Engineers, No. 2 Company
2nd Battalion 3rd Foot
99th Foot (6 companies)
Naval Brigade
No. 2 Squadron Mounted Infantry
Natal Hussars
Durban Mounted Rifles
Alexandra Mounted Rifles
Stanger Mounted Rifles
Victoria Mounted Rifles
2nd Regiment Natal Native Contingent
(2 Battalions)
No. 2 Company Natal Native Pioneer Corps

Column Strength: 20 Staff and Departments, 23 Royal Artillery, four 7pdrs., one Gatling gun, 2 rocket tubes and 1 trough, 1,517 infantry, 312 cavalry, 2,256 Native Contingent, 622 conductors, drivers and foreloopers, 3,128 oxen, 116 horses, 121 mules, 384 wagons and 24 carts.
Total officers and men 4,750.

No. 3 Column

Brevet Colonel R. Glynn, 24th Foot

N Battery 5th Brigade Royal Artillery
Royal Engineers, No. 5 Company
1st Battalion 24th Foot
2nd Battalion 24th Foot
No. 1 Squadron Mounted Infantry
Natal Mounted Police
Natal Carbineers
Newcastle Mounted Rifles
Buffalo Border Guard
3rd Regiment Natal Native Contingent
(2 Battalions)
No. 1 Company Natal Native Pioneer Corps

Column Strength: 20 Staff and Departments, 132 Royal Artillery, six 7pdrs., 2 rocket troughs, 1,275 infantry, 320 cavalry, 2,566 Native Contingent, 346 conductors, drivers and foreloopers, 1,507 oxen, 49 horses, 67 mules, 220 wagons and 82 carts.
Total officers and men 4,709.

No. 4 Column

Brevet Colonel E. Wood, V.C., C.B., 90th Foot

Royal Artillery, six 7pdrs
1st Battalion 13th Foot.
90th Foot
Frontier Light Horse
Wood's Irregulars

Column Strength: 15 Staff and Departments, one Krupp gun, two 6pdr. Armstrongs, 834 infantry, 553 cavalry, 338 Native Contingent, 25 conductors, drivers and foreloopers, 150 oxen, 10 horses, 12 mules, 17 wagons and 2 carts.
Total officers and men 1,565.

No. 2 Column

Lieutenant-Colonel A. Durnford, R.E.

Rocket Battery
1st Regiment Natal Native Contingent
(3 Battalions)
Natal Native Horse (5 Troops)
No. 3 Company Natal Native Pioneer Corps

Column Strength: 5 Staff and Departments, 3,488 Native Contingent, 315 mounted natives, 3 rocket troughs, 63 conductors, drivers and foreloopers, 480 oxen, 498 horses, 350 mules, 30 wagons.
Total officers and men 3,871.

No. 5 Column

Colonel H. Rowlands, V.C., C.B., late 34th Foot

80th Foot
Schutte's Corps
Transvaal Rangers
Border Horse
Ferreira's Horse
Eckersley's Contingent
one 4pdr. Krupp
two 6pdr. Armstrongs

Column Strength: 25 Staff and Departments, 108 Royal Artillery, six 7pdrs., 2 rocket troughs, 1,502 infantry, 208 cavalry, 387 Native Contingent, 48 conductors, drivers and foreloopers, 260 oxen, 20 horses, 123 mules, 41 wagons and 5 carts.
Total officers and men 2,278.

Despite the opposition of a sector of the settler community, who were afraid that the arming of the Colony's black population might pose a threat to their security, Lord Chelmsford had raised several regiments of the Natal Native Contingent. Each consisted of two or three battalions, each of ten companies of nine white NCOs and 100 levies. The men were drawn from clans that had suffered heavily from Zulu raids in past generations. They were in plentiful supply and were highly motivated, but such potential as they might have had was largely squandered. Although some attempt was

A Sergeant of the 24th Regiment in full marching order. Those experienced in African warfare soon learned to remove their helmet plates and dull their helmets to a less conspicuous neutral brown colour with dyes improvised from tea or coffee. At Isandlwana the 24th would not have been wearing their valises and rolled greatcoats. (Mike Chappell)

made to appoint NNC officers from amongst the ranks of those who spoke Zulu, the NCOs were drawn from the dregs of Colonial society, and inspired no confidence in their men. Only one man in ten was issued with a firearm – usually of obsolete pattern – and only four rounds of ammunition: the rest carried traditional shields and spears. There were no uniforms available, and the men were distiguished by a red rag worn around the head, and by a few items of cast-off European clothing. Both battalions of the 3rd NCC accompanied the Central Column.

Early in the course of the war, Chelmsford ordered Durnford's No. 2 Column up from the Middle Drift to support his command. Durnford's force was almost entirely composed of black troops, including the 1st Battalion, 1st NNC. It also included five troops of mounted Africans, each of about fifty men, known collectively as the Natal Native Horse. Three of these troops were drawn from the amaNgwane, a Natal clan with a tradition of hostility to the Zulus, and known as the Sikhali Horse, after their Chief. One of the

◀ *Top: Members of Major Bengough's battalion of the Natal Native Contingent. These men carry their own shields and spears and are distinguished by a red headband. The N. N. C. were poorly armed, equipped and organized and their performance suffered accordingly. They have often been blamed – unfairly – for the disaster at Isandlwana. (Buffs Museum, Canterbury)*

◀ *A British column on the march; the banks of a stream have had to be cut away to enable it to cross. The invasion of Zululand – a rugged country without roads – presented Chelmsford with a logistical nightmare. (Ian Knight Collection)*

remaining troops consisted of Sotho horsemen under their Chief, Hlubi, who were old friends of Durnford's and had fought with him at Bushman's Pass. The final troop was drawn from the Christian Edendale Mission in Natal. The NNH men wore European clothing, with red rags wound around their wide-brimmed hats. Most preferred to ride bare-foot, but the Edendale men were booted and spurred. All were armed with carbines, and some carried spears in quivers over their shoulders or attached to their saddles.

Durnford's only Imperial troops consisted of Brevet Major Russell of 11/7 Battery RA, with three 9pdr Hales rocket troughs. Rockets were notoriously unreliable weapons, inaccurate, erratic in flight and unpredictable on impact, but they were considered useful in Colonial warfare, where their fearsome screech and the shower of sparks they gave off in flight was considered to have a tremendous psychological effect.

▶ *Two constables of the Natal Mounted Police, 1879. The N. M. P. was the most organized and disciplined of the Natal units. It wore black corduroy uniforms. (National Army Museum)*

◀ *The British forces recruited large numbers of African auxiliaries from the black population in Natal, which was historically antagonistic towards the Zulu kingdom. By and large, however, this potential asset was squandered as the resulting Natal Native Contingents were badly armed and poorly led. Only one in ten was issued with a firearm, and the rest fought with their own spears and shields. Their only uniform was a red rag around the head. (Angus McBride)*

▶ *The original caption of this photograph merely says 'Transport problems'; these oxen were struck down by a freak storm. A graphic illustration of the difficulties Chelmsford faced. (John Young Collection)*

Of course, all of these units required considerable logistical support, and the transport situation remained a nightmare which tormented Chelmsford. Each infantry battalion needed to carry its own ammunition, tents, entrenching tools, signalling and medical equipment, and rations. On average, this amounted to seventeen wagon loads per battalion, without such luxuries as bottled beer and rum, and the officers' personal effects. There was a limited number of mule-drawn Army transport wagons available, but not nearly enough, and Chelmsford had to buy in civilian wagons at grossly inflated prices. These were large, heavy ox-wagons which, fully loaded, required as many as eighteen oxen to drag them. If they were to remain healthy, oxen needed up to sixteen hours' a day grazing and resting, or they dropped like flies. At best their progress might amount to about ten miles a day, and in bad weather, or across open country, or on roads damaged by erosion, it would be much less. Furthermore, Chelmsford had only a ludicrously small trained transport staff available, and had to make up the short-fall with volunteers, whose enthusiasm did not always compensate for their ineptitude. By the time hostilities began,

Chelmsford had amassed a total of 977 wagons, 56 carts, 10,023 oxen, 803 horses and 398 mules. The difficulties in managing such numbers can be easily imagined.

During the early stages of the war, too, there was a shortage of Royal Engineers, only one company – less than 200 officers and men – distributed throughout the entire column, and of medical staff, a handful of men of the Army Hospital Corps, augmented by volunteer civilian surgeons.

The Zulu Army

Unlike the British Army, the Zulu army was not a professional institution, but rather an armed citizenry. It was based on a system of age-grade regiments known as *amabutho* (sing. *ibutho*). Every few years the king would call together all youths throughout the country who had reached the age of eighteen or nineteen, and form them into an *ibutho*. They would be given a district where they built a barracks known as an *ikhanda*, which served as their headquarters. Each *ibutho* was given a distinctive name, and a uniform consisting of a

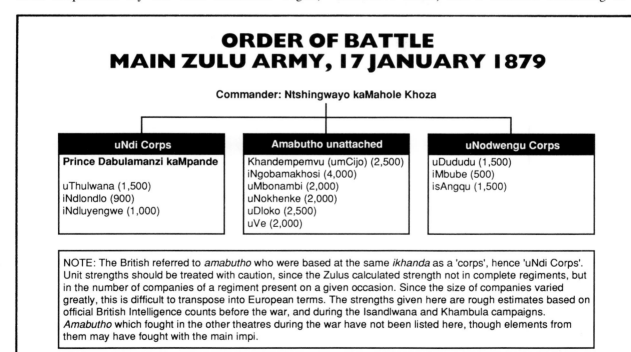

ORDER OF BATTLE
MAIN ZULU ARMY, 17 JANUARY 1879

Commander: Ntshingwayo kaMahole Khoza

uNdi Corps	Amabutho unattached	uNodwengu Corps
Prince Dabulamanzi kaMpande	Khandempemvu (umCijo) (2,500)	uDududu (1,500)
	iNgobamakhosi (4,000)	iMbube (500)
uThulwana (1,500)	uMbonambi (2,000)	isAngqu (1,500)
iNdlondlo (900)	uNokhenke (2,000)	
iNdluyengwe (1,000)	uDloko (2,500)	
	uVe (2,000)	

NOTE: The British referred to *amabutho* who were based at the same *ikhanda* as a 'corps', hence 'uNdi Corps'. Unit strengths should be treated with caution, since the Zulus calculated strength not in complete regiments, but in the number of companies of a regiment present on a given occasion. Since the size of companies varied greatly, this is difficult to transpose into European terms. The strengths given here are rough estimates based on official British Intelligence counts before the war, and during the Isandlwana and Khambula campaigns. *Amabutho* which fought in the other theatres during the war have not been listed here, though elements from them may have fought with the main impi.

▶ *A splendid study of a Zulu Chief in full regalia, photographed at the end of the nineteenth century. His body is almost totally obscured by cow-tails, and his head-dress consists of bunches of scarlet lourie and white ostrich feathers. This is typical of the ceremonial uniforms of the Zulu army in 1879, though most of it was not worn into battle. (Local History Museum, Durban)*

particular combination of feathers and furs, and a uniform shield-colour. They would remain in the king's service until he gave them permission to marry and disperse, at which point they passed from active service on to the national reserve list. Most warriors remained unmarried until their thirties, and marriage signalled the point at which they transferred their first allegiance from the king to their own families. This artificial prolongation of bachelorhood had nothing to do with channelling sexual frustration into military agression, as the British claimed; it was simply a means of

◀A young Zulu Warrior in 'war dress' – an abbreviated form of ceremonial dress – armed with a shield and knobkerry. This individual has frizzed his hair into an unusual style, a fashion among some young men in the 1870s. (Ian Knight Collection)

▶Zulu warriors looting the camp in the aftermath of victory at Isandlwana. Religious custom dictated that the enemy dead be disembowelled, and the victorious warrior had to wear part of his victim's clothing until various cleansing ceremonies had been undertaken. All of these warriors are wearing war dress. The regiments are: 1, the Mbonambi, 2, the iNdlondlo and 3, the iNgobamakhosi. (Angus McBride)

1 uMbonambi
2 umKhulutshane
3 umCijo

155

maximizing the period of national service, and in any case Zulu moral codes allowed for limited sexual activity outside marriage. In King Shaka's day, it was common for regiments to spend most of their time in the *amakhanda*, but by the 1870s the warriors lived mostly with their families, and only reported to their barracks when the king summoned them to perform a particular duty. When in service they were effectively the state labour-force; they tended the king's fields, took part in his hunts and the national ceremonies, policed his subjects and fought his wars.

In their military capacity, the *amabutho* functioned as battlefield tactical units. Each regiment was divided into two wings, right and left, and further sub-divided into companies of between fifty and seventy warriors apiece. Each company appointed its own leader from within its ranks, while wing commanders, the second-in-command and commander-in-chief were appointed by the king. Most *amabutho* were about 1,500 warriors strong, but some of the younger ones were much larger, reflecting Cetshwayo's success in revitalizing national institutions. The *amabutho* system fostered close ties between members of the same regiment, exaggerated by their common age and the fearsome reputation they enjoyed outside the kingdom. As a result, morale and *esprit de corps* was high, and rivalry between *amabutho* was common.

On ceremonial occasions each regiment wore a lavish uniform, but by 1879 very little of this was worn in battle, beyond perhaps a stuffed headband of animal-skin, and arm and leg ornaments made from the bushy part of cows' tails. Everyday dress consisted of a thin belt of hide around the waist, with strips of fur hanging at the front, and a square of softened cowhide over the buttocks.

Weapons consisted of a large oval cowhide war-shield, and a selection of spears. In Shaka's day the war shields were fully five feet high by almost three feet wide, but by 1879 a smaller variant, about 3.5 feet high by 2 feet wide, was more popular. War-shields were not the property of individual warriors, but were kept in special stores in the *amakhanda*. The hides were carefully matched for each regiment. Young regiments carried black shields; senior, usually married, regiments carried white or red shields. New shields seem to have been issued periodically in a regiment's lifespan, and the quantity and arrangement of white spots on a shield reflected its status.

The standard Zulu weapon remained the stabbing spear, apparently introduced by Shaka. This had a blade between 12 and 18 inches long, mounted in a stout haft, and was used with a powerful under-arm thrust. In addition, many warriors carried lighter spears, with smaller blades, which were used for throwing. These could be flung with some accuracy up to a maximum of fifty yards.

By 1879, the Zulu army had also acquired large numbers of firearms. King Cetshwayo's white adviser, John Dunn, had imported a number into the kingdom, and many more came in through Portuguese Mozambique in the north, or illegally across the Natal border. British observers were shocked to see that most warriors could lay their hands on some firearm or other, but most were obsolete percussion models or old Brown Bess types, usually in poor condition. With no training, regular ammunition supplies or spare parts, the Zulus were unable to make the most of their firepower, but subsequent reports stress its volume, and it was to boast a number of notable successes.

Unlike the British, the Zulu army was highly mobile, and required no baggage train. It normally could march twenty miles in a day, and twice that distance was not unknown. For the first few days it would be accompanied by civilians – usually boys too young to fight – who drove slaughter cattle and carried corn and beer. After that, it was expected to live by foraging. In Shaka's time, this was usually enough to see it beyond the kingdom's borders, but in 1879 it was fighting on home territory, which led to problems with provisions and a tension within the civilian population, whose crops were likely to suffer on the army's approach.

Tactically, the army was wedded to an agressive manoeuvre known as 'the beast's horns'. One formation, usually of senior warriors, and called 'the chest', would advance straight at the enemy, while on each side younger regiments, known as 'the horns', would rush out to surround him. The Zulus were able to perform this tactic in close formation, moving at great speed over broken

▲Zulu warriors in action in 1879. This illustration gives a good impression of their appearance in the field. They have discarded their ceremonial regalia, retaining only a few plumes. Note the number of firearms. (Ian Knight Collection)

▶The Zulu attack formation was called impondo zankomo, the 'beast's horns'. The centre, or 'chest', made a frontal assault on the enemy while the 'horns' rushed out to surround it on each side. (S Bourquin)

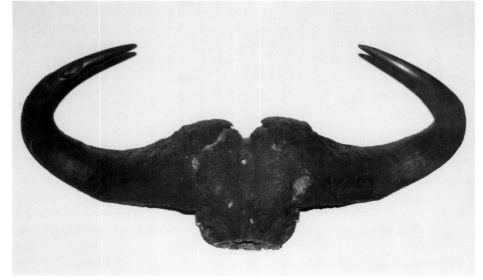

ground, as Chelmsford would soon discover to his cost.

The great army which left Ulundi consisted of twelve full regiments: the uDududu, isAngqu, iMbube, uNokhenke, Khandempemvu (umCijo), uMbonambi, iNgobamakhosi, uVe, uThulwana, iNdluyengwe, iNdlondlo and uDloko, augmented by small detachments from regiments that were fighting elsewhere. Several were regiments of married men, recalled to active duty at this time of national trial, but the majority were young unmarried warriors in their prime.

The First Phase of the War

Chelmsford's orders to Pearson's No. 1 Column were to advance north from the Lower Drift to the abandoned mission station of Eshowe, some 35 miles from the border. Because this had a number of buildings which could be used as stores, it had been selected as the most suitable base for future operations. After several days spent ferrying supplies across the Thukela, Pearson began his advance on 18 January. He had just crossed the Nyezane river on the 22nd when he was attacked in the open by a force of about 6,000 Zulus. Heavy fighting lasted for about an hour and a half before the Zulus were defeated. Pearson, who lost ten men killed and sixteen wounded, immediately pushed on to Eshowe which he reached the following day. Once in position he began to fortify the deserted mission.

Wood's No. 4 Column had not been allocated an immediate strategic objective, but was required to subdue the northern reaches of the Zulu kingdom. The area was home to a number of aggressive and semi-independent Zulu groups, including followers of the renegade Swazi prince Mbilini, and the abaQulusi, who were descendants of an *ibutho* established by Shaka, who had settled in the area. The Zulus operated from a chain of flat-topped mountain strongholds, Zungwini, Hlobane and Ityenka. Wood immediately organized a series of far-ranging patrols to harry the Zulus. It was during a skirmish near Hlobane on 24 January that he received a message from Lord Chelmsford telling him that the Centre Column had suffered a major set-back.

The Advance to Isandlwana

Lord Chelmsford crossed the Mzinyathi river into Zululand at Rorke's Drift early on the morning of 11 January. The Royal Artillery covered the crossing from the Natal bank while a line of

vedettes from the Natal Volunteers were the first across. One company of the 2/24th was left at Rorke's Drift to guard the supply depot and river crossing. Once the column was across, a new camp sprang up on the far bank, and the exhausting task of ferrying over the transport wagons began. There was no sign of the enemy.

Chelmsford intended to establish his first base inside enemy territory at Isiphezi mountain, but first he had a local problem to resolve. A few miles ahead along the line of his advance the track cut across a stream known as the Batshe, close to the homestead of an important Zulu Chief named Sihayo. His sons had been responsible for one of the border incidents that had provoked the war, and in any case Chelmsford could not afford to leave a potentially hostile force in his rear. Accordingly, on 12 January he undertook an attack on Sihayo's stronghold, which was in a gorge set into a line of cliffs overlooking the eastern bank of the Batshe. Sihayo and many of his men were absent at Ulundi, having attended the general muster, but a small force had been left to guard his homestead. Chelmsford's attacking force comprised four companies of the 2/24th, the 3rd N.N.C. and the mounted troops. The N.N.C. were instructed to carry out a frontal assault which, with some encouragement, they succeeded in doing. A line of 24th men followed them with fixed bayonets. The mounted men and the remainder of the infantry surrounded the stronghold by climbing the cliffs on either side, and the position was taken after a stiff skirmish which claimed the lives of about thirty Zulus. Chelmsford ordered Sihayo's homestead to be burnt and, having rounded up the Chief's cattle, the British returned to camp.

With this threat removed, Chelmsford was free to turn his attention once more to his advance. His route lay across country that was alternately rocky

The Isandlwana Campaign, 11 to 23 January 1879

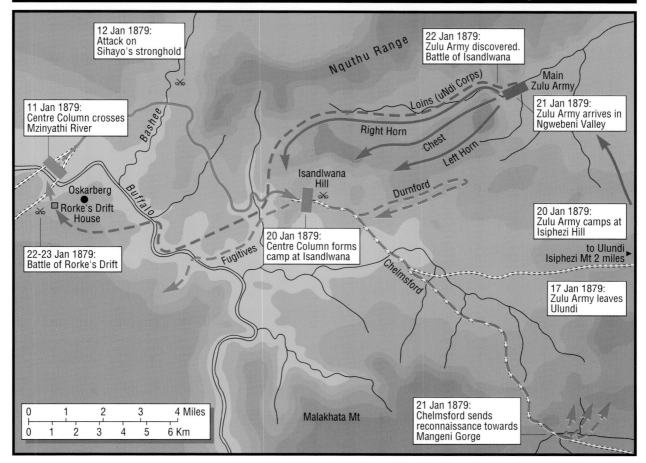

12 Jan 1879:
Attack on
Sihayo's stronghold

22 Jan 1879:
Zulu Army discovered.
Battle of Isandlwana

Main
Zulu Army

21 Jan 1879:
Zulu Army arrives in
Ngwebeni Valley

11 Jan 1879:
Centre Column crosses
Mzinyathi River

Nquthu Range

Loins (uNdi Corps)

Right Horn

Chest

Left Horn

Durnford

Isandlwana
Hill

20 Jan 1879:
Zulu Army camps at
Isiphezi Hill

Oskarberg

Rorke's Drift
House

Buffalo

22-23 Jan 1879:
Battle of Rorke's Drift

Fugitives

20 Jan 1879:
Centre Column forms
camp at Isandlwana

Chelmsford

to Ulundi
Isiphezi Mt 2 miles

17 Jan 1879:
Zulu Army leaves
Ulundi

0 1 2 3 4 Miles
0 1 2 3 4 5 6 Km

Malakhata Mt

21 Jan 1879:
Chelmsford sends
reconnaissance towards
Mangeni Gorge

---

and marshy, and which would therefore be very difficult for his transport wagons. It was necessary for Engineer parties to clear and repair the track, and while this work was going on, Chelmsford moved his camp to the ridge on the western bank of the Batshe. From here his scouts reported that the best place for his next camp site would be the eastern foot of a mountain known as Isandlwana.

At about this time, Chelmsford sent orders to Colonel Durnford, in command of No. 2 Column, instructing him to leave two battalions of his N.N.C. to guard the Middle Drift, to send one to the border magistracy at Msinga, and to move the rest of his forces up to Rorke's Drift. Chelmsford wanted Durnford on hand should he be needed to support the advance, and Durnford was delighted at the prospect of a more active role in the campaign. He arrived at Rorke's Drift on the 20th,

just as Chelmsford was pushing on to Isandlwana.

The track crested a rising nek which lay between Isandlwana mountain on the left and a stony kopjie on the right, then wound its way towards Isiphezi, and ultimately Ulundi, but Chelmsford's troops spilled off on either side, and at about noon began pitching their tents. Their camp was arranged in blocks running north to south along the base of the mountain; first the 2/3rd N.N.C., then the 1/3rd N.N.C., then the 2/24th, the Royal Artillery, mounted troops, and finally, south of the track below the stony kopjie, the 1/24th.

Throughout this time, Chelmsford had only the vaguest knowledge of the Zulu movements. The main *impi* had left Ulundi on 17 January and, following its orders, moved slowly towards the Centre Column. On the 20th it camped just north

against it. The ground was too stony for a proper entrenchment, he considered it only a temporary halt, and the wagons had to be free to keep up the flow of supplies between the camp and Rorke's Drift. Chelmsford intended to move on as soon as possible, and no sooner had he arrived on the 20th than he set off on a reconnaissance towards the Mangeni gorge, about twelve miles eastwards. This was the stronghold of a Chief named Matshana, and the General ordered that the hills that flanked his planned advance should be thoroughly searched for signs of the enemy.

Accordingly, early on the morning of 21 January, Commandant Rupert Lonsdale left camp with sixteen companies of the 3rd N.N.C., followed by Major John Dartnell with a party of Natal Mounted Police and Volunteers. At the far end of the range, where it overlooked the Mangeni, Dartnell encountered more than 1,000 Zulus blocking any further advance. As darkness fell Dartnell decided to make camp for the night, though neither his nor Lonsdale's men had tents or supplies. A note was sent back to Chelmsford asking for reinforcements so that an attack could be made in the morning, and the force settled down for an uneasy night.

Chelmsford received this note early on the morning of the 22nd and it took him by surprise; he had not expected Dartnell to engage the enemy, and now it appeared he had blundered into part of the main *impi*. Chelmsford decided that Dartnell and Lonsdale would not be strong enough to engage the *impi* alone, and he assembled a force to march to their relief. At about 4.00 a.m. he rode out of the camp with six companies of the 2/24th, four R.A. guns, a mounted infantry detachment, and the Natal Native Pioneers, heading for Mangeni.

The camp at Isandlwana was left in the hands of Lieutenant-Colonel Henry Pulleine, 1/24th, and the force at his disposal was still impressive: five companies of the 1/24th, one of the 2/24th, the two remaining 7pdr guns of N/5 Battery, more than a hundred mounted men from the Mounted Infantry and Natal Volunteers, and four companies of the N.N.C. Chelmsford's orders to Pulleine were that he should keep his cavalry vedettes advanced, draw in his line of infantry outposts, and

of Isiphezi hill, and on the following day it moved into the Nquthu hills north-east of Isandlwana. Here they rested in the valley of the Ngwebeni stream, about four miles from Isandlwana. They intended to remain there throughout the 22nd, because a new moon was imminent, and the night of a 'dead' moon was considered too ill an omen for so great an undertaking as an attack on a British camp.

The Battle of Isandlwana

Before the invasion had begun, Chelmsford had issued detailed regulations for the defence of all camps on the line of march, calling for wagon laagers or earth entrenchments at every stop. But when Colonel Glyn suggested protecting the camp at Isandlwana, Chelmsford himself decided defend the camp if attacked. Before leaving, he also sent orders to Durnford at Rorke's Drift, ordering him to move his column up to Isandlwana, and informing him of his (Chelmsford's) movements. Once Durnford reached Isandlwana, there would be a total of 67 officers and 1,707 men in the camp to carry out the General's orders.

After Chelmsford marched out, Pulleine organized his defensive arrangements. The mounted men were deployed as vedettes on the Nquthu plateau and towards the east of the camp, where some were posted on a conical kopjie about a mile away. A screen of infantry pickets was placed about 1,500 yards from the camp, in a curve which stretched from the right in the south, round to a lip of the Nquthu plateau in the north. This commanded a spur where the ground sloped down to join the tail of Mount Isandlwana itself.

Shortly after 8.00 a.m. a mounted vedette rode into camp with the news that a large body of Zulus was approaching across the plateau from the north-east. The 'Fall In' was sounded, the infantry pickets came in (except for an N.N.C. outpost on the lip of the plateau), and the whole force formed up in front of the tents. Pulleine sent a note to Chelmsford informing him that the Zulus were approaching the camp in force. No further developments were reported by the vedettes until a message was delivered over an hour later, which stated that the Zulus had divided into three

▼*A small diorama of the battlefield is dwarfed by the real Isandlwana behind. The great black arc on the model represents the Zulu* attack: the numbers are perhaps exaggerated, but it does convey the overwhelming strength of the Zulu army. (Ian Knight Collection)*

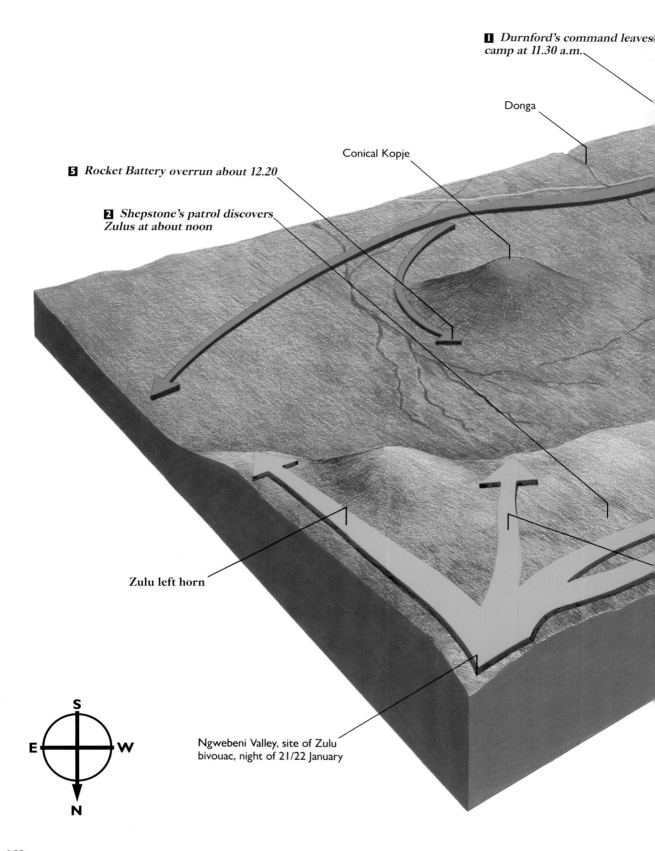

1 *Durnford's command leaves camp at 11.30 a.m.*

Donga

Conical Kopje

5 *Rocket Battery overrun about 12.20*

2 *Shepstone's patrol discovers Zulus at about noon*

Zulu left horn

Ngwebeni Valley, site of Zulu bivouac, night of 21/22 January

S

E   W

N

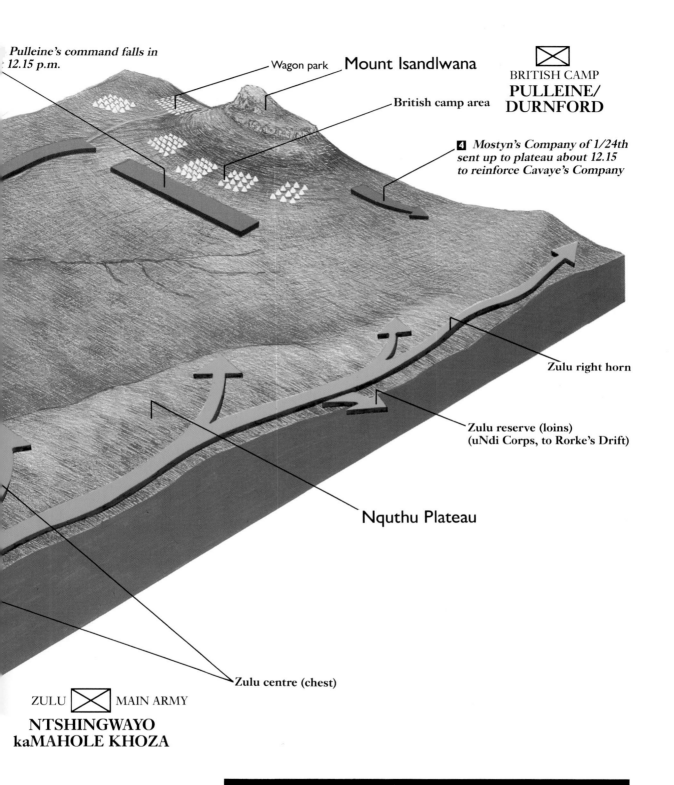

Pulleine's command falls in 12.15 p.m.

Wagon park

Mount Isandlwana

British camp area

4 *Mostyn's Company of 1/24th sent up to plateau about 12.15 to reinforce Cavaye's Company*

Zulu right horn

Zulu reserve (loins)
(uNdi Corps, to Rorke's Drift)

Nquthu Plateau

Zulu centre (chest)

ZULU MAIN ARMY
**NTSHINGWAYO
kaMAHOLE KHOZA**

THE BATTLE OF ISANDLWANA

The Zulu approach and Durnford's sortie, to 12.20 p.m., 22 January 1879

columns. Two retired to the north until they were lost from sight, while the other was even then moving north-west. This report had just come in when Durnford rode into the camp with his men. Pulleine informed Durnford of the situation.

Chelmsford's orders to Durnford had not told him what to do on arriving at the camp, and this created an awkward situation. He had presumably been brought up to reinforce the camp, but he felt that he was also to support the advance if necessary. Durnford was senior to Pulleine and so normal military procedure would mean that he now commanded the camp, but it is unlikely that Chelmsford had had this in mind since he expected the camp to be moved forward to join him shortly. In the circumstances, Durnford felt able to act independently. The sound of gunfire had been heard at Mangeni and this, coupled with news of the Zulu movements on the hills, suggested that Chelmsford was engaged with the main *impi*. Durnford was worried that the Zulus spotted by the vedettes were moving off to threaten Chelmsford's rear. He felt that it was essential to

counter this, and ordered two troops of the N.N.H., under Captain George Shepstone, up on to the plateau to drive any Zulus they encountered to the east. Durnford himself proposed to move out across the plain with the remainder of his column to cut the Zulus off. He asked Pulleine to give him two companies of the 24th, but Pulleine, mindful of his specific orders to defend the camp, refused. Durnford accepted the situation and the two parted amicably, Durnford commenting that he would none the less expect to be supported if he got into difficulties.

Pulleine sent up a company of the 1/24th under Lieutenant Cavaye to support the N.N.C. picket on the head of the spur. Cavaye detached a platoon under Lieutenant Dyson to a point 500 yards farther to their left, where it could watch the rear approaches to Isandlwana. At about 11.30

▼*Members of the Natal Native Horse skirmishing with Zulus, 1879. Members of Lieutenant Raw's troop discovered* *the* impi *resting in a valley less than five miles from Isandlwana on the fateful 22 January. (National Army Museum)*

a.m. Durnford rode out of Isandlwana, while his detached party fanned out to scout the plateau. About four miles from the camp, some of Lieutenant Raw's N.N.H. spotted a herd of cattle being driven by some Zulus, and they immediately gave chase. The herders promptly disappeared over a fold in the ground. Raw's men galloped up to the edge, then desperately reined in their horses. Dropping sharply away in front of them was the deep valley of the Ngwebeni, and below them, not miles away at Mangeni as they had thought, lay the 20,000 warriors of the main *impi*.

They were resting in silence, but the sight of British troops looking down on them was too much for the warriors, who, led by the nearest regiment, the Khandempemvu, immediately sprang up and began to clamber up the slopes towards the retreating horsemen. The senior *indunas* were powerless to stop them, and the regiments instinctively formed up in the traditional 'chest and horns' formation. The Khandempemvu and elements of the uMxhapo formed the chest, the uMbonambi, iNgobamakhosi and uVe the left horn, and the uDududu, iMbube, isAngqu and uNokhenke the right horn. Only the uNdi corps, consisting of the uThulwana, iNdluyengwe, iNdlondlo and uDloko regiments, were intercepted by the commanders and formed into the 'loins', or tactical reserve.

Raw's troop fell back, firing as they went. They met Shepstone, who sent a message to Durnford warning him of the Zulu approach, and then rode to pass the news to Pulleine himself. While Shepstone was delivering the message a note arrived from Lord Chelmsford, telling Pulleine to strike the tents and send on the baggage to join him. Pulleine, still not grasping the seriousness of the Zulu threat, merely sent back a note saying that he was unable to move the camp 'at present'. He sounded the 'Fall In' again and sent a second company, Captain Mostyn's, up to the plateau to reinforce Cavaye.

Durnford was advancing across the plain, below the Nquthu escarpment, when Shepstone's messenger reached him. He had no sooner halted his men than elements of the left horn appeared in strength on the rim of the plateau above. Durnford's men began to retire, halting every so

often to loose a volley. Meanwhile, Durnford's rocket battery and its escort, commanded by Major Russell, which was not mounted, had lagged behind. It had just passed the conical Kopje when news reached it of the Zulu approach. Russell turned to his left to climb the slope, but was stopped in his tracks by the sudden appearance of warriors on the skyline. Russell's men hastily set up their troughs, but had only managed to loose one salvo when a Zulu volley crashed down into them, causing the N.N.C. to flee. The Zulus then charged down and overran the battery. Russell was killed, but miraculously three of his men survived and escaped to safety.

As Mostyn's men reached the top of the spur they were greeted with a chilling sight. A massive column of Zulus, the right horn, was streaming across Cavaye's front at about 600 yards' distance. They were heading towards the rear of Isandlwana, and they took not the slightest notice of the fire Cavaye was directing at them. Mostyn placed his men between Cavaye and Dyson, and they joined in the shooting. At about this time, too, Shepstone's two troops of the N.N.H., who had been retiring in front of the Zulus, joined them on the spur. The N.N.C picket meanwhile had fallen back to the plain below.

Pulleine was still unaware of the extent of the attack, until more and more warriors began to appear on the skyline. Since that was obviously the direction of the main threat, he ordered Major Stuart Smith, RA to position his two 7pdrs on a low rocky knoll about 600 yards to the front of the camp. Here they opened fire on the Zulus spilling over the lip of the plateau. To support the guns, Lieutenant Porteus' company, 1/24th, formed up to their left, and Captain Wardell's company to the right. Lieutenant Pope's sole company of the 2/24th, which had been out on picket duty, was also on the plain in front of the camp, and took up a position facing the hills. The men were able to take advantage of the cover provided by a line of boulders which marked the point where the ground fell away towards a donga, or run-off gulley. Pulleine realised that he could not leave Mostyn and Cavaye exposed on the plateau, so he recalled them, and sent his last company of the 24th, Captain Younghusband's, to cover their

retreat. The N.N.H. and N.N.C. picket formed up on Younghusband's right, while Mostyn and Cavaye fell in line with Porteous. The infantry therefore formed a more or less continuous line from Younghusband on the left, stretching to Pope on the right, though they were spread dangerously thin. Exactly where the rest of the N.N.C. were no one is sure; one company was formed up in front of the camp itself; the rest seem to have been out on the right.

Durnford's men continued their retreat, picking up a vedette of the Natal Carbineers along the way. At about a mile from the camp they stopped in a deep donga and dismounted to open fire on their pursuers. Here they were joined by some of the mounted men from the camp. This placed Pulleine in a quandry. He remembered his promise to support Durnford if he got into difficulties, and sure enough Durnford was now under pressure way out to the right. Pulleine ordered Pope to fall back to direct some of his fire against the left horn facing Durnford, and the N.N.C. apparently filled the gap between them. The 24th were 'old, steady shots', but they were too scattered to concentrate their fire. Nevertheless they managed to slow the Zulu advance which stalled under the cover of a slight depression about 300 yards from the line. The frustrated Zulus, unable to move forward in the face of so murderous a fire, could be heard murmuring like a swarm of angry bees.

Durnford's men had been in action for some time now and were beginning to run out of ammunition. Attempts to resupply them were hampered by the fact that their runners could not find their own ammunition wagons, and the infantry quartermasters would not issue ammunition to Levies. Sensing the reduction in firepower, the iNgobamakhosi and uVe began to extend to their left, to outflank Durnford, and cross the donga farther down. Pulleine, aware of this, tried to counter it by having Smith turn his fire on the left horn. The climax of the battle had

◀ *Isandlwana battlefield, with the donga defended by Durnford in the foreground. Outflanked and running out of ammunition, Durnford* *retreated closer to the camp at the climax of the battle, allowing the Zulus to burst through the line. (Ian Knight Collection)*

approached, and suddenly the tide turned against the British. Durnford's position was critical and he could no longer hold the donga. He ordered his men to mount up and ride back to the camp. It was probably at this point that the N.N.C., seeing them go, threw down their weapons and fled to the rear. In a few minutes the situation had become desperate. Pope was hopelessly exposed, and

▲ *This late Victorian engraving portrays the 24th as an island swamped by the tide of the Zulu advance. Although it exaggerates the size of the Zulu impi, it does suggest something of the way the regulars were overwhelmed as they tried to retreat towards the camp. (Ian Knight Collection)*

▶ *The position occupied by the 24th companies at Isandlwana, looking towards Durnford's donga (marked by the white building in the distance). The boulders provided some cover, but the men were too thin on the ground to hold such a wide front. (Ian Knight Collection)*

▶ *Inset: Lieutenant C. Pope, who commanded the only company of the 2/24th present at Isandlwana during the battle. His men held the right of the firing line and were outflanked when Durnford's men withdrew. Pope was killed in the battle. (Ian Knight Collection)*

Pulleine tried frantically to pull his men back to a closer defensive position with the mountain at his back. The bugles sounded the retire, and the infantry stopped firing and began to fall back.

It was too late. An *induna* who had been observing the battle goaded the Khandempemvu in the centre into action, and, released from the galling fire, they rose and surged forward. The

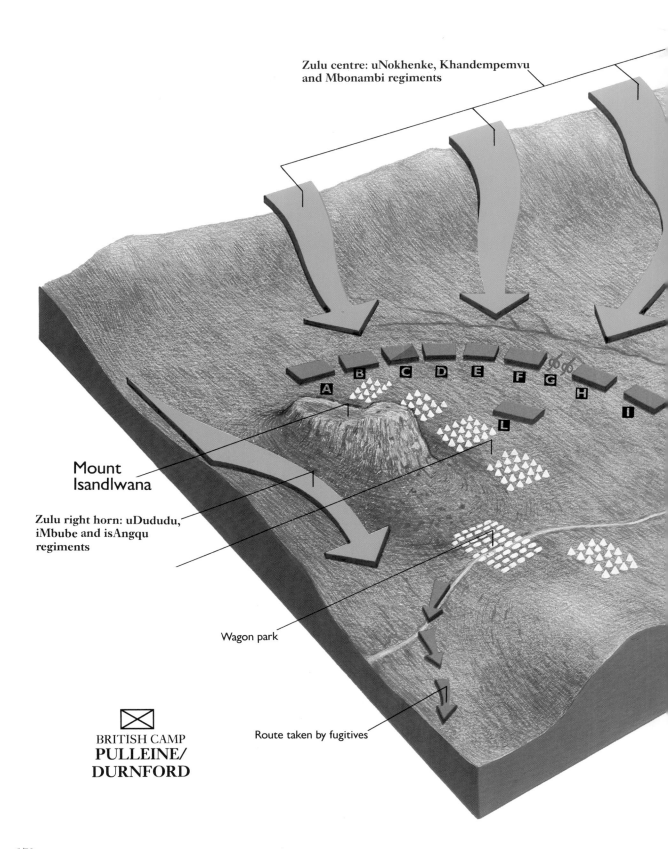

Zulu centre: uNokhenke, Khandempemvu
and Mbonambi regiments

A B C D E F G H I L

Mount
Isandlwana

Zulu right horn: uDududu,
iMbube and isAngqu
regiments

Wagon park

Route taken by fugitives

BRITISH CAMP
**PULLEINE/
DURNFORD**

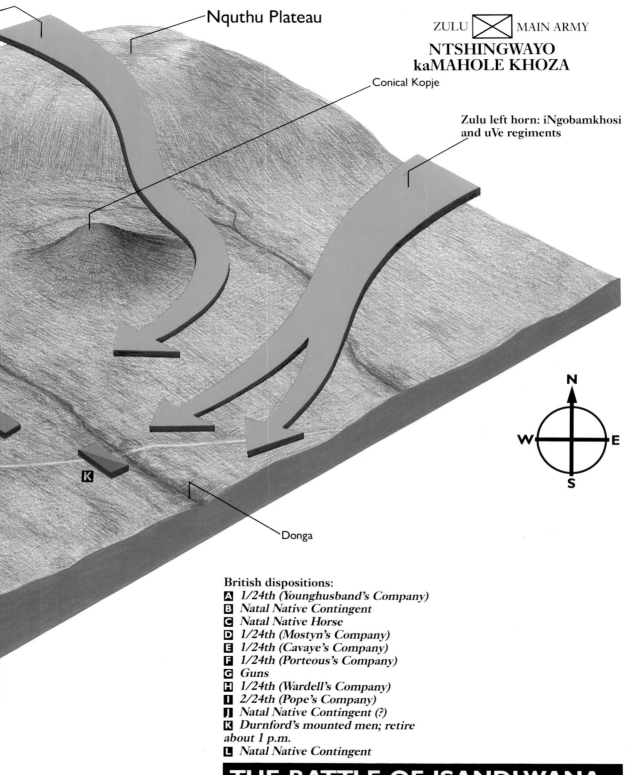

Nquthu Plateau

**NTSHINGWAYO
kaMAHOLE KHOZA**

Conical Kopje

Zulu left horn: iNgobamkhosi
and uVe regiments

N
W — E
S

Donga

British dispositions:
A *1/24th (Younghusband's Company)*
B *Natal Native Contingent*
C *Natal Native Horse*
D *1/24th (Mostyn's Company)*
E *1/24th (Cavaye's Company)*
F *1/24th (Porteous's Company)*
G *Guns*
H *1/24th (Wardell's Company)*
I *2/24th (Pope's Company)*
J *Natal Native Contingent (?)*
K *Durnford's mounted men; retire
about 1 p.m.*
L *Natal Native Contingent*

THE BATTLE OF ISANDLWANA
The climax of the battle, about 1 p.m., 22 January 1879

171

◄ *A rather romanticized view of Isandlwana. In fact, the 24th companies did not take up such a tight formation, and this was the reason for their downfall: nevertheless, the picture does suggest the fierce nature of the hand-to-hand fighting. (Ian Knight Collection)*

◄ *Below: C. E. Fripp's classic painting of the last moments of the 24th at Isandlwana. In fact, there was no Regimental Colour present in the firing line, but the picture is otherwise accurate. (National Army Museum)*

▼ *Brevet Major S. Smith., RA, who commanded the two guns at Isandlwana. Smith kept them firing for as long as possible, then tried to save them, but the guns became stuck in rough ground and were overrun. Smith himself was killed near the Fugitives' Drift.*

▲ *The two 7pdr guns of N/5 Battery, RA, which were captured by the Zulus at Isandlwana. At the end of the war they were found abandoned on the veld near Ulundi. The Zulus had tried unsuccessfully to make them work. (Ian Knight Collection)*

regiments on either side followed them, and suddenly the entire *impi* was in motion once more. The 7pdrs kept firing until the last minute, then limbered up and careered back towards the camp. One gunner was stabbed to death as he mounted the axle-tree. The infantry grouped together in rallying squares, but the Zulus rushed in right amongst them, and pushed them back through the camp. It was no longer possible to make any concerted defence. Men stood back to back or in small clusters, firing until their ammunition was spent, then keeping the Zulus at bay with the bayonet. Individuals took refuge in and around the wagons, lashing about them with rifle butt and bayonet. Durnford dismissed the N.N.H. men who had fought well under his command, and gave them permission to leave the camp. Together with a mixed group of Volunteers and 24th men he took up a position just below the nek, trying to hold back the left horn. Here he was killed. Pulleine, too, died somewhere in the camp, and knots of the 24th held out in the broken ground behind Isandlwana, until the Zulus overwhelmed them. The Zulu horns had closed, and the battle was over.

Those who had managed to escape the carnage in the camp crossed the nek hoping to ride to Rorke's Drift, but were horrified to find that the right horn had already blocked their route. They veered to the left, down-valley of a stream known

◀ The closing stages of Isandlwana: the firing line has collapsed, and the British infantry are pushed back into the camp, where much of the hand-to-hand fighting takes place. The two Zulus 1 are both of the uVe ibutho, the youngest in the Zulu army. They are wearing war-dress rather than full ceremonial regalia, although it is possible that more regalia was worn at Isandlwana than in later campaigns. The warrior on the right wears his hair fashionably styled with wax. 2 is an officer of the 24th, wearing the blue infantry-pattern patrol jacket, while 3 is a private with three 'long service and good conduct' chevrons, reflecting the seniority of many men in the 1st Battalion's ranks. (Angus McBride)

▲ 'The Pride of the 24th'; scattered infantry try to rally together as the Zulus overrun the line. A modern painting of the scene, by American artist Bud Bradshaw. (By Kind Permission of the Artist)

◀ Top: The flight along the 'Fugitives' Trail' was a running fight as the Zulus tried to finish off the survivors: without a horse the chances of escape were slender. (Ian Knight Collection).

◀ Lieutenant E. Anstey, one of the 1/24th officers killed at Isandlwana. His body was found on the banks of the Manzimyama stream behind the mountain, where he had organized a 'last stand'. (Ian Knight Collection)

▲ The valley of the Manzimyama stream, behind mount Isandlwana. The Zulu left horn passed down this valley in pursuit of the survivors of the battle: in the foreground is one of the graves on the 'Fugitives' Trail'. Many of the last stands took place on the far slope, nearer the mountain. (Ian Castle)

as the Manzimyama, chasing blindly after the fleeing N.NC. who seemed to know an escape route. The Zulus raced after them and a desperate struggle for survival developed over the rocky slopes. There are many tales of the lucky escapes, individual heroism, and horror of this tortuous journey. Many did not make it, including the gunners, whose guns became stuck in a gulley, and were overwhelmed.

Perhaps the most famous incident from the retreat concerns Lieutenant Melvill's attempt to save the Queen's Colour of the 1/24th. Melvill was the adjutant of his battalion, and it is thought that, as the line collapsed, he was ordered to take the Colour to a place of safety. He managed to fight his way across country and was joined by Lieutenant Coghill, also of the 1/24th. They descended into the steep valley of the Mzinyathi and plunged into the river which was in flood. Coghill crossed safely, but Melvill was pulled from his horse by the current, and clung to a rock mid-stream. Coghill turned back to help him, but his horse was immediately shot. Melvill was too exhausted to keep hold of the Colour and it slipped

▲Lieutenant and Adjutant T. Melvill, 1/24th. He attempted to save the Queen's Colour of his battalion, but was killed at Fugitives' Drift. Years later a posthumous VC was sent to his family. (Ian Knight Collection)

▲ Right: Lieutenant N. J. A. Coghill, 24th Regiment. He went to Melvill's aid at Fugitives' Drift, but was also killed. He too was awarded a posthumous VC years later. (Ian Knight Collection)

▶'Melvill's Ride to Glory': a recent study by artist Bud Bradshaw of Lieutenant and Adjutant Teignmouth Melvill, 1/24th, escaping from Isandlwana with the 1st Battalion's Queen's Colour. This picture, is more accurate than most contemporary studies, since it shows the colour furled and in its black leather case. (Reproduced by kind permission of the artist)

from his grasp. Together the two men managed to get across to the Natal bank and scrambled up the slope beyond. They reached a large rock and collapsed with their backs to it. There the Zulus found them and, after a sharp fight, killed them.

The camp was completely devastated. Bodies lay strewn about, black entwined with white. The bodies of the British soldiers were stripped and disembowelled in accordance with Zulu custom. Oxen and horses were killed, stores broken open and looted, tents and wagons set on fire. The Zulus took everything of value and by late afternoon they began to drift away, carrying their dead. More than a thousand had been killed and many corpses were simply dragged into dongas or nearby homesteads. Hundreds more would die later from the terrible wounds they had sustained.

The casualties among the defenders were the worst ever inflicted on a British army by a native foe. Not one member of the six 24th companies survived. Of the 1,700 men who were in the camp on the morning of the 22nd, only 60 whites and 400 blacks survived.

Lord Chelmsford, meanwhile, had remained unaware of the disaster until it was over. He had arrived at Dartnell's position at about 6.00 a.m. There was no evidence of the large enemy concentration that he had hoped to find, but there was a number of small groups on the hills surrounding the Mangeni. By 9.30 these had been cleared, and Chelmsford allowed his men to take breakfast. During the meal he received the first note from Isandlwana, reporting that Zulus were advancing on the camp. He was not unduly

worried by this news, being confidant that Pulleine's force was strong enough to defend itself, and nothing unusual could be observed through a staff officer's telescope. Chelmsford sent orders for the camp to be moved forward so that the search for the main *impi* could continue. Further messages arrived during the morning, but these failed to reveal the true extent of the attack. Artillery fire was heard, and shells could be seen bursting against the Nquthu escarpment, but the tents could be seen still standing, which was taken as a sign that all was well.

Earlier in the morning, Chelmsford had ordered the 1/3rd N.N.C. under Commandant Hamilton-Browne, back to camp. They had gone a few miles when a large mass of Zulus – the left horn – swept across their front some way off. In the far distance, Hamilton-Browne could see fighting among the tents. He withdrew his men to a safer position and sent a message to Chelmsford. Chelmsford had turned with his escort to see for himself what was happening. He gave no credit to

Hamilton-Browne's stories of disaster, until a lone figure approached him and convinced him of the dreadful truth. This was Commandant Lonsdale who, suffering from heatstroke, had ridden back to the camp to secure supplies for his men who had been out all night with no food. He was dozing in his saddle, and had ridden close to the tents before he noticed the victorious Zulus ransacking them. He had managed to turn around and gallop away in the nick of time.

Chelmsford was thunderstruck. In the open, unsupported, with a hostile force between him and Natal, he had little choice but to try to retrace his steps to Isandlwana, and thence back to Rorke's

▼*Perhaps the most famous battle of the Zulu War: the defence of Rorke's Drift, 22/23 January 1879. This rather lurid contemporary print suggests something of the desperate fighting during* *one of the night attacks, lit by the flames from the blazing hospital. The artist has erred in giving two Zulus (left) daggers, which were not a Zulu weapon. (Kenneth Griffith Collection)*

▶Lord Chelmsford's force leaves Isandlwana on the morning of 23 January after a night spent on the battlefield. The appearance of the mountain is not accurate, but the the awful devastation is. (Ian Knight Collection)

Drift. He formed his men up and began a long, slow, melancholy march back to the camp. It was dark by the time he arrived. He deployed his men in line and the artillery lobbed shells into the darkness in case the Zulus were still in possession. Three companies of the 24th were sent forward to clear the stony kopje south of the nek, then the whole force advanced. There was no opposition, for there was nothing living left in the camp. Chelmsford's men spent the night among the debris. Many found they were lying in the tall grass among the bodies of their fallen comrades. The night was interrupted by several scares, and a red glow in the sky above Rorke's Drift made matters worse. There was a fire at Rorke's Drift and the garrison was under attack.

Chelmsford had the men roused before dawn, wishing to spare them sight of the horrors that surrounded them. As they descended into the Batshe valley, an *impi* came into view on the their left. It was coming from the direction of the Oskarberg, the hill overlooking Rorke's Drift. Warily, the two sides watched each other, then passed at a safe distance, neither side seeking a confrontation. On reaching the Drift Chelmsford feared the worst, for a heavy pall of smoke could be seen hanging over the post. He sent forward some mounted men to reconnoitre and soon the sound of cheering broke out. The post was safe.

Chelmsford rode up eagerly, hoping to find that some part of the Centre Column had escaped to Rorke's Drift, but he was to be disappointed. The post had been defended with great tenacity by its original garrison, 'B' Company, 2/24th, under the command of Lieutenants Chard, RE, and Bromhead, 24th. One hundred and thirty-nine men, of whom 35 were sick, had withstood a relentless attack by 4,000 warriors for nearly twelve hours. These Zulus were members of the Undi corps, commanded by Prince Dabulamanzi kaMpande, who had been held back as the reserve at Isandlwana. They had swung wide of the right horn, taking no part in the battle, and had crossed the Mzinyathi near Fugitives' Drift. This was against the king's orders, but they were angry at having won no glory in the big battle. Chard had received an hour's warning of their approach, and had formed makeshift barricades around the mission station. The Zulu attack had begun at about 4.00 p.m. and had continued throughout the night. Having been unable to make any headway against the improvised fort, however, they withdrew at dawn on the 23rd.

Chelmsford congratulated the heroes of the fight, then left Colonel Glyn in charge to clear up the mess and secure the post, while he rode on to Pietermaritzburg, to cope as best he could with the consequences of the disaster.

◀ *Private, Newcastle Mounted Rifles, battle of Isandlwana. Natal boasted a number of small mounted volunteer corps drawn from the settler community, each with its own uniform, which contrasted smartly with the irregulars who fought with Wood's column. They were issued with Swinburne-Henry carbines shortly before the outbreak of the Zulu War. (Wynn Owen Lang)*

▶ *Troops from the 2nd Division revisit Isandlwana, May 1879. Serviceable wagons are being removed while troops search for the dead amidst the debris. (Ian Knight Collection)*

▼ *A sentry of the King's Dragoon Guards on duty among the wrecked wagons on the nek. Isandlwana, June 1879. (Ian Knight Collection)*

W.C. LANG.

The Aftermath of Isandlwana

The news of Isandlwana spread rapidly throughout Natal, carried by the fleeing survivors. The population, black and white, was gripped by panic, and the settlers made for the safety of improvised defensive laagers, or more secure centres such as Pietermaritzburg or Durban. For several days they feared the arrival of a Zulu army, but nothing happened. The victorious warriors had dispersed to take part in the necessary post-combat purification rituals and to recover.

From Pietermaritzburg, Chelmsford had the sorry task of sending messages to both the home government and his surviving columns, telling them of the disaster. To Wood and Pearson he could offer little advice beyond asking them to act as they saw fit, and to prepare for an attack by the entire Zulu army. With his initial invasion plan in ruins, Chelmsford must have felt despair, but he resolutely set about reorganizing his forces. It was imperative that he keep the war going while waiting for reinforcements. News of Isandlwana reached Britain on 11 February and created uproar. The goverment had not wanted a war, and now it had a serious defeat on its hands, but a cessation of hostilities under such circumstances was politically unacceptable, so Chelmsford would get his reinforcements.

The survivors of the Centre Column strengthened the post at Rorke's Drift, but life there was cramped, insanitary and unpleasant. Nevertheless they were able to mount a number of patrols in the direction of Isandlwana and Fugitives' Drift, and on 4 February one of these patrols found the bodies of Melvill and Coghill. Below them, among the debris trapped in the shallows of the river, they found the remains of the Queen's Colour. In March a new post was built overlooking the crossing at Rorke's Drift, and it was named Fort Melvill.

Wood received news of Isandlwana two days after the battle. Finding his camp at Fort Thinta exposed, he retired a few miles north to a new camp at Khambula. From here he continued to harass the local Zulus, and in particular the abaQulusi. It was here that Buller came into his own, constantly patrolling, skirmishing and driving off Zulu cattle. Towards the end of February, word came that news of Isandlwana had stirred republican elements within the Transvaal, and Colonel Rowlands was sent to Pretoria to guard against a possible uprising. His Column came under Wood's command, the mounted men were transferred to Khambula, and a garrison of the 80th was left at Luneburg.

On 12 March a supply convoy, escorted by a company of the 80th, which had been stranded by bad weather at Myer's Drift on the Ntombe river, was attacked by a large force of Mbilini's followers. That the preparations for defence were woefully inadequate was proved before dawn when the Zulus rushed right in among the wagons, before the escort had time to emerge from their tents and form up. There were 106 soldiers with the convoy, and 62 of them were killed, together with seventeen civilian drivers.

Buller raided the Ntombe valley as a reprisal, but failed to catch Mbilini, and Wood became convinced that stronger measures were needed.

Pearson, meanwhile, had been in Eshowe for several days when he received news of Isandlwana. He called his officers together, and after some consideration, decided to stay put. The mounted Natal Volunteers and the N.N.C. were sent back to Natal to conserve supplies, and the remaining garrison set about improving the defences. Trenches were dug, revetments built, firing steps and bastions constructed until the fort was considered impregnable. At first Pearson expected an attack daily, but it never materialized, and in fact the Zulus were content to lay siege to the post,

▲ *A dramatic illustration of Irregulars fighting Zulus. Under Buller's leadership, Irregular cavalry constantly harried local clans in the run-up to the Khambula campaign. (Rai England Collection)*

▶ *The 1/24th Queen's Colour, lost at Isandlwana, was found a month later in the shallows of the Mzinyathi river. Here, the patrol returns it to the regiment at Fort Helpmekaar. (Ian Knight Collection)*

hoping for the chance of a fight in the open when either Chelmsford tried to relieve it, or Pearson tried to fight his way out. Communications with Natal were cut, and skirmishes with pickets were a regular occurrence. It was only a question of time before supplies ran out, and the men's health deteriorated. A steady trickle of men succumbed to disease and were buried in a small cemetery outside the fort. Anxiously, the garrison waited for news of relief.

The Second Phase
of the War

Opposing Strategies

Chelmsford's Centre and No. 2 Columns had effectively been smashed, and what remained of them was very much on the defensive. The Right Flank Column was immobilized at Eshowe, and only Wood's Left Flank Column was able to act offensively. Once the initial panic after Isandlwana had subsided, it became clear that there was to be no major Zulu incursion across the border into Natal and Chelmsford had a period of grace during which to re-organize his forces. In response to his request the home government had dispatched no less than six infantry battalions, two regiments of regular cavalry, and two more artillery batteries to South Africa. These would take several months to arrive, however, and in the meantime Chelmsford had to regain the strategic initiative.

His first task was to extricate Pearson from Eshowe, and throughout February and March he assembled a relief colum at the Lower Thukela Drift. As his preparations drew near completion he sent orders to his commanders to mount a series of diversionary attacks wherever possible along the border. Garrison commanders accordingly made a number of raids into Zulu territory, but the most serious operation was mounted by Colonel Wood. Since the attack at Ntombe, Wood had become convinced that Mbilini and the abaQulusi would have to be deprived of their mountain retreats, and Chelmsford's directive offered an ideal opportunity.

Hlobane is an irregularly shaped flat-topped plateau, whose summit is ringed by a line of cliffs broken in only a few places by rugged paths. It is the centre link in a chain of such mountains, the nearest of which, Zungwini, lay only twelve miles from Wood's camp at Khambula. Mbilini had one of his homesteads on the side of Hlobane, and it served as an abaQulusi rallying point. Wood's

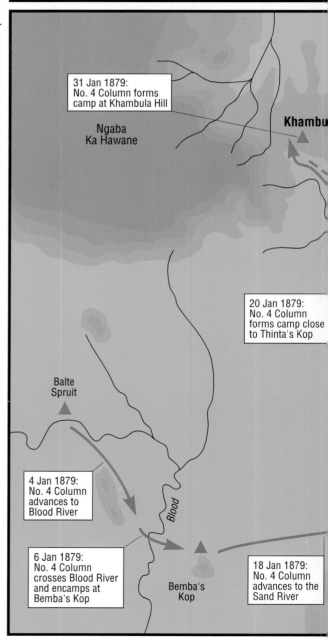

The Approach to Khambula

31 Jan 1879:
No. 4 Column forms camp at Khambula Hill

Ngaba Ka Hawane

Khambu

20 Jan 1879:
No. 4 Column forms camp close to Thinta's Kop

Balte Spruit

4 Jan 1879:
No. 4 Column advances to Blood River

Blood

6 Jan 1879:
No. 4 Column crosses Blood River and encamps at Bemba's Kop

Bemba's Kop

18 Jan 1879:
No. 4 Column advances to the Sand River

scouts had suggested that it was possible to ascend the mountain at its western and eastern ends, and Wood planned a pincer movement to catch the abaQulusi in the middle. During the night of 27 March he sent out two parties of mounted troops, one commanded by Lieutenant-Colonel J. C. Russell, and the other by Buller, with orders to

attack the mountain at each end. Buller's men rode to the far end of the mountain and began their ascent before dawn on the 28th. They succeeded in reaching the summit despite Zulu skirmishing, and rounded up a large herd of cattle which they began to drive across the top of Hlobane towards the rendezvous with Russell.

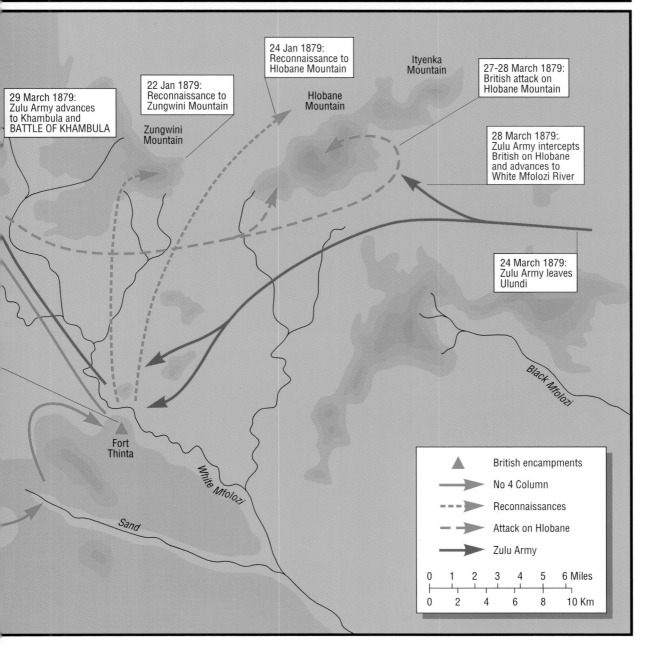

nuary to March 1879

24 Jan 1879:
Reconnaissance to Hlobane Mountain

Ityenka Mountain

27-28 March 1879:
British attack on Hlobane Mountain

22 Jan 1879:
Reconnaissance to Zungwini Mountain

Hlobane Mountain

29 March 1879:
Zulu Army advances to Khambula and BATTLE OF KHAMBULA

Zungwini Mountain

28 March 1879:
Zulu Army intercepts British on Hlobane and advances to White Mfolozi River

24 March 1879:
Zulu Army leaves Ulundi

Black Mfolozi

Fort Thinta

White Mfolozi

Sand

British encampments

No 4 Column

Reconnaissances

Attack on Hlobane

Zulu Army

| 0 | 1 | 2 | 3 | 4 | 5 | 6 Miles |

| 0 | 2 | 4 | 6 | 8 | 10 Km |

◀ Wood's camp on the Khambula ridge. The redoubt is in the centre of the picture, with the cattle laager below it on the right and the main laager in the foreground. Mount Zungwini is on the right skyline, and the valley occupied by the left horn is marked 'E' (right). The rocky outcrop where the iNgobamakhosi took shelter is marked 'C' (left). (Nottingham Castle Collection)

◀ A group of Mounted Infantrymen from the 90th L. I., who formed Wood's personal escort, and fought at both Hlobane and Khambula. They are wearing regimental jackets, with cord riding-breeches. They are armed with the Swinburne-Henry carbine and ammunition is carried in a bandolier. (S. Bourquin)

◀ A group of Irregular officers who served with Wood's Column. In the centre is Commandant Raaf of the Transvaal Rangers; the man standing left appears to be an officer of the Frontier Light Horse. That most Irregular units improvised their own uniform is is very clear from this photograph! (S. Bourquin)

► *The field smithy of Buller's Horse. To the disgust of some regular officers, Buller's men wore little in the way of uniform, and were usually distinguishable only by a red rag wound round a wide-brimmed hat. (S. Bourquin)*

► *Colonel Wood (seated centre) and his staff in the field during the Zulu War. Most of his officers are wearing comfortable and practicable blue patrol jackets, but Wood is wearing the scarlet undress frock. (S. Bourquin)*

► *Men of the commissariat of the 90th L. I., who were attached to Wood's column and were one of two infantry battalions present at Khambula. (S. Bourquin)*

Russell, however, had been defeated by the mountain's geography, and had been unable to get his men on to the plateau. He further misinterpreted a written order by Wood, and promptly withdrew from the scene of the action altogether. Furthermore, as Buller's men rode west, they looked to their left and saw a huge Zulu army moving parallel to them in a valley some miles away to the south. This was the main Zulu army from Ulundi, and it was en route to attack Khambula. It's appearance at that time was sheer coincidence, and the worst possible luck for the British. Encouraged by the presence of the *impi*, the abaQulusi stepped up their harrying attacks and Buller was driven from Hlobane in confusion. The main army dispatched one wing to join the fight, and it cut off one of Buller's parties and all but wiped it out. Buller himself was only able to extricate his men by leading them down a steep rocky staircase two hundred feet high, subsequently christened the 'Devil's Pass'. When night fell the bodies of fifteen officers and 79 men were left on the slopes of Hlobane and the Zulus were masters of the field.

Khambula: The Opening Moves

The Zulu army which had so disastrously affected Wood's action at Hlobane had been mustered at Ulundi in the middle of March. In the immediate aftermath of Isandlwana, King Cetshwayo had tried to use his position of strength to negotiate a political settlement of the war, but he had been frustrated by his army dispersing to recuperate, and by the British determination to avenge Isandlwana at all costs. By March it was clear from increased British activity that a new phase of fighting was about to begin. The king still hoped for a diplomatic settlement, but he had to be prepared for war. In council with his generals and advisers, he decided that Wood's Column presented the greatest threat. Chelmsford's reputation as an opponent was low, and the king had been bombarded with a stream of messengers from Mbilini and the abaQulusi, begging for help against Wood. Accordingly, he decided to dispatch the main army to the north, while local forces besieging Eshowe would check Chelmsford's advance.

The king was quite specific in his instructions to the *impi*. He ordered it not to attack fortified positions, but to try to lure the troops into the open. If that failed, it was to by-pass the camp altogether, and strike into the unprotected Transvaal, in the hope that Wood would be forced out to meet it. Once again command of the army was given to Ntshingwayo, with Mnyamana accompanying it as the king's representative. A number of other important *izinduna* were present, including Zibhebhu kaMapitha, but Prince Dabulamanzi was not there. He had left Ulundi under a cloud following his unsuccessful sortie against Rorke's Drift, and, since his personal homestead was near Eshowe, he was involved in the operations against Pearson. The army itself was at least as large as the *impi* that had attacked Isandlwana and the vast majority of the warriors were veterans of the earlier battle. Far from being disheartened by the terrible casualties they had suffered at Isandlwana, they

▼*An unusual photograph, thought to show the Frontier Light Horse, c.1877. The regiment originally wore a braided buff uniform and a hat with a red puggree, but by 1879 most of its men wore civilian dress, retaining only the hat. (Ian Knight)*

Trooper, Frontier Light Horse, Khambula. The Irregulars of the FLH proved to be tough and resiliant under the dynamic leadership of Redvers Buller, despite heavy casualties at Hlobane on 28 March. Their sortie provoked the Zulu attack at Khambula a day later, and they were particularly vengeful in the subsequent pursuit. The FLH seem to have worn either a buff braided jacket or a black patrol jacket, though many prefered civilian dress, with a red pugaree as the only uniform badge. (Wynn Owen Lang)

W.O. LANG.

◄Zulu commanders had great difficulty in restraining their men when they were provoked to attack, so the British often used Irregular cavalry to goad them into premature and unco-ordinated attacks. (Rai England Collection)

◄No. 4 Column did not include any of the battalions of the Natal Native Contingent, but did include a force of disaffected Zulus and Swazis, raised locally and known as 'Wood's Irregulars'. They were engaged at Hlobane where they were scattered, and many deserted on the night of the 28th, but about 100 remained to fight at Khambula. (Killie Campbell Library)

◄British infantry entrenching a laager in Zululand. Wood's laagers were protected by a ditch around the outside, with the soil banked up between the wagon wheels. Each wagon was chained to its neighbour and further barricaded with sacks and crates of provisions. (S. Bourquin)

were convinced that when they attacked in large numbers no British force could stand against them. This impression was probably enhanced by the fact that hundreds of breech-loading rifles captured at Isandlwana had been distributed amongst the *amabutho*, leading them to the belief that their fire-power was equal to that of the British. Few of the warriors shared the king's misgivings, but the fruit born of their over-confidence would be bitter indeed.

Following the action at Hlobane, the Zulus bivouacked on the White Mfolozi river, about fifteen miles from Wood's camp. If the action on 28 March had been a disaster for the British, it had at least given them ample warning of an impending attack, and Wood roused his men early on the 29th and set them to making his final preparations. His position was, in any case, a strong one, lying across the crest of a ridge the British called Khambula, but which the Zulus knew as Ngaba ka Hawana, 'Hawana's Stronghold'. To the north the ground fell away in a bare slope towards two converging streams about a mile away; to the south it dropped into a valley in a series of rocky terraces. The eastern anchor of Wood's position was a redoubt – a ditch with the earth thrown up inside to form a parapet – which was connected by a palisade to a small laager of wagons on a flat below it, which was used as a kraal for the transport oxen. A couple of hundred yards west of the redoubt was a large defensive laager, an irregular circle of wagons chained together, with a shallow ditch and rampart thrown up around them.

To defend this position Wood had 2,086 officers and men. These included eight companies of the 90th Light Infantry, and seven of the 1/13th Light Infantry. Like Chelmsford at Isandlwana, he had no regular cavalry, but the indomitable Buller commanded 99 men of the Mounted Infantry, 165 men of the Frontier Light Horse, 135 men of the Transvaal Rangers, 99 men of Baker's Horse, 40 men of the Kaffrarian Rifles, 16 men of the Border Horse, and 74 mounted Africans (some of whom had fought at Isandlwana). These units were outside the Natal Volunteer system, and most had been raised on the Cape Frontier or the Transvaal border. They were of a decidedly piratical appear-ance which did not always endear them to their regular counterparts, but the Frontier Light Horse in particular had earned a reputation for hard riding and tough fighting. They had suffered heavily at Hlobane, but were still a force to be reckoned with. Finally, Wood also had the services of about 180 black auxiliaries from Wood's Irregulars, four 7pdrs from 11/7 Battery, RA, augmented by two unattached guns, and eleven Royal Engineers.

All in all, it was a force comparable to Chelmsford's command during the Isandlwana campaign. Yet the outcome of the two battles was to be very different.

The Battle of Khambula

Wood's scouts spotted the Zulu army moving away from its bivouac at about 10.30 on the morning of the 29th. It appeared to be marching to the west, and for a while it seemed as it it were following the king's instructions not to attack the camp, and Wood was worried that it might be making for the unprotected Transvaal. Then it halted about four miles south of the camp and began to form up to attack. As to why the commanders were disobeying the king's orders cannot be explained with certainty, but in all probability the young warriors, who made up the bulk of the force, had no time for a waiting game, and believed it their duty to attack the British as soon as possible. Once again, as at Isandlwana, a crucial battle was to be fought against the wishes of the Zulu generals.

Wood made his final preparations. He had placed two of his guns in the redoubt, supported by a company of the 90th L.I. One and a half companies of the 13th were told off to guard the cattle laager, while the remainder of the infantry and the mounted men occupied the main laager. The other four guns were placed in the open between the redoubt and the laager. As the morning wore on, and the dense Zulu masses were manoeuvring on the hills around the camp, Wood allowed his men to eat lunch. He was fully aware of the importance of the coming battle, but he appeared cool and in control, and saw no reason to make the men fight on an empty stomach. Open ammunition boxes were placed close to the lines.

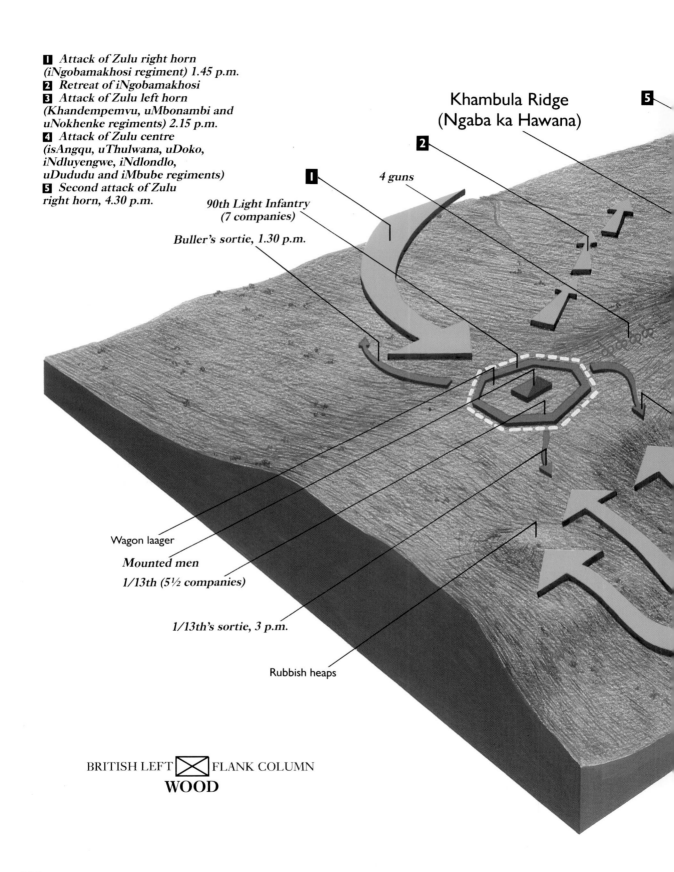

1 Attack of Zulu right horn
(iNgobamakhosi regiment) 1.45 p.m.
2 Retreat of iNgobamakhosi
3 Attack of Zulu left horn
(Khandempemvu, uMbonambi and
uNokhenke regiments) 2.15 p.m.
4 Attack of Zulu centre
(isAngqu, uThulwana, uDoko,
iNdluyengwe, iNdlondlo,
uDududu and iMbube regiments)
5 Second attack of Zulu
right horn, 4.30 p.m.

Khambula Ridge
(Ngaba ka Hawana)

4 guns

90th Light Infantry
(7 companies)

Buller's sortie, 1.30 p.m.

Wagon laager

Mounted men

1/13th (5½ companies)

1/13th's sortie, 3 p.m.

Rubbish heaps

BRITISH LEFT ⊠ FLANK COLUMN
WOOD

194

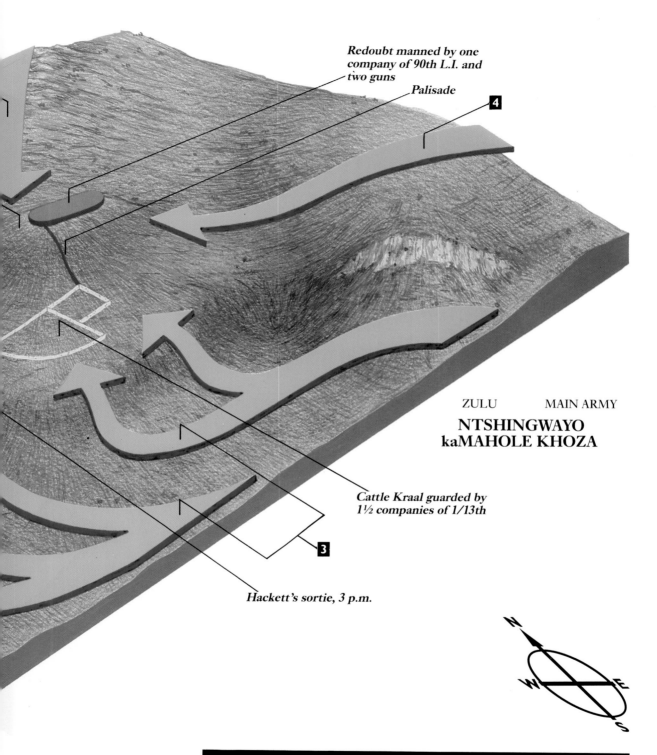

Redoubt manned by one company of 90th L.I. and two guns

Palisade

4

ZULU   MAIN ARMY
**NTSHINGWAYO
kaMAHOLE KHOZA**

Cattle Kraal guarded by 1½ companies of 1/13th

3

Hackett's sortie, 3 p.m.

THE BATTLE OF KHAMBULA
The Zulu attacks and the British sorties, 1.30 to about 5.30 p.m., 29 March 1879

Then, at about 12.45 p.m., he ordered the tents struck in preparation for the fight.

By that time, the Zulus were almost in position. The left horn (Khandempemvu regiment) moved towards the valley to the south of the camp, while the chest (the uMbonambi, iNdlondlo, uDududu, isAngqu, uThulwana, iMbube and iNdluyengwe regiments) ascended the eastern spurs of the ridge. The iNgobamakhosi regiment, which comprised the right horn, swung round to the north of the camp. The regular *amabutho* had been augmented by a large number of Qulusi clansmen from the local district, and the huge masses stretched for more than ten miles from tip to tip. To more than one anxious observer inside the laager, it seemed that the hills were black with warriors.

Curiously, considering it had had farthest to march, the right horn came into action first. It had halted its advance about a mile and a half from the camp, while the chest and centre were still moving into position. Wood was increasingly concerned

▼ *The Khambula battlefield today. This view was taken across the ground where the iNgobamakhosi charged. The rise on the skyline is the redoubt: the main laager was to the right of* *the trees. The slope is completely devoid of cover, apart from anthills. Many warriors threw themselves down behind these in a vain attempt to avoid the withering fire. (Ian Knight Collection)*

that a coordinated attack by such a large force would be more than his firepower could withstand, but he needn't have worried. At about 1.30 the iNgobamakhosi suddenly moved forward, and drew up in battle formation – a dense mass screened by clouds of skirmishers – less than a mile away. Apparently the warriors believed that the rest of the army was also advancing to attack; or perhaps they were vying with other regiments for the honour of being first into the red-coat camp. Certainly, it was not a move ordered by Ntshingwayo, who had taken up a position about 700 yards east of the redoubt, and who was apparently scarcely able to control his forces. In any case, Wood seized his opportunity, and ordered Buller to make a sortie to provoke the iNgobamakhosi into an unsupported attack.

The ground over which the first dramatic phase of the battle would take place sloped away from the laager towards a patch of marshy ground which marked the sources of the streams. It was completely bare grass, with no cover except for dozens of ant-heaps which scattered the slope like low boulders. Buller's sortie consisted of roughly a hundred men, and they rode to within comfort-

▼*Buller's sortie against the Zulu right horn at Khambula; the opening* *shots of the decisive battle of the War. (Ian Knight Collection)*

▶Two 7pdrs from an unidentified battery, photographed with Wood's Column later in the War. Wood had four guns of Major Tremlett's battery, and two unattached ones, at his disposal. Because the Zulu attacks were not coordinated, he was able to move them to meet each fresh threat. (S. Bourquin)

◀Sergeant, 1/13th Light Infantry, Khambula. Unlike the majority of infantry battalions, the Light Infantry wore their rank chevrons on both sleeves, rather than on the right sleeve only. Chevrons were white for NCOs below the rank of sergeant. Sergeants also carried a sword bayonet for the Martini-Henry rather than the usual triangular-section socket bayonet. The 90th's uniform would have been the same, apart from the difference in facing colour (buff for the 90th); the 90th did not, however, wear the facing colour on the cuff of the undress frock coat, which was therefore plain red. (Wynn Owen Lang)

▶Lieutenant F. Nicholson, RA, who commanded the two guns stationed in the redoubt at Khambula. He was directing the fire from an exposed position at the parapet when he was wounded. He died the next day. (Ian Knight Collection)

able rifle-range of the stationary warriors. Here they dismounted and loosed a volley. The effect was electric; with a great shout of the war cry 'Usuthu!', the Zulus surged forward. Buller's men hastily mounted up and fell back, pausing every fifty yards or so to deliver another volley. Several times the furious Zulu charge swept to within a few paces of the stragglers, but each time Buller managed to extricate his men. The Zulus called out in frustration 'Don't run away Johnny, we want

to speak with you!' and 'We are the boys from Isandlwana!' Most of the mounted men raced back to the laager, but the Native Horse retired to the west. Perhaps, after their experiences at Isandlwana, they distrusted British defended camps, and they spent the day in the open, harassing the Zulu flanks throughout the fight.

As Buller's men rode up the final approach to the laager, the guns boomed out, lobbing shrapnel over their heads and into the Zulu ranks. A wagon was rolled aside, and the mounted men raced in and dismounted, taking their place on the barricades. A tremendous volley burst out from the infantry, rippling down the side of the laager and across to the redoubt. The front ranks of the Zulus melted away in the face of this storm of fire and the charge faltered. A few madly brave warriors reached the wagons, spilling round the sides trying to find a way in, but the rest threw themselves down behind what pathetic cover they could find. They were terribly exposed, however, and could not sustain this position, and they reluctantly fell back, taking cover behind a rocky fold 'in the ground to the north-east.

They left the slope behind them strewn with bodies.

By provoking the attack of the right horn and defeating it, Wood had gained a tremendous tactical advantage. He had disrupted the Zulu plan, and it would be difficult now for them to avoid squandering their strength in uncoordinated piecemeal attacks, while he, in turn, would be free to concentrate his fire wherever it was most

199

needed. The whole movement had lasted less than three-quarters of an hour, and as the iNgobamakhosi fell back, so the left horn and chest moved rapidly foward in a belated attempt to support them. The chest came on in great waves, rippling over the contours, the warriors holding their shields high of the grass as they surged towards the redoubt. Their approach was hardly less open than that of the iNgobamakhosi, however, and the artillery opened up with shrapnel which blasted great gaps in their lines. At 800 yards the infantry opened fire, and by the time the distance closed to 300 yards, the devastation wrought in the ranks had been appalling. Nevertheless the centre pressed up almost to the walls of the redoubt before falling back.

It was the Zulu left horn which proved the most dangerous, however. Here the warriors could advance along the southern face of the camp, completely sheltered from fire by a steep, grassy valley. At the western end a small stream had cut a slope which offered a route up to the crest of the ridge. It opened out between the two laagers, almost in the centre of the camp. The Zulus could mass in the valley then charge up the slope, out of reach of British fire until they crested the rise less than a hundred yards from the laager. When they did so, of course, they ran into a hail of fire that was devastating at so close a range. The heavy Martini-Henry bullets sent warriors somersaulting back into their ranks, or tumbling over one another, but they kept coming, buoyed up by a very real hope of success. At about 3.00 p.m. a series of determined charges made Wood aware of the danger. The uNokhenke *ibutho*, on the left of the Zulu centre, moved down into the valley and carried on right up to the walls of the cattle kraal.

There was a flurry of hand-to-hand fighting with the men of the 1/13th stationed there, and the Zulus forced their way in. The kraal was still full of cattle, and the mêlée continued among the herd, which was surging and bellowing in fright. The British troops were in a dangerous position and Wood sent a messenger to order them to fall back. He and his staff took up a conspicuous position below the redoubt to encourage and support the men during the retreat. The jubilant uNokhenke poured into the positions they had vacated, and opened a heavy, but inaccurate, fire on the laager.

Exploiting this success, Zulu commanders could be seen frantically urging a new wedge of warriors into position on the slope. These were men of the uMbonambi *ibutho* and their attack threatened to punch a hole into the heart of Wood's defences. The rocky terraces prevented his fire from striking into the valley, so Wood ordered Major Robert Hackett of the 90th to take out two companies of his regiment and break up the Zulu concentration. To leave the protection of the laagers was a very risky business, but Hackett's men advanced swiftly and in good order, taking the Zulus by surprise. They formed up in a line at the top of the slope, and began firing steady volleys down into the valley. These chopped great swathes through the tightly packed uMbonambi, who gradually fell back before them, scrambling back into the valley or for the cover of the rocky outcrops on either side.

Hackett's sortie probably saved the day for Wood, but his men were completely exposed to Zulu return fire. Wood ordered the artillery and infantry in the redoubt to rake the cattle-laager, and the uNokhenke were gradually driven out, but a few snipers were still able to enfilade his line from the left. Worse, he came under a heavy cross-fire from his right, the extreme tip of the Zulu left horn. This, the Khandempemvu (umCijo) regiment, had pushed forward as far as the lip of the ridge to the west of the camp. A company of the 1/13th dashed out and drove them back with the bayonet, preventing them from forming up, but the British could not maintain this position, and the Zulus took possession of a small knoll about three hundred yards from the laager. This was the site of a camp rubbish dump, and was covered by a

◀ *Left: Major R. Hackett. His sortie was a turning-point in the Battle of Khambula, but he was severely wounded in the head by Zulu sniper fire. (Royal Collection)*

◀ *Lieutenant A. Bright, 90th L. I. He was wounded during Hackett's sortie, a bullet striking his thigh and passing through to his other leg. In the confusion of the battle, the surgeons failed to notice the extent of his injuries and he bled to death. (Ian Knight Collection)*

◀ *Hackett's sortie: his men line the crest of the slope and fire down at the warriors massing in the valley. The redoubt is on the rise, centre; the main laager is to the left. The number of casualties in this sketch suggest how vulnerable Hackett was to Zulu enfilading fire. (Ian Knight Collection)*

▶ *Major Robert Hackett, 90th Light Infantry. Hackett led the sortie of two companies of his regiment that broke up the Zulu left horn. He received a serious head wound during the retreat. We have shown him in the officers' undress frock coat, with regimental facing colour on the collar, and the collar badge and cuff braid of a major. (Wynn Owen Lang)*

W.O. LANG.

▲ After its initial repulse, the Zulu right horn took shelter behind the rocky outcrop seen on the left of this photograph. It made a final valiant attempt to charge the redoubt (skyline), but could make no headway against the hail of British fire. (Ian Knight Collection)

◄ The tide turns: during the closing stages of the battle, the 13th drive back the Zulu left for the last time. (Somerset L. I. Museum, Taunton).

heap of manure which had sprouted a covering of tall green grass. Warriors from the regiment dived into the grass and opened a galling fire at close range on both Hackett's men and the southern face of the laager. As the bullets began to strike down amongst the 90th men, several were hit. Hackett's subaltern, Lieutenant Bright, fell shot through both legs, and a minute later Hackett himself was hit in the face. Wood recalled the sortie and the men carried back their wounded officers. Hackett was to survive, though he lost the sight of both eyes; the surgeons failed to notice the extent of Bright's injury, and he bled to death during the night.

In the main laager, Redvers Buller noted the danger posed by the riflemen in the rubbish dumps and organized counter-fire. He urged his men not to waste time aiming at individual warriors, but to fire into the soft dung. The bullets passed clean through and struck the warriors behind. Volley after volley obliterated the heaps, and the Zulu fire was suppressed. The next day sixty-two bodies were found amongst the debris.

The narrow failure of the Zulu assaults on the south of the camp, and the success of the British sorties, was probably the turning-point of the battle, but there were to be several hours' hard fighting to come. The Zulu chest regrouped and advanced again and again along the crest of the ridge, each succeeding assault jockeying for a better position. On one occasion they came almost within reach of the artillery horses, in the open between the laagers, and in another the dead fell against the very wall of the redoubt. Each attack met with the same result, however; a concentrated storm of fire which nothing could withstand

At about 4.30, the iNgobamakhosi, on the Zulu right, having recovered from the shock of its initial repulse, came forward again. It was a spirited charge that surged out from the cover of the rocky outcrop and dashed towards the northern face of the redoubt. But the final approach to the ramparts was steep, and as the warriors struggled forward a furious rain of musketry and shrapnel fell on them, scything them down. The charge collapsed.

It was as if the Zulu tide had reached high-water mark. The warriors crouched or lay in a great semi-circle, taking whatever cover they could, surrounding the camp on three sides, firing their inadequate firearms. Now and then an *induna* would urge one regiment or another to screw up their courage for a final rush, but none was able to close. By 5 o'clock it was clear to Wood that the day was his, and he ordered a sortie of the 13th to clear the cattle laager of any surviving warriors. A company of the 90th was pushed out to the lip of the valley again, forming up where Hackett's men had once stood. They drove a few lingering

▶ *The original caption of this montage of incidents from the battle is 'Heroism at Khambula', and it is honest enough to include Zulu bravery. A warrior stabs himself (left) rather than die at the hands of a British sortie. In the centre a wounded man is snatched to safety in front of the Zulus during Buller's sortie, while (right) a wounded man is succoured during the retreat from the cattle laager. (Ian Knight Collection)*

HEROISM AT THE BATTLE OF KAMBULA

warriors out at bayonet point, and then began to fire down into the dark masses beginning to drift away down the valley. Everywhere, the Zulus were beginning to retire. For the most part they went slowly and in good order, still firing and carrying their wounded. The British infantry shouted and cheered as they went.

Now was the moment for Wood to close in for the kill. He ordered Buller to chase the warriors from the field, and his men hastily mounted up and streamed out of the laager in pursuit. The Irregulars had suffered heavily in the Hlobane débâcle of the day before, and they were in no mood to be merciful now. The effect of their charge on the disheartened Zulus was shattering. Any cohesion that remained collapsed under the pressure and the retreat disolved into a rout. A few Zulus turned and fought, but most were utterly exhausted. Many were so tired that they could not run, and some simply turned and stood, inviting their tormentors to shoot them down. Some even stabbed themselves rather than die at the hands of the British. The Irregulars were only too happy to be granted the opportunity for such slaughter. They shot warriors down at close range, 'butchering the brutes all over the place', as one officer later commented. Some even snatched up Zulu spears to skewer the warriors more efficiently. A few warriors tried to hide in long grass or ant-bear holes, but all were spotted and killed. 'The slaughter continued for as long as we could discover any human form before our eyes,' wrote another participant. Later, when details of the butchery reached the British press, they caused something of an outcry, yet in truth Wood had been given a golden opportunity to deliver a stunning blow to the Zulu army and he would have been foolish to pass it up. Nor could his troops have been much restrained in any case; they knew only too well that there was no quarter given in Zulu warfare, and they were hell-bent on revenge. Someone saw Buller himself in the thick of the fight, 'like a tiger drunk with blood'.

The chase continued to the slopes of the Zungwini mountain, about twelve miles away. In the early stages, the Zulu commanders made some attempt to rally their men. Mnyamana Buthelezi urged them to turn around once the British had

emerged from their laager, but Zibhebhu pointed out that it was hopeless. Once the rout had begun, there was no stopping it. Mnyamana tried to lead part of the army away, back to Ulundi, but most of the warriors would not follow him, and simply fled towards their homes. It is not known for certain

▲ As the Irregular cavalry emerge from the laager to chase the Zulus from the field, a warrior fires a last defiant shot. The Zulu retreat began in good order, but the Irregulars turned it into a rout. (S. Bourquin)

▶ The Zulu snipers in the rubbish heaps at Khambula. For once the Zulus were able to make the most of their firepower and effectively enfilade British sorties. Figures 1 and 2 are of the Khandempemvu (Mcijo) regiment, and are wearing the minimal war-dress of the later battles. Before the war, most Zulu guns were either Brown Bess flintlock patterns 2 or percussion models, but the Martini-Henrys

captured at Isandlwana 1 markedly improved the range and accuracy of Zulu fire. Figure 3 is one of Mbiline's followers, wearing an 80th Regiment jacket taken at Ntombe. Figure 4 represents a senior Zulu commander. His status is suggested by his single crane feather and lourie plume, and by the necklace of red beads and leopards' claws, worn only by important men. He also wears a 'bravery bead' necklace and a full waist-kilt. He has a revolver taken at Isandlwana: a number of officers' personal weapons were recovered after Khambula. The Zulus seem to have carried them more as trophies than for use. (Angus McBride)

how many casualties they had suffered, but when the British burial parties began to collect the dead, 785 bodies were brought in from the immediate confines of the camp. Many were badly knocked about by shell fire. They were buried in large pits 200 feet long, 20 feet wide and 10 feet deep.

Because of the severe nature of the pursuit, the ratio of killed to wounded was probably very high. Hundreds more lay out along the route of the retreat, and bodies kept turning up for days, hidden behind rocks or in tall grass where they had crawled to die. Of those who managed to escape, bearing the terrible wounds inflicted by the heavy lead bullets, few probably survived the journey to their family homesteads. Many men of rank and influence had been killed, for the officers had exposed themselves a good deal in leading the charges. Most of the dead were from the younger regiments, and the nation was to be stunned by their loss. Perhaps as many as 3,000 warriors died in total, and it is impossible to calculate the number who survived with minor injuries.

By comparison, Wood's losses were insignificant: eighteen NCOs and men killed, and eight officers, 57 NCOs and men wounded. Ten of the wounded later died and they were all buried in a

Zulus were capable of mounting a successful attack on the camp, until it was too late. His tactical decisions were based not only on this false premise, but also on poor Intelligence work. Thus he allowed his command to be split, and the further division between Durnford and Pulleine compounded this error. When the fighting began, the Zulus had the initiative and caught the British scattered over a wide area. Pulleine did not have the chance to do anything but react to their attacks. His opening dispositions were based on a misunderstanding of the threat – like everyone else, he believed the main army to be miles away confronting Chelmsford – and the Zulus never gave him the chance to correct his mistake. They won because they had out-generalled their enemy and caught them on the wrong foot.

Wood, who is held by many to have been a better general than Chelmsford, was nevertheless just as capable of under-estimating his enemy, as the Hlobane shambles proved. After Isandlwana, however, it was very clear to everyone in the British force that a massed Zulu attack had to be taken seriously. Wood had a day's warning of the attack on Khambula and he made the most of it. His camp was securely entrenched, and he was able to plan his dispositions knowing exactly the sort of attack he would face. Whereas Pulleine's firepower was scattered and diluted, Wood's was concentrated to devastating effect. Zulu commanders were extremely adept at spotting enemy weaknesses, but Wood left nothing to chance. Khambula was a rock on which the Zulu army dashed itself to pieces.

The extraordinary courage of the Zulus in attacking both camps should not be under-estimated. They sustained horrifying casualties at Isandlwana, but if they were disheartened, they were prepared to face British fire yet again in the belief that they could triumph in the end. Their own firepower was increased in the second battle, yet it made no difference to the outcome, and in the final analysis success still depended on coming to close quarters with the enemy. This was exactly what Wood prevented them from doing. The defeat was a particularly bitter one, because after Khambula the Zulu survivors understood that they were no match for the enemy.

small cemetery to the north of the camp.

There are a number of instructive comparisons to be drawn from the battles of Isandlwana and Khambula. There was not, on the whole, a great deal of difference in the troops involved in either campaign. Lord Chelmsford and Colonel Wood had commanded columns of roughly equal strength and, for the most part, the same Zulu warriors fought in both battles. Why then were the results so different?

There is no doubt that Chelmsford's over-confidence was a contributing factor to the disaster at Isandlwana. He simply could not accept that the

Aftermath

It was immediately apparent to both sides that the Zulu defeat at Khambula was of the greatest strategic importance. The victors of Isandlwana had been faced head on, and been crushed. British confidence was restored while Zulu morale collapsed. The *impi* would never again take the field with quite the same determination, and many warriors simply stayed at home for the duration of the war. King Cetshwayo, when he heard the news from his dispirited commanders, realized straight away that a successful military solution to the war was simply no longer an option. His view was confirmed a few days later with the report of a fresh defeat in southern Zululand.

On the same day that Wood had been engaged at Khambula, Lord Chelmsford had crossed the Thukela with the Eshowe relief column. On 2 April he had been attacked by an *impi* consisting largely of local troops near the site of the burnt-out military kraal of Gingindlovu. Chelmsford's men had formed a square and thrown up a ditch and rampart about it, and the Zulus had once again been unable to penetrate the wall of fire. The next day Eshowe was relieved. Chelmsford decided not to hold the post, and he began to evacute the garrison, which had withstood three months of siege. By the end of the month most of his men were back in Natal and he was more or less back where he started in January.

His reinforcements had been arriving, steadily, however, and Chelmsford planned a new campaign. He stuck to his original idea of advancing in several columns, but each column was much stronger, and they were to act in close cooperation with one another. The main thrust was to come from the new Second Division, which advanced from the border hamlet of Dundee and joined the old route of the Centre Column some miles beyond the fateful field of Isandlwana. Wood's column was to remain largely intact, but it was now to be called the Flying Column, and it was to move down to link up with the Second Division. The remaining column, the First Division, was to pacify the coastal strip.

The troops were in their start positions by the end of May, and the so-called Second Invasion began. The business of supplying the troops remained as much a nightmare as it had during the first invasion, and the advance was marked by a series of forts built as depots, and to protect the lines of communication. Cumbersome wagon trains constantly shuffled between them, tying down hundreds of troops on escort duty. The invasion had scarcely begun when it suffered a new disaster. The exiled Prince Imperial of France, Louis Napoleon, heir to the Bonapartist throne, who was attached to Lord Chelmsford's force as an observer, was killed while on patrol. The final advance took place in the face of constant skirmishing. The Zulus may have been reluctant to mount a full-scale attack in the open, but they harassed patrols and advance parties by sniping and ambush.

There was also an increase in diplomatic activity. King Cetshwayo sent repeated messages to Chelmsford, asking his terms. Chelmsford, knowing that Sir Garnet Wolseley was en route to replace him, demanded unconditional compliance with the terms of the Ultimatum. Cetshwayo was no more able to comply with that in June 1879 than he had been in January; nor did Chelmsford expect otherwise. He was hoping to win one final battle in an endeavour to restore his tarnished reputation.

It took place on 4 July. Chelmsford led the men of the Second Division and the Flying Column across the White Mfolozi river, and drew them up in a large square opposite the king's residence at Ulundi. Here the Zulus made their last dramatic gesture of defiance. More than 20,000 warriors

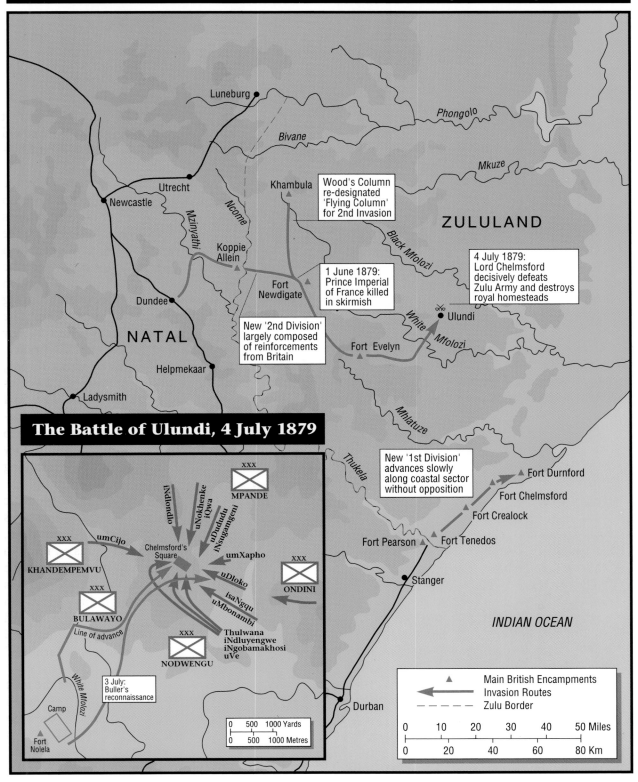

The Second Invasion of Zululand, May to July 1879

Luneburg

Phongolo

Bivane

Mkuze

Utrecht

Newcastle

Khambula

ZULULAND

> Wood's Column re-designated 'Flying Column' for 2nd Invasion

Koppie Allein

Mzinyathi

Ncome

Black Mfolozi

Fort Newdigate

> 1 June 1879: Prince Imperial of France killed in skirmish

> 4 July 1879: Lord Chelmsford decisively defeats Zulu Army and destroys royal homesteads

Dundee

White Mfolozi

Ulundi

NATAL

> New '2nd Division' largely composed of reinforcements from Britain

Fort Evelyn

Helpmekaar

Ladysmith

Mhlatuze

Thukela

> New '1st Division' advances slowly along coastal sector without opposition

Fort Durnford

Fort Chelmsford

Fort Crealock

Fort Pearson

Fort Tenedos

Stanger

INDIAN OCEAN

Durban

The Battle of Ulundi, 4 July 1879

XXX
MPANDE

uNokhenke
iQwa
iNdlondlo
uDududu
iNsugangeni

XXX
KHANDEMPEMVU

umCijo

Chelmsford's Square

umXapho

XXX
ONDINI

XXX
BULAWAYO

uDloko

Line of advance

isaNgqu

uMbonambi

XXX
NODWENGU

Thulwana
iNdluyengwe
iNgobamakhosi
uVe

White Mfolozi

> 3 July: Buller's reconnaissance

Camp

Fort Nolela

| 0 | 500 | 1000 Yards |
| 0 | 500 | 1000 Metres |

Main British Encampments
Invasion Routes
Zulu Border

| 0 | 10 | 20 | 30 | 40 | 50 Miles |
| 0 | 20 | 40 | 60 | 80 Km |

from right across the kingdom had mustered for the last great battle. They attacked with great daring, but their cause was lost before it began. After half an hour their charges petered out, and the 17th Lancers chased them from the field.

The British withdrew from Zululand as soon as the war was over. King Cetshwayo was hunted down, captured and sent into exile in Cape Town. Chelmsford returned home and was greeted as a conquering hero, though he never commanded troops in action again. Wood and Buller went on to pursue their successful careers, and spent a good deal of time fighting Africans the length and breadth of the continent. Buller was finally humbled by the Boers during his bungled attempts to relieve Ladysmith in 1900.

And Zululand? Once victory had been won, a new home government had no compunction in abandoning Frere's policy of Confederation. No attempt was made to annex the country taken at the cost of so much blood. Instead it was broken up into thirteen petty kingdoms and distributed amongst Africans thought to be loyal to Britain. Within a few years it had disolved into civil war. Cetshwayo was brought out of exile and given part of his own kingdom in an attempt to restore order, but he was defeated by Zibhebhu kaMapitha, who had become his implacable rival. He died in 1884. During the next twenty years there were two rebellions aimed at overthrowing white influence, but both were ruthlessly suppressed. Today Zululand is part of the Republic of South Africa.

◀ *The final defeat of the Zulu army: the battle of Ulundi, 4 July 1879. In the final analysis, Zulu courage and fighting spirit were every bit as good as those of the British, but, as this picture suggests, British firepower was crushingly superior. (Rai England Collection)*

◀ *The effect of Martini-Henry volley fire: a group of warriors cut down in a clump. This sketch was made at Ulundi, but there were many such scenes at Khambula, where the Zulus suffered terribly from British firepower. (Ian Knight Collection)*

▶ *King Cetshwayo was captured at the end of the War and sent into exile at Cape Town where he was lodged – as this photograph shows – at the castle. The post-war settlement of Zululand was such a disaster, however, that part of his old territory was restored to him. He was defeated in the civil war that followed and died in 1884. (Keith Reeves Collection)*

The Battlefields Today

For any one interested in the Anglo-Zulu War, a trip to the battlefields offers a fascinating chance to see them largely unchanged by the passing of more than a century. In some sectors commercial farming has altered the landscape, but the two battles featured in this book, Isandlwana and Khambula, look almost as they did when brave men crossed rifle with assegai, seeking to destroy or defend a royal dynasty. There are a number of organized tours, based both in the UK and South Africa. A good set of maps, such as the Laband and Thompson *Field Guide*, is essential for anyone exploring on his own, as Zululand is still quite rugged in places!

The nearest modern town to Isandlwana is Dundee – which for the military historian is interesting in itself, being the site of the Boer War battle of Talana – and from here it is 5 kilometres to the junction with the R68 Nquthu road. Follow this towards Nquthu, a distance of about 45 kilometres, then turn right, following the R68 towards Babanango. About 14 kilometres along this road is a turn off to the right leading to Isandlwana, a further 10 kilometres away.

Your first view of the battlefield is as this dirt road crests the lip of the Nquthu plateau and begins to descend to the plain. This is the view the attacking *impi* would have had, and it is worth stopping here and walking to a high-point, a knoll named Itusi, on the left. From here one can see the whole area of the Isandlwana campaign, from the distant Oskarberg on the right, round to the new camp site at Mangeni on the left. The road dips past the spot where the rocket battery came to grief, skirts the Conical Kopje, and crosses the donga where Durnford made his stand. It then runs up to the nek beneath Isandlwana, where much of the fighting took place. Leave your car here and explore the camp site, where there are a number of monuments to the fallen, and numerous

white-washed cairns that cover their bones. A road leads across the front of the mountain towards the small settlement of St. Vincent's. Here a foot-track leads up to the spur, where Mostyn and Cavaye were posted. Back on the plain, one can walk out to the firing line, which is a surprisingly long way from the camp. It is easy to imagine how exposed the men must have felt. Walking back to the mountain and ascending the lower slopes, one finds a large cairn marking the spot where Captain Younghusband made his last stand. This position gives a good view of the battlefield as a whole. Behind the mountain, a line of cairns marks the trail to Fugitives' Drift.

Moves are currently under way to ensure the preservation of the battlefield and to prevent any encroachment on the site by expanding local settlements. It is intended to move the current road, making it less obtrusive, and establish a visitors' centre at St. Vincent's. A new school for local children is to be built. These additions will not damage the dignity of the area, but will aid visitors in their understanding of the battle. Only by standing on the slopes of Isandlwana and experiencing the brooding atmosphere is it possible fully to appreciate the factors which shaped the decisions of that fateful day in January 1879.

The most suitable base for exploring the battlefield of Khambula is the town of Vryheid in northern Natal. Driving out of Vryheid, follow the R33 Paulpietersberg road and after 12 kilometres turn left along a dirt road, the D486, to the site of the battle. Passing through a farm gate, the road runs along the southern base of the redoubt and curves right to the military cemetery. The best overall view of the battlefield can be gained from the redoubt itself. From here you can see in all directions. The area has hardly changed, apart from a wattle grove which grows near the site of the main laager, where the British guns once stood. Having taken in the general view, one can examine specific areas of the battlefield. Walking away from the redoubt, crossing the track, you will see a valley open up before you, lined in places with cliffs. This is where the Zulu left horn advanced, completely sheltered from British fire. Turn to the right and you will see the slope where the valley runs up to the ridge. This is where Hackett made his sortie. There is a Zulu homestead nearby, and above it is the knoll where the Zulu snipers took shelter. Following the track one passes the laager side, and winds down towards the cemetery where British soldiers killed in the battle are buried. From here one can walk across the north face of the laager and redoubt. The country is just as open as it was during the battle, and it is easy to imagine the terrifying ordeal of the right horn, as it ran up the slopes in the face of withering fire. This ascent is deceptive; viewed from the redoubt, it appears gentle, but viewed from the Zulu position, the final stretch is a stiff climb, and the redoubt towers above you on the skyline. There are still antheaps on the site, and their inadequacy as cover is a poignant reminder of the plight of those brave warriors.

Of the other sites connected with the war, Hlobane and Ntombe are largely unchanged, but Nyezane and Gingindlovu, nearer the coast, are in the heart of the sugar-cane district and have been affected accordingly. There is little at Gingindlovu to remind one of the battle other than a small cemetery. The battlefield of Ulundi is largely surrounded by the rapidly growing capital of KwaZulu. The site of Chelmsford's square is marked by an ornamental garden which contains the graves of British troops killed in the battle, and

by a large dome. Plaques on its walls constitute what was, for many years, the only memorial to the Zulu dead. Nearby is the site of King Cetshwayo's Ondini homestead (an alternative name for Ulundi, and so called to distinguish it from the modern town), where archaeologists have reconstructed some of the huts over the original floors. The complex also holds the Museum of Zulu Cultural History. Perhaps the most famous site of the war, Rorke's Drift, is still a working mission and there are a number of modern buildings on the site. Plans are progressing, however, to develop a museum on the site of the original defensive position, the exact location of which has been recently determined by archaeologists.

As well as the battlefields, there are numerous forts marking the British advance, and a scattering of lonely graves, each with a story to tell.

Note: If you are interested in visiting the battlefields, you may like to know that the authors of this book organize regular tours, which visit all the sites connected with the war. For further details, write to Ian Castle, 49 Belsize Park, London, NW3 4EE.

Battlefield Relics

The issue of removing relics from South African battlefields is currently the subject of intense debate, following the illegal excavation of part of Khambula, and the subsequent sale of relics. Readers are advised that it is ILLEGAL to dig on South African battlefields, and hefty fines may be imposed on anyone found guilty of breaking this law.

Chronology

11 December 1878: Ultimatum delivered to Zulu representatives.

6 January 1879: No. 4 Column crosses River Ncome into Zululand.

11 January: Expiry of Ultimatum.

11 January: No. 3 Column crosses into Zululand at Rorke's Drift.

12 January: No. 1 Column begins to cross into Zululand at Lower Thukela.

12 January: No. 3 Column attacks Sihayo's stronghold.

17 January: Main Zulu army leaves Ulundi to attack No. 3 Column.

18 January: No. 1 Column begins advance on Eshowe.

20 January: No. 4 Column establishes base at Fort Thinta.

20 January: No. 3 Column arrives at Isandlwana.

22 January: Battle of Nyezane; No. 1 Column defeats 6, 000 Zulus.

22 January: Battle of Isandlwana.

22/23 January: Battle of Rorke's Drift.

24 January: No. 4 Column receives first news of Isandlwana.

27 January: No.1 Column receives news of Isandlwana.

28 January: No. I Column decides to hold Eshowe.

31 January: No. 4 Column moves camp to Khambula Hill.

11 February: Chelmsford's dispatch detailing defeat at Isandlwana reaches London.

11 February: Communications with Eshowe cut.

3 March: Heliograph commmunication opened between Thukela and Eshowe.

11 March: First reinforcements authorized by UK government arrive.

12 March: Attack on 80th Regimental convoy at Ntombe river.

28 March: Battle of Hlobane; mounted troops of No. 4 Column defeated.

29 March: Advance of Eshowe Relief Column.

29 March: Battle of Khambula.

1 April: Prince Imperial of France arrives in Natal to join Lord Chelmsford's staff.

2 April: Battle of Gingindlovu. Eshowe Relief Column defeats large Zulu army.

3 April: Eshowe relieved.

11 April: Last of Chelmsford's reinforcements arrive.

13 April: Chelmsford reorganizes his forces into 1st Division, 2nd Division and Flying Column.

21 May: Reconnaissance in force to Isandlwana, bodies buried except those of 24th. Wagons removed.

31 May: 2nd Division crosses into Zululand.

1 June: Prince Imperial killed in ambush while on patrol.

16 June: Chelmsford receives news that he is to be superseded by Sir Garnet Wolseley.

17 June: Flying Column and 2nd Division link for advance on Ulundi.

20 June: 1st Division advances from depots previously established in southern Zululand.

20 June: Bodies of 24th Regiment at Isandlwana buried.

27 June: Combined 2nd Division and Flying Column arrive at Mthonjaneni heights, for final march on Ulundi.

28 June: Sir Garnet Wolseley arrives in Durban.

1 July: 2nd Division and Flying Column camp on White Mfolozi river.

4 July: Battle of Ulundi; final defeat of the Zulu army.

8 July: Chelmsford resigns his command.

15 July: Chelmsford hands over command to Wolseley.

28 August: Capture of King Cetshwayo.

Index

(References to illustrations are in **bold**. Plates are shown with page and caption locators in brackets)